AIDS, drugs, and prostitution

Edited by Martin A. Plant

London and New York

First published 1990
by Routledge
11 New Fetter Lane, London EC4P 4EE

Simultaneously published in the USA and Canada
by Routledge
29 West 35th Street, New York, NY 10001

Reprinted 1991

First published in paperback 1993

Typeset in Times by LaserScript Limited, Mitcham, Surrey

Printed and bound in Great Britain by
Biddles Ltd, Guildford and King's Lynn

British Library Cataloguing in Publication Data

A catalogue record for this book is available from the British
Library

Library of Congress Cataloging in Publication Data

AIDS, drugs, and prostitution / edited by Martin Plant.
  p. cm.
  Includes bibliographical references.
  1. AIDS (Disease)—Epidemiology. 2. Prostitutes–
Diseases. 3. Prostitutes–Health and hygiene.
  4. Prostitutes–Drug use. 5. Prostitutes–Alcohol
use. I. Plant, Martin A.
  [DNLM: 1. Acquired Immunodeficiency Syndrome–
transmission. 2. Prostitution. 3. Substance Abuse–
complications. WD 308 A288]
  RA644.A25A358 1990
  616.97′92071–dc20
  DNLM/DLC   89-70219
  for Library of Congress   CIP

ISBN 0–415–04109–0

'HIV transmission requires the active participation of two persons.'[1]

[1]World Health Organization (1988) *Global Programme on AIDS* (Progress Report November 4), Geneva: World Health Organization, October, p.4.

This book is dedicated to the women and men of the sex industry. Without their trust and help the research described in this book would have been impossible.

Contents

Contents

Tables

Contributors

Martin Plant Director, Alcohol Research Group, Department of Psychiatry, University of Edinburgh, Scotland, UK.

William Darrow Chief, Behavioral and Prevention Research Branch, Division of STD/HIV Prevention, National Center for Prevention Services, Centers for Disease Control, Atlanta, Georgia, USA.

Sophie Day Research Fellow, Department of Anthropology, London School of Economics and Political Science, London, England, UK.

Pilar Estebanez Estebanez Ministerio de Sanidad y Consumo, Instituto de Salud Carlos III, Madrid, Spain.

Christine Harcourt Research Co-ordinator, Sydney STD Centre, Sydney Hospital, Sydney, New South Wales, Australia.

Dagmar Hedrich Psychologist, Jugendberatung und Jegendhilfe (Research Project AMSEL), Frankfurt, Federal Republic of Germany.

Lyn Matthews Outreach worker, Maryland Centre (HIV and Prevention Unit), Mersey Regional Health Authority, Liverpool, England, UK.

Ruth Morgan Thomas Research Associate, Alcohol Research Group, Department of Psychiatry, University of Edinburgh, Scotland, UK.

Sheigla Murphy Project Director, Institute for Scientific Analysis, San Francisco, California, USA.

Alfred Neequaye Senior Lecturer/Consultant Physician, Department of Medicine, Ghana Medical School, Accra, Ghana.

Ross Philpot Director, Sydney STD Centre, Sydney Hospital, Sydney, New South Wales, Australia.

Petrien Uniken Venema Research Associate, Epidemiology Department, Municipal Health Department, Rotterdam, Holland.

Jan Visser Research Director, Mr A. de Graaf Foundation, Amsterdam, Holland.

Dan Waldorf Principal Investigator, Institute for Scientific Analysis, Alameda, California, USA.

Helen Ward Research Fellow in Epidemiology, Department of Community Medicine, St Mary's Hospital Medical School, London, England, UK.

Preface

This book is concerned with the interrelations between prostitution or 'sex work', HIV infection and AIDS, and the use and misuse of psychoactive drugs such as alcohol, cannabis (marijuana), cocaine, and the opiates. For the purposes of this book 'prostitution' may be defined as the provision of sexual services in exchange for some form of payment such as money, drink, drugs, or other consumer goods.

Millions of people are involved in prostitution. Such individuals, both males and females, are commonly labelled with terms such as 'hooker', 'whore', 'call girl', 'hustler', 'courtesan', 'rent boy', 'call man', as well as by a host of local variations. The term 'sex work' is preferred by some researchers because it is both general and non-pejorative, unlike some of the labels in the preceding sentence. Even so, most of the contributors to this volume use other terms, most commonly that of 'prostitute'.

The whole topic of AIDS is emotive and value laden and the controversies related to this terrible disease are further clouded by its association with 'high-risk behaviours' and with people such as drug users, gay men, sex workers and their clients, and more generally with sexuality. Conant has recently drawn attention to the dangers of applying labels which may be not only pejorative but also inappropriate or sexist:

> Scapegoating women by labelling is extensive. In the cities of both East Africa and eastern United States women as prostitutes are seen as central to virus transmission. In the epidemiological literature for East and Central Africa the labels 'prostitute', 'free woman' or *femme libre* are being used for women who are sexually active outside a monogamous marriage relationship. The prostitute label is being applied regardless of the multiple,

complex roles of women not only in the 'barracks' cities of East
Africa but also in some cities of the eastern United States . . . it is
evident that continued use of the prostitute label not only distorts
the complexity of the social factors in HIV transmission but also,
because of the pejorative nature of the label, directs attention to
women's immorality as a source of HIV transmission rather than
men's sexual adventuring.

(Conant 1988: 149)

As the AIDS pandemic has spread its sinister reach through society it
has become clear that the two major modes of transmission are: first,
through penetrative sexual contact, anal, vaginal, and possibly oral, and,
second, through the sharing of infected injecting equipment by intravenous drug users. As re-emphasized throughout this book, it has for
several decades been clear that at least a minority of the men and women
who provide sex for payment are intravenous drug users. Moreover, as
elaborated in Chapter 1, many sex workers and their clients are heavy
users of alcohol and other drugs. Drinking and drug use are commonplace accompaniments of sex worker–client contact. The disinhibiting
effect of these substances may have considerable relevance to levels of
compliance with 'safer sex' or 'harm minimization' guidelines.

AIDS is still a relatively new phenomenon. Research activities
related to AIDS have proliferated at a remarkable rate. This book is an
attempt to bring together a group of reviews which relate to studies of
AIDS risks among sex workers and in some cases their clients. These
reviews, from ten research groups or researchers, originate from four
continents: Africa, Australia, Europe, and North America. The material
presented does not purport to be a complete global account of ongoing
research in this field. It is not, for other important studies are not
included here because of lack of space. Even so, it is hoped that this
collection provides an introduction to the AIDS/sex work/drug connection. In addition, the information presented is intended to furnish readers
with a fairly clear account of the objectives, scope, and preliminary
results of several very different initiatives in varied geographical and
institutional settings.

Some of the contributors to this book took part in a three-day workshop in Edinburgh during February 1989. This small, informal event
was jointly sponsored by the Alcohol Research Group in the University
of Edinburgh and the Scottish Health Education Group. As one of the
participants I was heartened by the commitment of those working in this

field not only to the production of research results but also to the far more important goal of curbing the spread of HIV infection and AIDS. It is always difficult to carry out research in a 'new area' if one does so in isolation. The Edinburgh workshop provided those present with an opportunity to exchange ideas and conclusions, to discuss research problems, and to identify public health strategies. It is hoped that this book will serve a similar purpose for a wider audience.

The original version of this book was published as a hardback in 1990. Since that date the AIDS pandemic has continued its relentless progress.

In many areas of the world the AIDS situation is far graver now than it was in 1990. Efforts to curb the spread of HIV/AIDS have met with only limited success in relation to some sub-groups and the general picture is gloomy in the extreme.

As noted by Morgan Thomas et al. (1990), Swaddiwudhipong et al. (1990), Bwayo et al. (1991), Chetwynd (1992), and Goldsmith (1992) even in areas in which the dangers of AIDS have been highly publicized there is a persistent and strong demand by sex industry clients for *unprotected* sex. More generally most young sexually active people in Britain, the USA and in most other countries do not appear to have adapted their behaviours in the light of AIDS. In fact in some localities levels of sexual activity among the young appear to have been increasing (Plant and Plant 1992).

The situation in some developing centres is particularly grave. As noted by Potts et al. (1991: 608): 'In some areas of Sub-Saharan Africa, between one tenth and one third of all sexually active adults harbour HIV-1.'

The connection between HIV/AIDS and the sex industry has attracted extensive clinical and scientific attention during recent years. Prostitutes and their clients have been identified as 'high frequency transmitters' of sexually transmitted diseases (Cameron et al. 1991). Reports have described levels of HIV infection and AIDS and other sexually transmitted diseases among male or female prostitutes or their clients from many countries. These include: Australia (Philpot et al. 1991; Crofts et al. 1992); Benin (Bigot et al. 1992); Brazil (Caterino-de-Araujo and De-Los-Santos-Fortuna 1990; Peterson and Szterenfeld 1992); Cameroon (Kaptue et al. 1991); Denmark (Melbye and Biggar 1992); France (Gayet-Mengelle et al. 1991); Gambia (Pickering et al. 1992); Ghana (Neequaye et al. 1991); Honduras (Venegas et al. 1991); India (Seth and Sharma 1991); Israel (Modan et al. 1992); Italy (Tirelli et al. 1991; Gattari et al. 1992); Kenya (Kreiss et al. 1992; Plourde et al. 1992); Mexico (Guerena-Burgueno et al. 1991); The Netherlands (Van den Hoek 1991); Nigeria (Williams *et al.* 1992); Somalia (Burans *et al.* 1990); Spain (Estebanez *et al.* 1992); Thailand (Ryan, 1991; Ford and Koetsawang 1991); the United Kingdom (McKegany and Barnard 1992); and the USA (Campbell 1991; Magana 1991; Morse *et al.* 1991; Rosenblum *et al.* 1992; Dorfman *et al.* 1992).

This burgeoning evidence underlines the facts that the sex industry may involve a very high risk of HIV infection. In addition in some areas a notable proportion of sex workers have used drugs intravenously and are heavy users of alcohol or other non-injected drugs. Even so it is emphasized that in many areas, especially in developing countries where HIV appears to be most widespread, intravenous drug use is by no means common. In most of Africa, for example, recreational drug injection is rare.

Available evidence (e.g. Plant and Plant 1992) suggests that some people take more risks than others. Heavy use of alcohol or other psychoactive drugs is often associated v ith unprotected sex. In addition the use of alcohol and other drugs is often associated, for many social, cultural and psychological reasons, with the sex industry. Nevertheless it has not yet been demonstrated that non-intravenous psychoactive drug use, through disinhibition or other effects, increases the probability that a man or woman will engage in risky sex (Plant 1993). The latter is influenced by a host of factors, not the least of which are the relative bargaining positions of those engaged in sexual acts.

Martin Plant
February 1993

STATISTICAL NOTE

In order to make the text of this book comprehensible to readers who are not researchers or who are not familiar with statistical procedures, statistical test results are omitted. When 'significant' associations or differences are cited these refer to confidence intervals of at least $p < 0.05$.

REFERENCES

Bigot, A., Bodeus, M., Burtonboy, G., Ahouignan, G., and Zohoun, I. (1992) 'Prevalence of HIV infection among prostitutes in Benin (West Africa)', *Journal of Acquired Immune Deficiency* 5: 317–19.

Burans, J.P., Fox, E., Omar, M.A., Farah, A.H., Abbass, S., Yusef, S., Guled, A., Mansour, M., Abu-Elyazeed, R., and Woody, J.N. (1990) 'HIV infection surveillance in Mogadishu, Somalia', *East African Medical Journal*, July: 466–72.

Bwayo, J.J., Mutere, A.N., Omari, M.A., Kreiss, J.K., Jaoko, W., Sekkade-Kigondu, C., and Plummer, F.A. (1991) 'Long distance truck drivers 2: knowledge and attitudes concerning sexually transmitted diseases and sexual behaviour', *East African Medical Journal*, September: 714–19.

Cameron, D.W., Ngugi, E.N., Ronald, A.R. Simonsen, J.N., Braddick, M., Bosire, M., Kimata, J., Kamala, J., Ndinya-Achola, J.A., Waiyaki, P.G., and Plummer, F.A. (1991) 'Condom use prevents genital ulcers in women working as prostitutes', *Sexually Transmitted Diseases* 18: 188–91.

Campbell, C.A. (1991) 'Prostitution, AIDS and preventive health behavior', *Social Science and Medicine* 32: 1367–78.

Caterino-de-Araujo, A. and De-Los-Santos-Fortuna, E. (1990) 'Seropositivity to *chlamydia trachomatis* in prostitutes: relationship to other sexually transmitted diseases', *Brazilian Journal of Medical and Biological Research* 23: 697–700.

Chetwynd, J. (1992) 'HIV/AIDS and sex workers', *New Zealand Medical Journal* 105: 227.

Conant, F.P. (1988) 'Social consequences of AIDS: implications for East Africa and the Eastern United States', in R. Kulstad (ed.) *AIDS 1988*, Washington, DC: American Association for the Advancement of Science, pp. 147–58.

Crofts, N., Russell, D., Breschkin, A., and Hatch, B. (1992) 'Heterosexual transmission of HIV in Victoria: implications for tracing and sex tourism', *Medical Journal of Australia* 156: 137.

Dorfman, L.E., Derish, P.A., and Cohen, J.B. (1992) 'Hey girlfriend: an evaluation of AIDS prevention among women in the sex industry', *Health Education Quarterly* 19: 25–40.

Estebanez, P., Sarasqueta, C., Najera, R., Contreras, G., Perez, L., Fitch, K., and Vicente, A. (1992) 'Prevalence of HIV-1, HIV-2 and HTLV-111 in Spanish seamen', *Journal of Acquired Immune Deficiency Syndromes* 5: 316.

Ford N. and Koetsawang, S. (1991) 'The socio-cultural context of the transmission of HIV in Thailand', *Social Science and Medicine* 33: 405–14.

Gattari, P., Spizzichino, L., Valenzi, C., Zaccorelli, M., and Rezza, G. (1992) 'Behavioural patterns and HIV infection among drug using transvestites practising prostitution in Rome', *AIDS Care* 4: 83–7.

Gayet-Mengelle, C., Puel, J., Averous, S., and Bazex, J. (1991) 'AIDS virus infection in Toulouse prostitutes (France)', *Journal of Acquired Immune Deficiency Syndromes* 4: 443–5.

Goldsmith, M. (1992) 'Rapid spread of pandemic in Asia dismays experts, spurs efforts to fight transmission', *Journal of the American Medical Association* 266: 1048–53.

Guerena-Burgueno, F., Benesson, A.S., and Sepulveda-Amor, S. (1991) 'HIV-1 prevalence in selected Tijuana sub-populations', *American Journal of Public Health* 623–5.

Kaptue, L., Kekeng, L., Djournessi, S., Monny-Lobe, M., Nichols, D., and

Debuysscho, R. (1991) 'HIV and chlamydia infections among prostitutes in Yasunde, Cameroon', *Genitourinary Medicine* 67: 143–5.

Kreiss, J., Ngugi, E., Holmes, K., Ndinya-Achola, J., Waiyaki, P., Roberts, P.L., Ruminjo, I., Sajabi, R., Kimata, J., Fleming, T.R., Anzala, A., Holton, D., and Plummer, F. (1992) 'Efficacy of nonoxynol 9 contraceptive sponge use in preventing heterosexual acquisition of HIV in Nairobi prostitutes', *Journal of the American Medical Association* 268: 477–82.

McKegany, N. and Barnard, M. (1992) *AIDS, Drugs and Sexual Risk*, Buckingham: Open University Press.

Magana, J.R. (1991) 'Sex, drugs and HIV: an ethnographic approach', *Social Science and Medicine* 33: 5–9.

Melbye, M. and Biggar, R.J. (1992) 'Interactions between persons at risk of AIDS and the general population in Denmark', *American Journal of Epidemiology* 135: 593–602.

Modan, B., Goldschmidt, R., Robinstein, E Vonsover, A., Zinn, M., Golan, R., Chetrit, A., and Gottleib-Stematzky, 1. (1992) 'Prevalence of HIV antibodies in transexual and female prostitutes', *American Journal of Public Health* 82: 590–2.

Morgan Thomas, R., Plant, M.A., Plant, M.L., and Sales, J. (1990) 'Risk of HIV infection amongst clients of the sex industry in Scotland', *British Medical Journal* 301: 525.

Morse, E.V., Simon, P.M., Osofsky, H.J., Balson, P.M., and Gaumer, H.R. (1991) 'The male street prostitute: a vector for transmission of HIV infection into the heterosexual world', *Social Science and Medicine* 32: 535–9.

Neequaye, A.R., Neequaye, J.E., and Biggar, R.J. (1991) 'Factors that could influence the spread of AIDS in Ghana', *Journal of Acquired Immune Deficiency Syndromes* 4: 914–19.

Peterson, C. and Szterenfeld, C. (1992) 'Organizing a project with community-based health agents recruited from prostitutes in Rio de Janeiro', *Public Health* 106: 217–23.

Philpot, C.R., Harcourt, C.L., and Edwards, J. M. (1991) 'A survey of female prostitutes at risk of HIV infection and other sexually transmissible diseases', *Genitourinary Medicine* 67: 384–8.

Pickering, H., Todd, J., Dunn, D., Pepin, J., and Wilkins, A. (1992) 'Prostitutes and their clients: a Gambian survey', *Social Science and Medicine* 34: 75–88.

Plant, M.A. (1993) 'Alcohol, AIDS and sex', in: L. Sherr (ed.) *Heterosexual AIDS*, London: Harwood (in press).

Plant, M.A. and Plant, M.L. (1992) *Risk-Takers: Alcohol, Drugs, Sex and Youth*, London: Tavistock/Routledge.

Plourde, P.J., Plummer, F.A., Pepan, J., Agoki, E., Moss, G., Ombette, J., Ronald, A.R., Cheang, M., Decosta, L., and Ndinya-Achola, J.O. (1992) 'Human immunodeficiency virus type 1 in women attending a sexually transmitted diseases clinic in Kenya', *Journal of Infectious Diseases* 166: 86–92.

Potts, M., Anderson, R., and Boily, M-C. (1991) 'Slowing the spread of human immunodeficiency virus in developing countries', *Lancet* 338: 608–13.

Rosenblum, L., Darrow, W., Witte, J., Cohen, J., French, J., Gill, P.S., Potterat, J., Sikes, K., Reich, R., and Hadler, S. (1992) 'Sexual practices in the transmission of hepatitis B virus and prevalence of hepatitis delta virus infection in female prostitutes in the United States', *Journal of the American Medical Association* 267: 2477–81.

Ryan, M.P. (1991) 'AIDS in Thailand', *Medical Journal of Australia* 154: 282–4.

Seth, P. and Sharma, U.K. (1991) 'Recovery of human immunodeficiency virus from asymptomatic prostitutes from Tamil Nadu', *Indian Journal of Medical Research* 93: 277–9.

Swaddiwudhipong, W., Nguntra, P., Lerdlukanavonge, P., Chaovakiratipong, C., and Koonchote, S. (1990) 'A survey of knowledge about AIDS and sexual behavior in sexually active men in Mae Sot, Tak, Thailand', *Southern Asian Journal of Tropical Medicine and Public Health* 21: 447–52.

Tirelli, V., Vaccher, E., and Covre, P. (1991) 'Condom use among transvestites in Italy', *Journal of Acquired Immune Deficiency Syndromes* 4: 302–3.

Van den Hoek, J.A.R., Van Haastrecht, H.J.A. and Countinho, R.A. (1991) 'Homosexual prostitution among male drug users and its risk of HIV infection', *Genitourinary Medicine* 67: 303–6.

Venegas, V.S., Madrid, J.P., Lorenzana, I., Griller, L., Cosenza, H., and Bygdeman, S. (1991) 'Human immunodeficiency virus infection and syphilis in Honduran female prostitutes', *International Journal of STDs and AIDS* 2: 110–13.

Williams, E., Lamson, N., Efem, S., Weir, S., and Lamptey, P. (1992) 'Implementation of an AIDS prevention program among prostitutes in the Cross River State of Nigeria', *AIDS* 6: 229–30.

Chapter one

Sex work, alcohol, drugs, and AIDS

Martin Plant

Introduction

As noted in the Preface, 'prostitution' or 'sex work' relates to the provision of sexual services for payment. One of the contributors to this book, Dr William Darrow, has provided a cogent account of the historical connection between prostitution and sexually transmitted diseases (Darrow 1984). As this account graphically describes, 'prostitutes' (until recently this term has overwhelmingly been confined to females) have long been associated with and often 'blamed for' the spread of syphilis, gonorrhoea, and other sexually transmitted diseases. As Darrow notes, studies from many centres confirm the view that prostitutes do have high rates of sexually transmitted diseases. It has frequently been concluded that prostitutes are an extremely high-risk group in this respect and that, accordingly, prostitutes pose a major public health problem. The advent of AIDS has greatly increased concern about the possible health implications of commercial sex. This concern has both been stimulated by and given impetus to the studies described in the following pages. This chapter attempts to provide a selective review of available evidence relating sex work to the use and misuse of psychoactive drugs and to both HIV infection and AIDS.

Sex, alcohol, and drugs

There is an extensive literature indicating that, in many societies, sexual behaviours are interwoven with the recreational use of mind-altering drugs. In societies where alcohol is legally available, bar-rooms, hotels, and other licensed premises are popular places for seeking sexual partners. Several authors have further emphasized the influence of drugs such as alcohol and cannabis as 'social lubricants' or as disinhibitors

1

(e.g. Soloman and Andrews 1973; O'Farrell *et al*. 1983; Room 1985; Reinarman and Leigh 1988). Many of the connections between alcohol, other drugs, and sex are attributable to the coalescence of social and cultural patterns, especially those related to leisure. One of the classic social science studies of alcohol use in bar-rooms bears the deliberately ambiguous title of *Liquor License* (Cavan 1966).

Ridlon has provided general comments on the subject of alcohol consumption by women. The following quotation comes from a paragraph entitled 'Sexual promiscuity: the drunken slut':

> From the beginning of civilization, there has been a connection between drinking and involvement with sex. Wine drinking by women was punishable by death in early Rome because it was believed to be linked directly with adultery. It was feared that if a woman opened herself to one male vice, drinking alcohol, she might open herself to another, sexual promiscuity.
>
> (Ridlon 1988: 27–8)

Psychoactive drugs, depressants, stimulants, and hallucinogens, also exert clear pharmaceutical effects. These influence mood and physical arousal (e.g. Wilson and Lawson 1976a, 1976b; Beckman 1979; Harvey and Beckman 1986).

The role of alcohol and other drugs as disinhibitors has been widely discussed (e.g. Bush 1980; Room and Collins 1983; Coles and Stokes 1985). An earlier review by M.L. Plant *et al*. noted:

> In many contexts drug use is believed to be and defined as a vehicle of disinhibition which implies a constellation of sequelae ranging from platonic good humour to sexual approaches, aggression and violence, including rape (MacAndrew and Edgerton 1969; Rada 1975; Johnson, Gibson, and Linden 1978; Collins 1982; Richardson and Campbell 1982; Lang 1985; Room 1985; Leigh 1988). Some drugs, such as amyl nitrate (poppers), are often used because it is believed they enhance sexual experiences. In countries in which alcohol is legally available it is commonplace for people to frequent bar-rooms and clubs in which drinking and sexual dalliance co-mingle.
>
> (Plant *et al*. 1989: 53–4)

Klassen and Wilsnack (1986) have suggested that women who regard alcohol as having disinhibiting effects may drink to become sexually freer. Unwanted pregnancies, sexually transmitted diseases, and unprotected sex have all been linked with the disinhibiting effects of alcohol and other drugs. Probably the most detailed study of their relationship which explicitly relates to AIDS risks has been reported by Stall and his co-workers (Stall *et al.* 1986, Stall 1988, Stall and Ostrow 1989). These researchers found a clear connection between the use of alcohol and illicit drugs during sexual activity and failure to comply with 'safer sex' guide-lines intended to minimize AIDS risks. The survey, which related to a study group of 463 gay males in the USA, indicated that 'high-risk' sexual activity was significantly more likely to have been reported by those who had used alcohol, poppers, cannabis, or 'other drugs' during their sexual encounters. He further noted that: 'Significantly more potentially unsafe sexual activity occurs within primary gay relationships than between men who are not as seriously involved' (Stall 1988: 75). Stall concluded that:

Depending on the specific drug, the men at high risk are from 2 to 3.5 times more likely to have used drugs during sexual activity than the men at no risk. The men at medium risk are approximately 1.5 times more likely to have used drugs during sexual activity than the men at no risk. In each case, the differences in probability of drug use by risk category are highly significant... Together these findings indicate that there is a strong cross-sectional relationship between high risk sexual activity and the use of drugs during sexual encounters. It appears that the use of drugs and/or alcohol during sexual contacts is one condition under which individuals sometimes decline to comply with risk reduction guidelines.

(Stall 1988: 78)

A Scottish study by Robertson and Plant (1988) has produced results which broadly reinforce Stall's findings. This exercise related to young men and women who had married as teenagers, clearly an atypical group of people. Fifty-eight per cent of the males and 48 per cent of the females reported having consumed alcohol immediately before their first experience of sexual intercourse. Only 31 per cent of males and 46 per cent of females in the study group reported the use of any type of contraception during their first sexual encounters. Males who had not consumed alcohol were more than three times as likely to have used contraception than were those who had consumed alcohol, 57 per cent and 13 per cent respectively. The corresponding proportions among females were 68 per cent and 24 per cent.

3

Hingson *et al.* (1989) conducted a telephone survey of 1773 people aged 16 to 19 in Massachusetts during 1988. This indicated that teenagers who were heavier drinkers or marijuana (cannabis) users were 2.8 and 1.9 times less likely to use condoms. Among those who were drinkers and illicit drug users 16 per cent reported using condoms less after drinking and 29 per cent reported such a decline after drug use.

Available evidence clearly supports the conclusion that alcohol and other drugs are associated with sexual behaviour for a host of social and psychological reasons. Further, it is apparent that high-risk sexual activities are frequently associated with heavy alcohol and drug use. The AIDS-related risks of psychoactive drug use are compounded by the fact that high levels of alcohol and some other drugs depress the immune system.

Alcohol and other forms of drug use are related to sexual behaviour and AIDS risks in two important ways: first, the use of such substances, due to their relaxing or disinhibiting effects, may increase the prospect of high-risk sexual activity. Second, people who have a predilection for indulging in some risky activities are also predisposed to indulge in others (Jessor and Jessor 1977; Room and Collins 1983; Adlaf and Smart 1983; Flavin and Frances 1987).

Alcohol and drug use among sex workers and their clients

As noted above, there is a well-established link between bar-rooms or other drinking locales and sexuality. Many bars are frequently used as pick-up places and some are clearly defined as singles bars, gay bars, or in relation to other specific sexual categories. Goldstein's study *Prostitution and Drugs* examined the links between commercial sex and illicit drugs in detail. Goldstein concluded that there was little empirical support for the beliefs that prostitution somehow 'drives' people into drug use or that female addicts turn to prostitution to support the costs of drug use.

Goldstein nevertheless wrote:

A literature search for estimates of the proportion of female drug users who were also prostitutes uncovered a range from about 30 per cent to about 70 per cent. Conversely, there was a reported range from about 40 per cent to about 85 per cent with regard to the proportion of prostitutes who were also drug users.

(Goldstein 1979: 6)

Weisberg, author of another important study on prostitution, drew the following conclusions:

Drug use is common among adolescent prostitutes, and few can say they never use drugs. They experiment with a variety of drugs. Most have tried marijuana; and many are frequent marijuana users. Half have experimented with psychedelic drugs, and many have used narcotics at some time. In addition, at least occasionally, a substantial number have been drunk....The frequency of drug use amongst young prostitutes is high. Studies reveal that one-fifth to one-half of them use drugs all the time. A considerable number feel they have drug problems....Estimates of juvenile prostitutes who use drugs at work range from about one-fifth to two-thirds. The prostitutes indicate that drugs relax them and make their work more bearable. They claim, for example, that drug use 'takes your mind off what you're doing', 'makes it bearable', 'calms me down so I can go through with it', 'makes me feel less miserable' and that 'otherwise I'd kill myself'.

(Weisberg 1985: 117–18)

Such conclusions are not universally supported. Weisberg cites a study by Bracey which indicated a low level of drug use by juvenile prostitutes. In this study fewer than 20 per cent of respondents reported using drugs other than cannabis and alcohol.

Goldstein's US study of sixty female drug users supported the view that different types of prostitutes used different types of drugs:

Among high-class prostitutes, prostitution was most likely to precede addiction, and the most common addiction was to stimulants....Among low class prostitutes, addiction tended to predate prostitution. The most common addiction was to heroin. The causal linkage between addiction and prostitution was most likely to be based on economic necessity.

(Goldstein 1979: 45)

Weisberg (1985) has inferred that 'lower-class' female drug users may engage in prostitution to pay for drugs. Weisberg has suggested several ways whereby drug use and commercial sex may be connected. Some sex workers use drugs to help them to cope with making contacts with clients. Some sex workers use drugs to compensate for their mixed feelings about their occupation. This is because some dislike their work, find it stressful or frightening. Also some sex workers have contact with

5

alcohol and other drugs because these are commonly used in many pick-up locales such as public bars. In addition some people engage in prostitution to pay for drug habits.

Goldstein concluded from reviewing available published evidence that a number of specific functions have been suggested of drug use by sex workers:

> Heroin use may help a prostitute adjust to a life that she resents; increase her ability to withstand emotional and physical stress; help her relax. Winick and Khissie report what must be a completely unintended function of narcotics use. They state that since heroin seems to relax the anal sphincter muscles, prostitutes who are heroin addicts are likely to have minimal problems in engaging in anal intercourse. (Thi.. study found no correlation between heroin use and a willingness to engage in anal sex.) Cocaine and other stimulants have been reported to increase the confidence of streetwalkers to solicit strangers on the street and to enable massage parlour prostitutes to maintain their 'energy level'. Hashish helped Israeli prostitutes forget 'the dirt' of their work. Valium aided some call girls in 'getting through the day'. Peruvian brothel prostitutes were able to 'time themselves out' while working by getting drunk each night. New York call girls got 'protection from insults to their bodies and minds' by drinking steadily.
>
> (Goldstein 1979: 117–18)

Goldstein's own work led him to conclude that alcohol was mainly used by female prostitutes to 'enhance sociability' with clients. He also noted that the most commonly reported problem attributable to alcohol was 'losing consciousness or control'. He emphasized that different prostitutes use drugs in different ways and to achieve varied functions. Alcohol, cannabis, and cocaine were used as social lubricants or ice breakers. Stimulants are sometimes used to ward off fatigue. Goldstein asserted that upper-class prostitutes are more inclined than lower-class prostitutes to socialize with clients. Lower-class prostitutes are, he concluded, less likely to use drugs to enhance sociability. The heroin users in his study group either worked to buy drugs or used heroin to 'deaden the realities of prostitution'.

Several authors have found, like Goldstein, that prostitution is commonplace among heavy users of illicit drugs and heavy drinkers, particularly if these are lower-class females. It must be noted that recent attention has been paid to male prostitution and to 'upper-class' female prostitution which may simply be less obvious and harder to investigate than that among low socio-economic groups (Lisansky 1957; Maerov 1965; Ellinwood *et al.* 1966; Perlmulter 1967; Medhus 1975; Connaughton *et al.* 1977; James *et al.* 1979; Martin and Martin 1980; Allen 1980; Datesman 1981; Rosenbaum 1981; Wilsnack 1984; Marshall and Hendtlass 1986). A 1987 survey of street prostitutes in New York City suggested that approximately half had at some time used drugs intravenously (Des Jarlais *et al.* 1987).

Other authors have drawn attention to the importance of bars, hotels, clubs, and other drinking localities as sexual contact points (e.g. Cavan 1966; Goldstein 1979; McLeod 1982; Weisberg 1985). Some sex workers meet many or even all of their clients in such places and, as noted by several authors, many of the clients of sex workers are intoxicated and some are aggressive or violent (e.g. JIF 1947; Silbert and Pines 1981; Smart 1985).

The literature on both prostitution and sexually transmitted diseases contains numerous references to military personnel, tourists, seafarers, and other groups of transients and travellers. In addition, the literature on alcohol problems has also identified some of these groups, such as the military and seafarers, as having high rates of heavy drinking and alcohol problems. It must be emphasized that far less has been documented about the clients of sex workers than has been written about the workers themselves.

Sex workers, HIV infection, and AIDS

The first person in the USA who was officially recorded as infected with HIV was not, contrary to popular belief, a gay man but was a female prostitute (Shilts 1987). More recently, the first officially recorded death of a USSR citizen due to AIDS (in 1988) also involved a female prostitute. In between these dates it has been established that the two major methods of transmitting HIV infection are through penetrative sexual contacts and intravenous drug use. As already indicated, there is ample evidence indicating that intravenous drug use is commonplace among some groups of sex workers. Such people, by definition, also have multiple sexual partners and have emerged, *together with their far more numerous clients*, as potential high-risk groups in relation to the spread of HIV infection. Moreover, it has been widely speculated during recent years that drug-using prostitutes and their clients may be, or could become, the major means through which HIV infection is passed into the general population. The connection between the sex industry and HIV infection is the central theme of this book. This section reviews some of the evidence that is already available on this topic. In so doing the general background to the studies which are described in detail in the following chapters is outlined.

The historical association between prostitution and sexually transmitted diseases has already been widely discussed and has been reviewed elsewhere (e.g. Darrow 1984).

Johnson (1988) concluded from a review of European studies that female prostitutes have low levels of HIV infection unless they also happen to be intravenous drug users. The evidence she reviewed showed zero levels of HIV infection among prostitutes in Copenhagen, London, Nuremberg, and Paris. Even so, some of the prostitutes in other localities had been exposed to HIV infection: Athens (6 per cent), the Federal Republic of Germany (1 per cent), and Pordenone (near Venice) (71 per cent). Half of the infected women in the Federal Republic of Germany and all of those in Pordenone were intravenous drug users. A multi-centre US study has been reported by the Centers for Disease Control (1987). This is elaborated by Dr Darrow in Chapter 2. This investigation indicated that sixty-two (10.9 per cent) of a study group of 568 prostitutes were HIV seropositive. Lange *et al.* (1987) have reported that 34 per cent of a subsample of Baltimore prostitutes with heavy drug use histories were found to be HIV seropositive. They further noted that HIV infection was highest in the predominantly black centre-city areas. Lange *et al.* also cite evidence from the Centers for Disease Control (1987) indicating HIV infection among 0–57 per cent of female prostitutes in nine selected US cities. They report that the corresponding position among male prostitutes remains unclear.

Coutinho *et al.* (1988) have reported the results of a study of thirty-seven male prostitutes working in brothels in Amsterdam. They also collected data from thirteen male prostitutes attending a clinic for sexually transmitted diseases. Four out of thirty-two men who were tested were HIV seropositive. Only one of these was an intravenous drug user. The authors concluded:

> Apparently the prevalence of infection in male prostitutes is no higher than in other groups of homosexual men with multiple partners. This indicates that male prostitutes do not play a special part in the spread of STDs and HIV among homosexual men in

Amsterdam. The clientele of male prostitutes may, however, include a relatively high number of bisexual men who want to hide their homosexuality, and in this way male prostitution could be a bridge for the spread of STDs and HIV into the general population.

(Coutinho *et al.* 1988: 207–8)

Van den Hoek *et al.* (1987) have described the results of another Amsterdam study. This revealed that 28 per cent of a study group of intravenous drug users and drug-using prostitutes were HIV seropositive. These authors noted that one HIV seropositive female prostitute had transmitted HIV infection to her non-intravenous-drug-using lover. They had not been using condoms. The authors further concluded:

The majority of women in this study engaged in prostitution. Many of the males were also prostitutes. Heterosexual transmission from infected drug using prostitutes to their clients is an alarming possible means of spreading HIV to the general population.

(Coutinho *et al.* 1988:59)

Goldberg *et al.* (1988) have reported that among HIV seropositive people in Glasgow twenty-six women (all of whom were drug users) were prostitutes. Much publicity was given to a female prostitute in Edinburgh who, though allegedly HIV seropositive, continued to have sex with approximately thirty men each week (Sarler 1987). Smith and Smith (1986) have reported that licensed prostitutes in the Federal Republic of Germany had an HIV infection rate of 1 per cent while unlicensed prostitutes had a rate of 20 per cent. They noted that this difference has not been explained, although unlicensed prostitutes are more likely than licensed prostitutes to have used drugs intravenously. Cooper and Dodds (1986) have described an Australian case in which a man allegedly contracted HIV infection during sex with a female prostitute.

The topics of sexually transmitted diseases and prostitution should not be discussed without due attention being given to those who purchase sexual services, the 'clients', 'punters', 'johns', 'tricks', etc. Masterton and Strike (1988) have produced an interesting review of rates of sexually transmitted diseases among British armed service personnel stationed in Europe. These authors emphasize that male service personnel, largely unmarried and living away from home, are likely to be more promiscuous than they would be in other settings. They further recall:

> During the Boer War as many as half the British troops suffered from venereal disease and in the First World War the proportion reached 20% in some military troops. This risk associated with combatant troops was identified again during the Second World War and a 1973 study of 400 Australian soldiers serving in Vietnam showed an STD incidence of 27%.
>
> (Masterton and Strike 1988: 56)

Masterton and Strike emphasize the importance of prostitution in the spread of sexually transmitted dise ses among service personnel. Several studies have reached similar conclusions. For example Bradbeer *et al.* (1988) have reported that in Singapore most men who have sexually transmitted diseases cite prostitutes as the source of such infections. Conversely it has also been suggested that HIV infection among Italian female prostitutes may have been caused by sharing injecting equipment with infected US service personnel (Dan and Rock 1987). James *et al.* (1986) reported that 5 per cent of US military personnel attending a venereal disease clinic in Berlin were HIV positive. They also noted that only 3 per cent of a group of US military personnel with gonorrhoea reported having contact with a prostitute.

Rosenberg and Weiner (1988) have drawn a distinction between the connections with prostitution and sexually transmitted diseases in general and with HIV in particular:

> Prostitutes are considered a reservoir for transmission of certain sexually transmitted diseases (STDs). However a variety of studies suggest that human immunodeficiency virus (HIV) infection in prostitutes follows a different pattern than that for STDs: HIV infection in non-drug using prostitutes tends to be low or absent, implying that sexual activity alone does not place them at high risk, while prostitutes who use intravenous drugs are far more likely to be infected with HIV....Prostitutes who do not use intravenous drugs probably face their highest risk from steady partners who may be infected with HIV and other STDs and with whom barrier protection is generally not used.
>
> (Rosenberg and Weiner 1988: 418)

These conclusions related only to the USA and Europe. Rosenberg and Weiner drew quite different conclusions in relation to Africa where they noted: 'infection rates are high among female prostitutes and appear to be related only to sexual activity. However, there may be other relevant factors which affect susceptibility in that population' (p. 420).

The African pattern is indeed very different from that noted in Europe and North America. Intravenous drug use does not appear to be associated with this phenomenon; nevertheless HIV infection has been detected in blood samples taken from female prostitutes in Africa. One of the contributors to this book, Dr Alfred Neequaye, reported that a study of ninety-eight female Ghanaian prostitutes revealed that only one was HIV seropositive (Neequaye et al. 1986). Other African studies have indicated higher levels of HIV infection among female prostitutes. These include 26 per cent in Kinshasa, Zaire (Mann et al. 1987), between 16–46 per cent and 66 per cent in Nairobi, Kenya (D'Costa et al. 1985; Kreiss et al. 1986), and 82 per cent in Rwanda (Van de Perre et al. 1985).

While, in general, the African situation is quite different from that in Europe or the USA, there are exceptions to the link between non-African prostitutes with HIV infection and drug use. Papaevangelou et al. (1985) have reported that none of a group of HIV seropositive female prostitutes in Athens have used intravenous drugs. Simoes et al. (1987) have also reported that ten out of 102 female prostitutes in Tamil Nadu (India) were found to be HIV seropositive. None of these had used intravenous drugs and all denied having engaged in anal sex. More recently, HIV infection has been reported among female sex workers in several areas of Thailand.

Conclusions

Available evidence clearly indicates that sex workers and their clients are 'high-risk groups' in relation to long-established sexually transmitted diseases. In many areas of the work varying proportions of sex workers have already been exposed to HIV infection or have developed AIDS. In some areas, notably in Europe and North America, HIV infection among sex workers is attributable to intravenous drug use (sharing infected injecting equipment) rather than to sexual contacts. Even so, elsewhere, notably in Africa and in some other localities (e.g. Athens), intravenous drug use does not appear to be a factor.

Gagnon et al. have provided an important reminder that 'hard information' in this field remains, as yet, relatively sparse: 'Although these factors suggest that female prostitution could play a role in the

AIDS epidemic, there is very little actual evidence about the role of prostitution in the transmission of HIV' (Gagnon *et al.* 1989: 137).

It is also apparent that in many settings the buying and selling of sexual services is often associated with the use of alcohol and other psychoactive drugs. Drug use, due to its disinhibiting effect, may and clearly sometimes does reduce rates of compliance with 'safer sex' guide-lines designed to prevent the transmission of HIV infection. These general conclusions are the point of departure for the following ten chapters, which describe sex workers (and in some cases their clients) in relation to alcohol and other drug use and the growing risks of HIV infection.

Acknowledgements

Some of the material cited in this chapter has previously been published in a review in the *British Journal of Addiction* (Plant, M.L., *et al.* 1989). The Journal's Editor, Professor Griffith Edwards, is thanked for permission to reproduce and paraphrase from that review.

References

Adlaf, E.M. and Smart, R.G. (1983) 'Risk-taking and drug use behaviour: an examination', *Drug and Alcohol Dependence* 11: 287–96.

Allen, D.M. (1980) 'Young male prostitutes: a psychosocial study', *Archives of Sexual Behavior* 9: 399–425.

Beckman, L.J. (1979) 'Reported effects of alcohol on the sexual feelings and behavior of women alcoholics and non alcoholics', *Journal of Studies on Alcohol* 40: 272–82.

Bradbeer, C.S., Thin, R.N., Tan, T., and Thirumoorthy, T. (1988) 'Prophylaxis against infection in Singaporean prostitutes', *Genitourinary Medicine* 64: 52–3.

Brain, P.E. (ed.) (1986) *Alcohol and Aggression*, London: Croom Helm.

Bush, P.J. (1980) *Drugs, Alcohol and Sex*, New York: Marek.

Cavan, S. (1966) *Liquor License: An Ethnography of Bar Behavior*, Chicago: Aldine.

Centers for Disease Control (1987) 'Antibody to human immunodeficiency virus in female prostitutes', *Morbidity and Mortality Weekly Report* 157–61.

Coles, R. and Stokes, G. (1985) *Sex and the American Teenager*, New York: Harper & Row.

Collins, J.J., jun. (ed.) (1982) *Drinking and Crime*, London: Tavistock.

Connaughton, J.F., jun., Reeser, D., Schut, J. *et al.* (1977) 'Perinatal addiction: outcome and management', *American Journal of Obstetrics and Gynaecology* 129: 679–86.

Cooper, D.A. and Dodds, A.J. (1986) 'AIDS and prostitutes' (letter), *Medical Journal of Australia* 145: 59.

Coutinho, R.A., van Andel, R.L.M., and Rysdyk, T.J. (1988) 'Role of male prostitutes in spread of sexually transmitted diseases and human immunodeficiency virus' (letter), *Genitourinary Medicine* 64: 207–8.

Dan, M. and Rock, M. (1987) 'HIV antibodies in drug-addicted prostitutes' (letter), *Journal of the American Medical Association* 257: 1047.

Darrow, W.W. (1984) 'Prostitution and sexually transmitted diseases', in K.K. Holmes, P.-A. Mardh, P.E. Sparling, and P.J. Wiesner (eds) *Sexually Transmitted Diseases*, New York: McGraw-Hill, pp. 109–15.

Datesman, S.K. (1981) 'Women, crime and drugs', in J.A. Inciardi (ed.) *The Drugs-Crime Connection*, Beverly Hills, Calif.: Sage, pp. 85–104.

D'Costa, L.J., Plummer, F.A., Bowmer, I., Fransen, L., Piot, P., Ronald, A.R., and Nsanze, H. (1985) 'Prostitutes are a major reservoir of sexually transmitted diseases in Nairobi, Kenya', *Sexually Transmitted Diseases* 12: 64–7.

Des Jarlais, D.C., Wish, E., Friedman, S.R., Stoneburner, R.L., Yancovitz, F., Midlhan, D., El-Sadr, W., Brady, E., and Cuadrado, M. (1987) 'Intravenous drug users and the heterosexual transmission of the acquired immunodeficiency syndrome', *New York State Journal of Medicine* 87: 283–6.

Ellinwood, E.J., jun., Smith, W.G., and Vaillant, G.E. (1966) 'Narcotic addiction in males and females: a comparison', *International Journal of the Addictions* 1: 33–45.

Flavin, D.K. and Frances, R.J. (1987) 'Risk-taking behavior: substance abuse disorders and the acquired immune deficiency syndrome', *Advances in Alcohol and Substance Abuse* 6: 23–32.

Gagnon, J.H., Lindenbaum, S., Morton, J.L., May, R.M., Menkin, J., Turner, C.F., and Zabins, L.S. (1989) 'Sexual behaviour and AIDS', in C.F. Turner, H.G. Miller, and L.E. Moses (eds) *AIDS, Sexual Behavior and Intravenous Drug Use*, Washington, DC: National Academy Press, pp. 63–185.

Goldberg, D.J., Green, S.T., Kingdom, J.C.P. *et al.* (1988) 'HIV infection among female drug-abusing prostitutes in Greater Glasgow', *Communicable Diseases (Scotland)*, Bulletin 88/12: 1–3.

Goldstein, P.J. (1979) *Prostitution and Drugs*, Lexington: Lexington Books.

Harvey, G.M. and Beckman, L.J. (1986) 'Alcohol consumption, female sexual behavior and contraceptive use', *Journal of Studies on Alcohol* 47: 327–32.

Hingson, R.W., Strunin, L., Berlin, B.M., and Meeren, T. (1989) 'Beliefs about AIDS, use of alcohol, drugs and unprotected sex among Massachusetts adolescents', paper presented at Alcohol Epidemiology Symposium, Kettil Bruun Society, Maastricht, June.

James, J., Gosho, C., and Wohl, R.W. (1979) 'The relationship between female criminality and drug use', *International Journal of the Addictions* 14: 115–229.

James, J.J., Morgenstern, M.A., and Hatten, J.A. (1986) 'HTLV III/LAV antibody-positive soldiers in Berlin' (letter), *New England Journal of Medicine* 314: 55.

Jessor, R. and Jessor, S.L. (1977) *Problem Behavior and Psychosocial Development: A Longitudinal Study of Youth*, New York: Academic Press.

JIF (1947) 'Alcoholism: an occupational disease of seamen', *Quarterly Journal of Studies on Alcohol* 8: 498–505.

Johnson, A.M. (1988) 'Heterosexual transmission of human immune deficiency virus', *British Medical Journal* 296: 1017–20.

Johnson, S.D., Gibson, L., and Linden, R. (1978) 'Alcohol and rape in Winnipeg 1966–1975', *Journal of Studies on Alcohol* 39: 1877–94.

Klassen, A. and Wilsnack, S.C. (1986) 'Sexual experience and drinking among women in a U.S. national survey', *Archives of Sexual Behavior* 15: 363–92.

Kreiss, J.K., Koech, D., Plummer, F.A., Holmes, K.K., Lightfoote, M., Piot, P., Ronald, A.R., Ndinya-Achola, J.O., D'Costa, L.J., Roberts, P., Ngugi, E.N., and Quinn, T.C. (1986) 'AIDS virus in Nairobi prostitutes', *New England Journal of Medicine* 314: 414–18.

Lang, A. (1985) 'The social psychology of drinking and human sexuality', *Journal of Drug Issues* 15: 273–89.

Lange, W.R., Snyder, F.R., Lozovsky, D., Kaistha, V., Kaczaniuk, A., and Jaffe, J.H. (1987) 'HIV infection in Baltimore: antibody seroprevalence rates amongst parenteral drug abusers and prostitutes', *Maryland Medical Journal* 36: 757–61.

Leigh, B.C. (1988) 'Drinking and sex: background issues', paper presented at Alcohol Epidemiology Section, Kettil Bruun Society/ICAA, Berkeley, California, June.

Lisansky, E.S. (1957) 'Alcoholism in women: social and psychological concomitants, 1. Social history data', *Quarterly Journal of Studies on Alcohol* 18: 588–623.

MacAndrew, C. and Edgerton, R.R. (1969) *Drunken Comportment: A Social Explanation*, Chicago: Aldine.

McLeod, E. (1982) *Women Working: Prostitution Now*, London: Croom Helm.

Maerov, A.S. (1965) 'Prostitution: a survey and review of 20 cases', *Psychiatric Quarterly* 39: 675–701.

Mann, J., Quinn, T.C., Piot, P., Bosenge, N., Nzilambi, N., Kalala, M.,

Francis, H., Colebunders, R.L., Byers, R., Kasa Azila, P., Kabeya, N., and Curran, J.W. (1987) 'Condom use and HIV infection among prostitutes in Zaire', *New England Journal of Medicine* 316: 345.

Marshall, N. and Hendtlass, J. (1986) 'Drugs and prostitution', *Journal of Drug Issues* 16: 237–48.

Martin, C.A. and Martin, W. (1980) 'Opiate dependence in women', in O.J. Kalant (ed.) *Alcohol and Drug Problems in Women*, New York: Plenum, pp. 465–85.

Masterton, R.G. and Strike, P.W. (1988) 'Sexually transmitted diseases in a British military force in peacetime Europe, 1970–83', *Genitourinary Medicine* 64: 54–8.

Medhus, A. (1975) 'Venereal diseases among female alcoholics', *Scandinavian Journal of Social Medicine* 3: 29–33.

Neequaye, A.R., Neequaye, J., Mingle, J.A., and Ofori Adjei, D.O. (1986) 'Preponderance of females with AIDS in Ghana' (letter), *Lancet* 2: 978.

O'Farrell, J.J., Weyand, C.A., and Logan, D. (1983) *Alcohol and Sexuality: An Annotated Bibliography on Alcohol Use, Alcoholism and Human Sexual Behavior*, Phoenix, Ariz.: Oryx.

Papaevangelou, G., Roumeliotou-Karayannis, A., Kallinikos, G., and Papoutsakis, G. (1985) 'LAV/HTLV-III infection in female prostitutes' (letter), *Lancet* 2: 1018.

Perlmutter, J.F. (1967) 'Drug addiction in pregnant women', *American Journal of Obstetrics and Gynaecology* 99: 569–72.

Plant, M.L., Plant, M.A., Peck, D.F., and Setters, J. (1989) 'The sex industry, alcohol and illicit drugs: implications for the spread of HIV infection', *British Journal of Addiction* 84: 53–9.

Rada, R.T. (1975) 'Alcoholism and forcible rape', *American Journal of Psychiatry* 132: 444–6.

Reinarman, C. and Leigh, B.C. (1988) 'Culture, cognition and disinhibition: notes on sexuality and alcohol in the age of AIDS', *Contemporary Drug Problems* 14 (in press).

Richardson, D.C. and Campbell, J.L. (1982) 'Alcohol and rape: the effect of alcohol on attributions of blame for rape', *Personality and Social Psychology Bulletin* 6: 51–5.

Ridlon, F.V. (1988) *A Fallen Angel: The Status Insularity of the Female Alcoholic*, London: Bucknell University Press.

Robertson, J.A. and Plant, M.A. (1988) 'Alcohol, sex and risks of HIV infection', *Drug and Alcohol Dependence* 22: 75–8.

Room, R. (1985) *AIDS and Alcohol: Epidemiological and Behavioral Aspects*, paper prepared for National Institute on Alcohol and Alcoholism Consultation on AIDS and Alcohol, 4–5 November, Berkeley, California, Alcohol Research Group.

Room, R. and Collins, G. (eds) (1983) *Alcohol and Disinhibition: Nature and*

Meaning of the Link, Research Monograph No. 12, Rockville, Md: National Institute on Alcohol Abuse and Alcoholism.

Rosenbaum, M. (1981) *Women on Heroin*, New Brunswick: Rutgers University Press.

Rosenberg, M.J. and Weiner, J.M. (1988) 'Prostitutes and AIDS: a health department priority', *American Journal of Public Health* 78: 418–23.

Sarler, C. (1987) 'A city at risk', *Sunday Times Magazine* (London) 21 June: 24–8.

Shilts, R. (1987) *And the Band Played On*, Harmondsworth, Middx: Penguin.

Silbert, M.H. and Pines, A.M. (1981) 'Occupational hazards of street prostitutes', *Criminal Justice and Behaviour* 8: 395–9.

Simoes, E.A.F., Babu, P.G., John, T.J., Nirmala, S., Solomon, S., Lakshminarayana, C.S., and Quinn, T.C. (1987) 'Evidence for HTLV-III infection in prostitutes in Tamil Nadu (India)', *Indian Journal of Medical Research* 85: 335–8.

Smart, C. (1985) 'Researching prostitution: some problems for feminist research', *Humanity and Society* 8: 407–13.

Smith, G.L. and Smith, K.F. (1986) 'Lack of HIV infection and condom use in licensed prostitutes', *Lancet* 2: 1392.

Soloman, D. and Andrews, G. (eds) (1973) *Drugs and Sexuality*, St Albans, Herts: Panther.

Stall, R. (1988) 'The prevention of HIV infection associated with drug and alcohol use during sexual activity', in L. Siegal (ed.) *AIDS and Substance Abuse*, New York: Harrington Park Press, pp. 73–88.

Stall, R., McKusick, L., Wiley, J., Coates, T., and Ostrow, D. (1986) 'Alcohol and drug use during sexual activity and compliance with safer sex guidelines for AIDS: the AIDS Behavioral Research Project', *Health Education Quarterly* 13: 359–71.

Stall R. and Ostrow, D.A. (1989) 'Intravenous drug use, the combination of drugs and sexual activity and HIV infection among gay and bisexual men: the San Francisco Men's Health Study', *Journal of Drug Issues* 19: 57–73.

Van den Hoek, J.A.R., Coutinho, R.A., Van Haastrecht, H.J.A., Van Zadelhoff, A.W., and Goudsmit, J. (1987) 'Prevalence and risk factors of HIV infections among drug users and drug-using prostitutes in Amsterdam', *AIDS* 2: 55–60.

Van de Perre, P., Clumeck, N., Careal, M., Nzabihimana, E., Robert-Guroff, M., De Mol, P., Freyens, P., Butzler, J.-P., Gallo, R.C., and Kanyamupira, J.-B. (1985) 'Female prostitutes: a risk group for infection with human T-cell lymphotropic virus type III', *Lancet* 2: 524–7.

Weisberg, D.K. (1985) *Children of the Night: A Study of Adolescent Prostitution*, Lexington: Lexington Books.

Wilsnack, S.C. (1984) 'Drinking, sexuality and dysfunction in women', in S.C. Wilsnack and L.J. Beckman (eds) *Alcohol Problems in Women*, New

York: Guilford Press, pp. 187–227.

Wilson, G.T. and Lawson, D. (1976a) 'The effects of alcohol on sexual arousal in women', *Journal of Abnormal Psychology* 89: 489–97.

Wilson, G.T. and Lawson, D.G. (1976b) 'Expectancies, alcohol and sexual arousal in male social drinkers', *Journal of Abnormal Psychology* 89: 587–94.

Chapter two

Prostitution, intravenous drug use, and HIV-1 in the United States

William Darrow and the Centers for Disease Control Collaborative Group for the Study of HIV-1 in Selected Women[1]

Introduction

Prostitution has been defined as the exchange of sexual services for money or things of monetary value, such as drugs (Darrow 1984: 109–16). One of the things of no monetary value that can be exchanged between a prostitute and a client is a sexually transmitted disease. To prevent venereal infections, novice prostitutes are taught to inspect clients for signs of gonorrhoea, syphilis, and other sexually transmitted diseases (Heyl 1979). If a suspicious discharge or lesion in the genital area is observed, the prostitute often asks for a second opinion (if a madam or co-worker is available). In many instances, clients are instructed to obtain treatment at a clinic or from a doctor before they are serviced. This system of sexually transmitted disease prevention seems to be most effective in brothels where venereal infections seldom occur (Nayyar *et al.* 1986; Ruijs *et al.* 1988).

[1] Deborah A. Deppe, Charles A. Schable, Stephen C. Hadler, Sandra A. Larsen, Rima F. Khabbaz, Harold W. Jaffe, Center for Infectious Diseases, Centers for Disease Control, Atlanta, Georgia 30333.
Judith B. Cohen, Constance B. Wofsy, University of California, San Francisco, California 94110.
John F. French, New Jersey State Department of Health, Trenton, New Jersey 08625-0362.
Parkish S. Gill, University of Southern California Cancer Center, Los Angeles, California 90033.
John J. Potterat, El Paso County Health Department, Colorado Springs, Colorado 80909.
Otto Ravenholt, Clark County Health District, Las Vegas, Nevada 89127.
R. Keith Sikes, Georgia Department of Human Resources, Atlanta, Georgia 30309.
John J. Witte, Florida Department of Health and Rehabilitative Services, Tallahassee, Florida 32301.
Note Correspondence should be directed to Dr William Darrow, Chief, Social and Behavioral Studies Section, Epidemiology Branch, Division of HIV/AIDS, Center for Infectious Diseases, Centers for Disease Control, Atlanta, Georgia 30333, USA.

Sexually transmitted diseases are more frequently found among female prostitutes who are street-walkers than among other women who have unprotected coitus with large numbers of men (Wooley *et al.* 1988; Reeves and Quiroz 1987). Recent outbreaks of penicillinase-producing *Neisseria gonorrhoeae* (PPNG) in Los Angeles (CDC 1983), Rotterdam, Netherlands (Nayyar *et al.* 1980), and Shreveport, Louisiana (Handsfield *et al.* 1982), have involved female prostitutes. As noted in Chapter 1, infection with human immunodeficiency virus type 1 (HIV-1), the virus that causes AIDS, has occurred in prostitutes in many parts of the world (Day 1988; Padian 1988; Piot *et al.* 1987). This chapter describes the methods and presents results from a multicentre study of HIV-1 infection in female prostitutes in the USA.

Heterosexual transmission of HIV-1

Studies of spouses of transfusion recipients (Peterman *et al.* 1986) and the sexual partners of other heterosexual men and women (Fischl *et al.* 1987) have shown that HIV-1 can be transmitted from men to women, and from women to men, during unprotected vaginal intercourse (Padian 1987). Some uninfected spouses have had hundreds of sexual exposures with their HIV-1 seropositive sex partners and not become infected, but one wife developed antibodies to HIV-1 after a single vaginal exposure to her infected husband (Peterman *et al.* 1986). The reasons for varying susceptibility are unknown at this time, but may be related to trauma, coexisting genital ulcer disease, or other co-factors in either the host or the uninfected partner (Holmberg *et al.* 1989).

Seroprevalence surveys for antibody to HIV-1 in women with histories of prostitution have shown varying results since testing began in 1984. This is elaborated in Table 2.1. In sub-Saharan Africa, where HIV-1 is thought to have been transmitted primarily through hetero-sexual exposure, levels of infection have ranged from none of thirty prostitutes in Monrovia, Liberia (Mintz *et al.* 1988), and none of fifty-six in Johannesburg, South Africa (Schoub *et al.* 1987), to twenty-nine (88 per cent) of thirty-three female prostitutes recruited from a sexually transmitted disease clinic in Ngoma, Rwanda (Van de Perre *et al.* 1985), HIV-1 seropositive. HIV-1 seroprevalence appears to be higher among prostitutes in central and east Africa[1] than elsewhere, and lower among those who use condoms frequently (for at least half of sexual exposures) (Mann *et al.* 1987), have higher socio-economic status (Kreiss *et al.* 1986), and have not been recruited from sexually transmitted disease clinics in areas with high levels of HIV-1 infection.

Table 2.1 Antibody to human immunodeficiency virus type-1 in female prostitutes

Investigators	Study site	HIV-1 seropositive N	Total tested N	HIV-1 seropositive %
Africa				
Mintz *et al.*	Monrovia, Liberia	0	30	0
Schoub *et al.*	Johannesburg, RSA	0	56	0
Chikwem *et al.*	Borno, Nigeria	4	767	0.5
Neequaye *et al.*	Accra, Ghana	1	98	1
Fox *et al.*	Djibouti			
	October 1987	3	66	5
	June 1987	7	78	9
Nzilambi *et al.*	Equateur, Zaire	32	283	11
Denis *et al.*	Ivory Coast			
	Tortiya	9	131	7
	Abidjan	20	102	20
Hudson *et al.*	South-west Uganda	9	36	25
Mann *et al.*	Kinshasa, Zaire	101	377	27
Kreiss *et al.*	Nairobi, Kenya			
	High status	8	26	31
	Lower status	42	64	66
Chiphangwi *et al.*	Southern Malawi	77	167	46
Van de Perre *et al.*	Ngoma, Rwanda	29	33	88
Asia and Western Pacific				
Chen *et al.*	Taipei, Taiwan	0	615	0
Philpot *et al.*	Sydney, Australia	0	387	0
Traisupa *et al.*	Bangkok, Thailand	0	2880	0
Yoshida *et al.*	Fukuoka, Japan	0	237	0
John *et al.*	Tamilnadu, India	31	1369	2
Europe				
Barton *et al.*	London, England: 1985	0	50	0
Day *et al.*	London, England: 1987	3	187	2
Brenky-Faudeux *et al.*	Paris, France	0	56	0
Krogsgaard *et al.*	Copenhagen, Denmark	0	101	0
Smith and Smith	Nuremberg, W. Germany	0	399	0

Table 2.1 (continued) Antibody to human immunodeficiency virus type-1 in female prostitutes

Investigators	Study site	HIV-1 seropositive N	Total tested N	HIV-1 seropositive %
Tirelli *et al.*	Pordenone, Italy			
	No intravenous drug use	0	10	0
	Intravenous drug user	10	14	71
Luthy *et al.*	Zurich, Switzerland			
	No intravenous drug use	1	103	1
	Intravenous drug user	14	18	78
Schultz *et al.*	Six W. German cities	17	2000	1
Papaevangelou *et al.*	Athens, Greece	12	350	3
Van den Hoek *et al.*	Amsterdam, Netherlands			
	Intravenous drug user: 1983–84	12	52	23
	Intravenous drug user: 1985–87	34	110	31
North America				
Hammond *et al.*	Manitoba, Canada	1	1446	0.07
Seidlin *et al.*	New York City, USA	1	78	1
South America				
Bartoloni *et al.*	Santa Cruz, Bolivia	0	295	0
Golenbock *et al.*	Callao, Peru	0	140	0
Reeves *et al.*	Panama City, Panama	0	183	0
Cortes *et al.*	Mines Gerais, Brazil	0	86	0
	Rio de Janeiro			
	Upper Class	0	47	0
	Middle Class	0	20	0
	Lower Class	3	34	9

In Europe, where homosexual exposures and intravenous drug abuse are major risk factors for HIV-1 infection, none of fifty prostitutes tested in London (Barton *et al.* 1985), none of fifty-six tested in Paris (Brenky-Faudeux and Fribourg-Blanc 1985), and none of 101 tested in Copenhagen, Denmark (Krogsgaard *et al.* 1986), had antibody to

21

HIV-1, but ten (71 per cent) of fourteen prostitutes who used drugs intravenously in Pordenone, Italy (Tirelli *et al.* 1985), and fourteen (78 per cent) of eighteen intravenous drug users in Zurich, Switzerland (Luthy *et al.* 1987), were infected. A more recent study in London found three HIV-1-infected prostitutes, one of whom had no history of needle sharing (Day *et al.* 1988). Seventeen (less than 1 per cent) of nearly 2000 registered prostitutes in six West German cities were HIV seropositive; half the infected women used drugs intravenously (Schultz *et al.* 1986). In Athens, Greece, twelve (3 per cent) of 350 registered prostitutes were HIV seropositive; none had injected drugs (Papaevangelou *et al.* 1988).

Data regarding HIV-1 seropositivity in men who have had sexual exposures with female prostitutes have shown inconsistent results. Among HIV-1 seropositive male sexually transmitted disease clinic patients in Nairobi (Simonsen *et al.* 1988) and heterosexual European men with AIDS who had returned from Africa, sexual contact with a prostitute was a common finding (Vittecoq *et al.* 1987). However, few HIV-1 positive heterosexual men in New York City sexually transmitted disease clinics have reported sexual exposures with prostitutes (Rabkin *et al.* 1987).

Centers for Disease Control multi-centre study

To assess the prevalence of antibody to HIV-1 in female prostitutes and to identify risk factors for HIV-1 infection in this population, officials at the Centers for Disease Control (CDC) proposed a multi-centre, cross-sectional comparative study of women with recent histories of prostitution. The Centers for Disease Control called for this line of inquiry as the Federal public health agency responsible for surveillance, epidemiological and laboratory studies, and the prevention of HIV-1 disease in the United States. An announcement of available funds to support this research was published in the Federal Register on 25 July 1985. State and municipal agencies, public and private organizations were eligible to compete for a limited number of co-operative agreements.

Sufficient resources were available to make awards to the five applicants with the highest priority ratings: the University of California at San Francisco, Florida Department of Health and Rehabilitative Services, New Jersey Department of Health, University of Southern California Cancer Center, and the Georgia Department of Human Resources. In addition, the El Paso County Health Department (Colorado Springs, Colorado) and the Clark County Health District (Las Vegas,

Nevada) agreed to participate without Federal support. After co-operative agreements were negotiated, investigators were invited to participate in a workshop at the Centers for Disease Control in Atlanta in October 1985 to develop a research protocol and standardized data-collection instruments that could be used in all research sites.

Drafts of the protocol and instruments were submitted to the Institutional Review Board at the Centers for Disease Control in November 1985. Reviews by local Institutional Review Boards were also requested to ensure that the rights of human subjects would be adequately protected by researchers in all study sites. The Institutional Review Board at the Centers for Disease Control approved a revised protocol and instruments in February 1986, but requested additional reviews from the Office for Protection from Research Risks for the two sites that sought to recruit incarcerated women. Data collection commenced at all sites in May 1986 after an amended protocol and consent forms were approved by the Office for Protection from Research Risks.

Study participants

Any woman, 18 years of age or older, who reported engaging in prostitution at least once since 1 January 1978 was eligible to participate. 'Prostitution' was defined as the exchange of physical sexual services for money or drugs. No attempt was made to obtain a representative sample of prostitutes because there was no way such a sample could be drawn. However, each site was encouraged to enrol as many eligible women as possible from a variety of settings.

Although the request for proposals published in the Federal Register stressed the importance of recruiting a diversity of research subjects, and collaborators were subsequently encouraged to try a variety of recruitment strategies, investigators tended to select potential partici-pants in limited ways. In northern New Jersey, women were most likely to be recruited from a methadone maintenance clinic in Jersey City and from a sexually transmitted diseases clinic or off the street in Newark, Paterson, Trenton, and Atlantic City. Advertisements were placed in tabloid newspapers in Atlanta, but most women were recruited while on the streets or through a social network of call girls in Georgia (Leonard *et al.* 1988). Almost all of the Florida respondents were enrolled while incarcerated at the Women's Detention Center in Miami. Most of the women enrolled in Colorado Springs were seen at a public clinic for the treatment of sexually transmitted diseases. Prostitutes tested in southern Nevada were either applying for a licence to work in a brothel or were already employed. In the San Francisco Bay area, eligible participants were primarily recruited off the street. In Los Angeles County, women who, while incarcerated at the Sybil Brand Institute, admitted to experiences in prostitution were invited to participate. Interpretation of results from the Centers for Disease Control multi-centre study must be made with extreme caution because of the varied methods used by different investigators to recruit potential participants.

Eligible women who expressed an interest in participating in the study were told that they would not be identified by name. In New Jersey and San Francisco, participants were offered modest reimbursement for their involvement. No pecuniary compensation was given in other places. Investigators who provided money to research subjects felt it was important to reward women for their time and trouble; those who chose not to pay participants felt that AIDS prevention messages, private counselling, and anonymous testing services provided sufficient incentive for enrolment. Anecdotal information suggests that most women appreciated the concern expressed by research staff members and would have participated without monetary inducement. However, all who were offered payment took it.

Data were not collected on the number of eligible women available for study or the number who were approached and then refused. Most of those who were given the opportunity to participate in the study agreed to do so. Those who had never injected drugs were more likely to object to the requirement that a specimen of blood be obtained by venipuncture. Few seemed to be concerned about the confidentiality of the personal information collected during interviews. Almost all were worried about the possibility that they might be infected with HIV-1.

Informed consent

Formal procedures were used to assure each potential participant that participation in the study was entirely voluntary. Furthermore, investigators were obliged to make every effort to protect research subjects from potential harm. After the consent form and procedures were modified to meet the concerns of all the Institutional Review Boards involved and also of the special panel assembled by the Office for the Protection from Research Risks to safeguard the rights of prisoners, the consent form was printed and distributed to potential participants. To avoid stigmatization, potential research subjects were told they should not participate if they were uninterested or thought they were ineligible.

The consent form contained all the elements required for research with human subjects. It identified the local agency and the Centers for Disease Control as co-sponsors of the study. It described the purposes of the investigation and procedures used to collect data: personal interview, limited physical examination, and blood specimen (about one tablespoon) to be collected by sticking a needle into a vein in the arm. It listed possible benefits and harm, and told the potential participant where she could go for further information about the study, her test results, and her health status.

Participants were repeatedly told that the interview guide, clinical findings sheet, and tube of blood would be identified by a pre-assigned patient number. No names or other personal identifiers would be recorded. To obtain her results, each participant would be required to know the number she was given, or would have to give a study team member some other identification. For example, investigators in San Francisco suggested a code number composed of elements of the mother's first name, father's first name, state of birth, month and day of birth. If an eligible woman chose to participate, she was asked to check a box on the consent form. The study staff member was then required to sign his or her name to the form to certify that informed consent had been obtained. A copy of the consent form, with the pre-assigned patient number stamped on it, was given to the participant.

Data collection and analysis

After the conditions for participation were explained to eligible women and informed consent was obtained, a specimen of blood (10 ml) was drawn by venipuncture. The mouth, face, hands, arms, and lymph nodes were examined for signs of HIV-1 infection and needle marks suggesting intravenous drug use, and a private, confidential interview was conducted. The tube of blood was identified by the patient number assigned to the participant, the Centers for Disease Control AIDS project number (72), and the date the specimen was collected. Findings from a brief medical history and examination were recorded on a clinical findings sheet. Socio-demographic characteristics and self-reported behaviours were indicated on an interview guide. The clinical findings sheet and interview guide also identified the respondent by her pre-assigned patient number.

Instruments

The clinical findings sheet showed the study participant's number, date of examination, self-reported symptoms that might be associated with HIV-1 infection, and results of a very limited physical examination. Symptoms noticed in the past five years by the respondent, such as 'shortness of breath, so bad that you could not walk up stairs, for two weeks or longer' and 'unintentional weight loss (10 or more lbs) which was not regained', were recorded by the month and year first noted, and by whether the participant still had the symptoms. If any one of the thirteen symptoms reviewed had been noticed, the respondent was asked if medical care had been sought and, if so, what diagnosis she had been given. Then height, weight, and clinical observations were noted. Signs were restricted to palpable nodes at least 1 cm in diameter, skin lesions, needle tracks, and white patches in the mouth suggesting thrush or oral candidiasis. Adenopathy was specified by right or left cervical, occipital, supraclavicular, axillary, or epitrochlear node. If any abnormality was detected, the participant was advised to seek a more thorough examination at her earliest convenience. Treatment was not provided as part of the study.

The interview guide began with questions about the sociodemographic characteristics of the respondent: date and place of birth, race and ethnicity, and possible occupational exposure to blood as a health care worker. In the medical history section, questions were asked about previous tests for HIV-1 antibody, receipt of blood products or transfusions since 1978, and histories of hepatitis B, syphilis, and gonorrhoea. Questions were also raised about number of pregnancies, pregnancy outcome, and the use of contraceptive agents in the past five years. Few questions were asked about drug use: attendance at a 'shooting gallery', injection practices, and history of needle sharing. No questions were asked about the consumption of alcoholic beverages or use of specific psychoactive substances. Over half the questions focused on the participant's sexual history and sexual practices with both clients and 'non-paying' partners.

Most of the questions in the sexual history and practices section required a numerical response. For example, respondents were asked to give their age (in years) at first intercourse with a male and the number of months that they had 'worked as a prostitute'. Although it was difficult for many to give the precise number of different males with whom they had ever engaged in sexual intercourse, they could usually count the number who never paid.

Instructions were provided to assist the interviewers in arriving at estimates of total numbers of partners and frequencies of specific sexual activities. For example, interviewers would generally begin by talking with the respondent about a recent week or typical month, and then try to trace the respondent's history by noting changes in residence, marital status, or other critical life events. After an estimate was made, the interviewer would probe further until the respondent would agree with a number or per cent that seemed accurate, or 'about right'. The estimate was then recorded on the interview guide.

Analyses

Line listings of laboratory data from the Centers for Disease Control were reported to collaborators by patient number once a week and compared by investigators to results obtained in local laboratories. Differences were resolved by retesting specimens, usually in both places. Confirmed results were available to study participants who contacted investigators and gave their patient numbers or other appropriate identifiers. Laboratory results were subsequently linked to clinical findings and self-reports recorded on the interview guides sent to the Centers for Disease Control for key-punching and computer-assisted analyses. These three files were merged by patient number and analysed using univariate and other statistical procedures described in the Statistical Analysis System.

Laboratory tests

Aliquots of blood (at least 5 ml) were sent to the Centers for Disease Control for laboratory analyses and storage. Serum was tested for antibody to HIV-1 by the enzyme immunosorbent assay (Abbott Laboratories or Genetic Systems); all positive enzyme immunosorbent assays were repeated and confirmed by Western blot (CDC 1989b). Evidence of syphilitic infection was determined by the rapid plasma reagin test (American Public Health Association in press) and microhemagglutination assay; discrepancies were resolved by a fluorescent treponemal antibody absorption test. Commercially available radioimmunoassays (Abbott Laboratories) attempted to detect hepatitis B surface antigen (Ausria III), hepatitis B surface antibody (Ausab), and hepatitis B core antibody (Corab). Residual specimens were also tested for HTLV-I/II by an enzyme immunoassay, and reactive sera were further tested by

Western blot and radioimmunoprecipitation assays for antibody to *gag* and *env* gene products (Khabbaz in press). Finally, selected specimens from all sites except Miami were screened for herpes simplex virus by enzyme immunoassay; sera positive by enzyme immunosorbent assay were then tested for type 1 and type 2 antibodies by immunodot assays using affinity-purified glycoprotein G from type-specific antigens (Lee *et al.* 1985).

Results

Over half (56 per cent) of the 1396 research participants had a seromarker for hepatitis B, 26 per cent of those tested for syphilis had been infected, and 12 per cent were seropositive for antibody to HIV-1. This is shown in Table 2.2. However, seropositivity for HIV-1 ranged from zero in southern Nevada, where most of the women enrolled were employed in brothels outside Las Vegas, to almost 50 per cent in northern New Jersey, where most of the women studied were street-walkers, and many of the street-walkers were enrolled through a methadone maintenance clinic.

Table 2.2 CDC collaborative study of female prostitutes in the United States: antibody to HIV type-1 by reported drug use

Study site	Intravenous drug use		No intravenous drug use		HIV-1 seropositive	Total tested	
	N	%	N	%	N	N	%
Southern Nevada	0/10	(0)	0/27	(0)	0	37	(0)
Atlanta	1/65	(1.5)	0/58	(0)	1	123	(0.8)
Colorado Springs	2/52	(3.8)	0/46	(0)	2	98	(2.0)
Los Angeles	6/163	(3.7)	6/137	(4.4)	12	300	(4.0)
San Francisco	10/101	(9.9)	0/111	(0)	10	212	(4.7)
Miami	46/173	(26.6)	20/267	(7.5)	66	440	(15.0)
Southern New Jersey	6/14	(42.9)	0/14	(0)	6	28	(21.4)
Northern New Jersey	67/115	(58.3)	8/43	(18.6)	75	158	(47.5)
Total	138/693	(19.9)	34/703	(4.8)	172	1396	(12.3)

Risk factors for antibody to HIV-1 included many variables associated with intravenous drug use, especially attendance at a 'shooting gallery', injecting drugs thirty or more times in a month of drug use, and having injected drugs for at least twelve months during the past five years. After controlling for study site in multivariate analysis, the most significant variables associated with HIV-1 antibody were (1) a history of intravenous drug use, (2) a seromarker for hepatitis B, and (3) being a member of a racial or ethnic minority group (Black or Hispanic). However, variations were noted by research site. For example in Los Angeles, white, Asian, and Native American women who had no evidence of intravenous drug abuse had the same prevalence of HIV-1 infection (7.0 per cent seropositive) as Black and Hispanic women who had used drugs parenterally (6.3 per cent seropositive).

To understand levels of HIV-1 infection in different communities, it is necessary to appreciate the social and behavioural processes that facilitate or impede disease transmission. The CDC multi-centre study was designed to gather elementary descriptive data on social and behavioural variables, particularly the sexual, intravenous drug use, prophylactic, and contraceptive behaviours that might be related to HIV-1 acquisition or prevention. Women who engaged in prostitution to support their drug habits were found to have different sociodemographic characteristics and behavioural patterns from those who had no evidence of intravenous drug use. Some of these self-reported patterns of behaviour appeared to put intravenous drug-using prostitutes at increased risk of HIV-1 infection.

Drug-injecting prostitutes enrolled in the CDC multi-centre study were significantly older women who were more likely to seek clients in public places and were more likely to be white (not black or hispanic) than prostitutes who had no evidence of active drug use. This is elaborated in Table 2.3.

Importantly, they were also more likely (51.4 per cent) than women with no evidence of intravenous drug use (12.2 per cent) to have a husband or boy-friend who injected drugs. Additionally, they were significantly less likely to report condom use during vaginal intercourse with clients and were slightly more likely to report a history of anal intercourse. However, no differences were found between the two groups with respect to numbers of sexual partners per month or frequencies of orogenital exposures. Thus, drug-injecting women who had engaged in prostitution in the United States appeared to be at greater risk of HIV-1 infection than non-injectors for four reasons: (1) their own use of possibly contaminated needles and syringes; (2) unprotected sexual contacts with husbands and boy-friends who were more likely to inject drugs; (3) unprotected vaginal exposures with clients; and (4) anogenital exposures to the retrovirus that causes AIDS.

Table 2.3 Socio-demographic characteristics and sexual practices of prostitutes with evidence and no evidence of intravenous drug use

Self-reported variable	Intravenous drug use %	No intravenous drug use %	Total %
Sociodemographic characteristics			
Born in the USA	95.8	92.8	94.3˙
Black or hispanic	50.8	59.0	54.9˙
25 years or older	68.8	50.5	59.5˙
Sexual practices			
Street prostitution	84.0	74.3	79.2˙
At least 13 years sexually active	58.2	38.6	48.4˙
At least 10 clients per month	82.2	84.7	83.4
At least 33% orogenital past 5 years	86.8	87.9	87.4
Anal intercourse (ever)	38.9	33.7	36.3˙
Husband or boy-friend intravenous drug user	51.4	12.2	31.8˙
Contraception or prophylaxis			
Used oral contraceptive	22.2	29.8	26.0˙
100% condom use last 5 years	3.3	4.8	4.0
100% condom use with clients	33.9	47.8	40.9˙
Pregnant when enrolled	8.4	6.4	7.4

˙ Differences significant.

Another major variable considered in the CDC multi-centre study was location. HIV-1 infections were more common among women enrolled in New Jersey than elsewhere. The higher prevalence observed in prostitutes enrolled there may have reflected the higher rates of AIDS and HIV-1 infection in the north-eastern United States or may have been attributable to a bias in selecting for study more prostitutes infected with HIV-1.

Differences in injection practices reported by drug-injecting prostitutes were examined to see if those in New Jersey might have engaged more frequently in high-risk injection practices. This is shown in Table 2.4.

Table 2.4 Patterns of intravenous drug use in New Jersey and elsewhere

Variable	New Jersey %	Other sites %	Total %
Ever shared a needle	70.7	77.6	76.2
Ever visited a 'shooting gallery'	83.0	55.0	60.3[*]
30 or more injections per month	84.6	68.3	71.4[*]
At least 12 months injecting in past 5 years	92.9	74.3	78.0[*]

[*] Differences significant.

Interestingly, prostitutes in New Jersey were *not* more likely to report ever sharing injecting paraphernalia, but were significantly more likely to have visited a 'shooting gallery' where previously used needles and syringes could be leased, were significantly more likely to have used drugs intravenously at least 30 times per month in the past five years, and were significantly more likely to have injected drugs for at least twelve out of the sixty months before study enrolment. These observations suggest that women who were intravenous drug users were at increased risk of HIV-1 infection because of their unsafe injection practices in places where HIV-1 was prevalent. Preventing intravenous drug-related HIV-1 transmission would help to avoid subsequent perinatal and heterosexual transmission in the United States.

Prospective research

The sample of prostitutes in the CDC multi-centre study was not representative of prostitutes in the United States; the design was cross-sectional and could not measure changes in behaviours or disease trends in response to societal changes; and the validity of data collected during personal interviews could not be assessed. Some women were under the influence of alcohol or illicit drugs at the time of interview (Hampton 1988) and may not have been able to recall events and experiences as clearly as others. Investigators were aware of these and other problems and tried to limit their effects, but could not completely control them. Therefore, findings from the eight-centre study were to be challenged by more rigorous prospective studies designed to take a closer look at prostitutes and their needle-sharing and sexual partners. Funds were available to support follow-up studies in three places: Atlanta, Colorado Springs, and San Francisco.

Researchers in the Department of Sociology at Georgia State University in Atlanta are gathering data on the sexual and drug-using behaviours of male as well as female prostitutes who work in a variety of settings. After consent is obtained, blood is drawn for serological testing; research participants are urged to obtain results twenty-eight days later by their pre-assigned patient numbers from the Fulton County Health Department. In addition, named sex partners are invited (with the consent of the person who identified them) to provide a specimen of blood as well as their histories. Six-month follow-up interviews with enrollees are planned to measure changes in HIV-1 incidence and behaviour. Preliminary baseline results indicate that forty-one (27 per cent) of 152 male 'street hustlers' recruited from two different locations in Atlanta have antibody to HIV-1 (Elifson et al. 1989). The most apparent risk for HIV-1 infection in this population is receptive anal intercourse, not intravenous drug use.

Social networks of sexually transmitted disease (Klovdahl 1985) are the primary focus of intensive research efforts in Colorado Springs to identify the friends, sexual, and drug-sharing partners of women who engage in prostitution. In this prospective study, sociological and epidemiological concepts are being combined with traditional sexually transmitted disease casefinding techniques to learn about possible routes of HIV-1 and other disease transmission. Prostitutes and their clients are recruited from a methadone maintenance clinic, sexually transmitted diseases clinic, and county jail, but their named sexual partners and associates will be selected at random from lists provided by participants. To date, approximately 200 study participants have named over 1400 residents who might be at risk of HIV-1 and other sexually transmitted diseases.

The third study is being conducted in the San Francisco Bay area where investigators are now following women in the sex industry and their steady sex partners. During 1986–87, ten prostitutes were infected with HIV-1; all used drugs intravenously. Recently, prostitution has spread to inner-city neighbourhoods where women report exchanging sexual services for the 'crack' derivative form of cocaine or for money to buy crack. Some of these women have antibody to HIV-1, and no evidence of intravenous drug use. This study is documenting the diffusion of crack smoking throughout the Bay area, and the increasing incidence of prostitution and HIV-1 infections that seem to follow.

Summary and recommendations

Research on prostitution, intravenous drug use, and HIV-1 infection in the United States is showing great variations in seroprevalence rates among women who practise prostitution in different locales. Rates are clearly higher in the New York City metropolitan area than elsewhere. Furthermore, antibody to HIV-1 infection in the CDC multi-centre study showed that the risks for HIV-1 infection increased with more frequent intravenous drug use and opportunities for using unsterile injection paraphernalia. Public health interventions must address the problem of intravenous drug use to prevent further transmission of HIV-1 in the United States.

Implications for public policy

Although the prevalence of HIV-1 infection in prostitutes with no evidence of intravenous drug use is relatively low in the United States, compared to the prevalence among other women of reproductive age it is high (CDC 1989a: 8–9). Therefore, prostitutes and their sexual partners must become aware of the increased risk of HIV-1 infection and be encouraged to take adequate precautions. One obvious way of reducing the risk would seem to be to leave prostitution, but earlier analyses of the CDC multi-centre data suggested that the more likely source of HIV-1 infection sexually transmitted to a prostitute was the woman's HIV-1-infected husband or boy-friend, not her client (CDC 1987a). If further analyses support this conclusion, finding another source of income for a prostitute will not significantly reduce her risk of HIV-1 infection as long as she maintains her sexual relationship with her husband or boy-friend. Attempts to abolish prostitution and reform the prostitute will not necessarily reduce her chances of HIV-1 infection.

Many eligible women participated in the CDC multi-centre study because they were concerned about AIDS and wanted to learn more about how to avoid HIV-1 and other sexually transmitted diseases. Most took condoms when offered and reported using condoms frequently with clients (Darrow 1989). Using condoms with their husbands or boy-friends was far more problematic. Their husbands and boy-friends felt they could not become infected from their wives or girl-friends because they believed that women always used condoms with all other men. Since there was no incentive for the man to use a condom, the woman had a difficult task in convincing her lover to change his ways to protect herself. Public policies and condom promotion campaigns designed to curtail the spread of HIV-1 through heterosexual intercourse must be developed to persuade sexually active men to take more responsibility for the health of their sexual partners.

Effective public health intervention must be implemented for HIV-1-infected men and women who continue to put their sex partners and others at risk (Bayer 1989). A less restrictive approach has been practised in the United States in which HIV-1-infected persons are first instructed to warn their sex partners and not endanger the lives of others (Gostin and Curran 1987). In a few cases, however, HIV-1 infected prostitutes have been held in custody. The effectiveness of this strategy has not been assessed.[2] The Public Health Service has encouraged male and female prostitutes to be counselled, tested, and made aware of the risks of HIV-1 infection to themselves and others. In addition, the Public Health Service has recommended that 'particularly prostitutes who are HIV-antibody positive ... discontinue the practice of prostitution' (CDC 1987b). No other specific recommendations have been made for prostitutes or their clients because they are subject to various state and local statutes, and to the same guide-lines as everyone else.

Directions for future research

Besides those questions about the relative effectiveness of public health interventions are the more basic questions about *how* HIV-1 and other sexually transmitted agents spread in human communities, and *why* some persons at risk of HIV-1 transmission change their behaviour while others do not. Most of the research on prostitution, drugs, and AIDS to this point has attempted to describe *who* is at risk, *what* they report doing, and *where* and *when* they do it. These questions must continually be asked to monitor changes over time, but the more important questions of how and why must be answered if we are to arrive at the most rational, humane, and effective solution for stopping the spread of HIV-1 and other sexually transmitted diseases.

Notes

1   Although the prevalence of antibody to HIV-1 appears to be relatively low in many parts of West Africa, rates of antibody to human immunodeficiency

virus type 2 (HIV-2) can be relatively high. In Bissau, Guinea-Bissau, for example, eleven (37 per cent) of thirty prostitutes were infected with HIV-2; none were infected with HIV-1 (Naucler *et al.* 1989). Other countries, such as the Ivory Coast, have shown that humans can be infected with one or both of these retroviruses, and infection with either virus can lead to AIDS. In Tortiya, Ivory Coast, HIV-2 was twice as common (14 per cent HIV-2 antibody positive) among prostitutes as HIV-1 (7 per cent HIV-1 antibody positive), but in Abidjan, prostitutes were as likely to have one virus as the other (Denis *et al.* 1987). However, in four suburban and rural provinces of the Ivory Coast, prostitutes were more likely to have antibody to HIV-1 than HIV-2 (Ouattara *et al.* 1989).

2 Only two interventions with prostitutes have been evaluated. Both emphasized personal contact with prostitutes and positive reinforcement rather than impersonal messages and threats of punishment. Both were designed to increase condom use with clients and both were successful. The one in Greece was designed to protect both the prostitute and her sex partners (Roumeliotou *et al.* 1988), but the one in Kenya was designed primarily to protect the male partners of prostitutes who had become infected with HIV-1 (Ngugi *et al.* 1988).

References

American Public Health Association (1989) *The 1989 Manual of Tests for Syphilis*, Washington, DC: American Public Health Association (in press).

Bartoloni, A. *et al.* (1989) 'Absence of HIV infection in low- and high-risk groups in the Santa Cruz region, Bolivia' (letter), *AIDS* 3 (3): 184–5.

Barton, S.E., Underhill, G.S., Gilchrist, C., Jeffries, D.J., and Harris, J.R.W. (1985) 'HTLV-III antibody in prostitutes' (letter), *Lancet* 2: 1424.

Bayer, R. (1989) *Private Acts, Social Consequences: AIDS and the Politics of Public Health*, New York: Free Press.

Brenky-Faudeux, D. and Fribourg-Blanc, A. (1985) 'HTLV-III antibody in prostitutes' (letter), *Lancet* 2: 1424.

Centers for Disease Control (1983) 'Penicillinase-producing *Neisseria gonorrhoeae* – Los Angeles', *Morbidity and Mortality Weekly Report* 32: 181–3.

Centers for Disease Control (1987a) 'Antibody to human immunodeficiency virus in female prostitutes', *Morbidity and Mortality Weekly Report* 36: 157–61.

Centers for Disease Control (1987b) 'Public health service guidelines for counselling and antibody testing to prevent HIV infection and AIDS', *Morbidity and Mortality Weekly Report* 36: 509–15.

Centers for Disease Control (1989a) 'AIDS and antibody to human immunodeficiency virus infection in the United States: 1988 update', *Morbidity and Mortality Weekly Report* 38 (supplement S–4): 1–38.

Centers for Disease Control (1989b) 'Interpretation and use of the Western blot assay for serodiagnosis of human immunodeficiency virus type-1 infections', *Morbidity and Mortality Weekly Report*, 38, Supplement S–7: 1–7.

Chen, C.J. *et al.* (1988) 'Seroepidemiology of human T lymphotropic viruses and hepatitis viruses among prostitutes in Taiwan', *Journal of Infectious Diseases* 15(3): 633–5.

Chikwem, J.O., Mohammed, I., Ola, T.O., Bajami, M., Mambula, S., and Gashau, W. (1988) 'Prevalence of human immunodeficiency virus (HIV) infection in Borno state of Nigeria', *East African Medical Journal* 65 (5): 342–6.

Chiphangwi, J., Liomba, G., Ntaba, H.M., Schmidt, H., Deinhardt, F., Eberle, J., Frosner, G., Gurtler, L., and Zoulek, G. (1987) 'Human immuno-deficiency virus infection is prevalent in Malawi' (letter), *Infection* 15 (5): 363.

Cortes, E. *et al.* (1989) 'HIV-1, HIV-2 and HTLV-I infection in high-risk groups in Brazil', *New England Journal of Medicine* 320 (15): 953–8.

Darrow, W.W. (1984) 'Prostitution and sexually transmitted diseases', in K.K. Holmes, P.-A. Mardh, P.F. Sparling, and P.J. Wiesner (eds) *Sexually Transmitted Diseases*, New York: McGraw-Hill, pp. 109–16.

Darrow, W.W. (1989) 'Condom use effectiveness in high-risk populations', *Sexually Transmitted Diseases*, 16 (3): 157–60.

Day, S. (1988) 'Prostitute women and AIDS: anthropology', *AIDS* 2 (6): 421–8.

Day, S., Ward, H., and Harris, J.R.W. (1988) 'Prostitute women and public health', *British Medical Journal* 297: 1585.

Denis, F. *et al.* (1987) 'Prevalence of human T-lymphotropic retroviruses type III (HIV) and type IV in Ivory Coast', *Lancet* 1(8530): 408–11.

Elifson, K.W., Boles, J., Sweat, M., Darrow, W.W., Elsea, W., and Green, R.M. (1989) 'Seroprevalence of human immunodeficiency virus among male prostitutes' (letter), *New England Journal of Medicine* 321 (12): 832–3.

European Study Group (1989) 'Risk factors for male to female transmission of HIV', *British Medical Journal* 298: 411–15.

Fischl, M.A., Dickinson, G.M., Scott, G.B., Klimas, N., Fletcher, M.A., and Parks, W. (1987) 'Evaluation of heterosexual partners, children, and household contacts of adults with AIDS', *Journal of the American Medical Association* 257: 640–4.

Fox, E., Abbatte, E.A., Said-Selah, A., Constantine, N.T., Rodier, G., and Woody, J.N. (1989) 'Incidence of HIV infection in Djibouti in 1988' (letter), *AIDS* 3 (4): 244–5.

Golenbock, D.T. *et al.* (1988) 'Absence of infection with human immunodeficiency virus in Peruvian prostitutes', *AIDS Research and Human Retroviruses* 4 (6): 493–9.

Gostin, L. and Curran, W.J. (1987) 'AIDS screening, confidentiality, and the duty to warn', *American Journal of Public Health* 77 (3): 361–5.

Hammond, G.W. *et al.* (1988) 'Seroprevalence and demographic information of patients at risk for human immunodeficiency virus (HIV) infection in Manitoba, Canada', *Journal of Acquired Immune Deficiency Syndromes* 1 (2): 138–42.

Hampton, L. (1988) 'Hookers with AIDS – the search', in I. Rieder and P. Ruppelt (eds) *AIDS: The Women*, Pittsburgh, Pennsylvania: Cleis Press, pp. 157–64.

Handsfield, H.H. *et al.* (1982) 'Epidemiology of penicillinase-producing *Neisseria gonorrhoeae* infections', *New England Journal of Medicine* 306 (16): 950–4.

Heyl, B.S. (1979) *The Madam as Entrepreneur*, New Brunswick, NJ: Transaction.

Holmberg, S.D. *et al.* (1989) 'Biologic factors in the sexual transmission of human immunodeficiency virus', *Journal of Infectious Diseases*, 160: 116–25.

Hudson, C.P. *et al.* (1988) 'Risk factors for the spread of AIDS in rural Africa: evidence from a comparative seroepidemiological survey of AIDS, hepatitis B and syphilis in southwestern Uganda', *AIDS* 2 (4): 255–60.

John, T.J., Babu, P.G., Jayakumari, H., and Simoes, E.A.F. (1987) 'Prevalence of HIV infection in risk groups in Tamilnadu, India' (letter), *Lancet* 1 (8525): 160–1.

Khabbaz, R.F. (in press) 'Seroprevalence and risk factors for HTLV-I/II infection in prostitute women in the United States', *Journal of the American Medical Association*.

Klovdahl, A.S. (1985) 'Social networks and the spread of infectious diseases: the AIDS example', *Social Science and Medicine* 21 (11): 1203–16.

Kreiss, J.K. *et al.* (1986) 'AIDS virus infection in Nairobi prostitutes: spread of the epidemic to East Africa', *New England Journal of Medicine* 314 (7): 414–18.

Krogsgaard, K., Gluud, C., Pedersen, C., Nielsen, J.O., and Juhl, E. (1986) 'Widespread use of condoms and low prevalence of sexually transmitted diseases in Danish non-drug addict prostitutes', *British Medical Journal* 293: 1473–4.

Lee, F.K. *et al.* (1985) 'Detection of herpes simplex virus type 2 specific antibody, with glycoprotein G', *Journal of Clinical Microbiology* 4: 642–4.

Leonard, T., Sacks, J.J., Franks, A.L., and Sikes, R.K. (1988) 'The prevalence of human immunodeficiency virus, hepatitis B, and syphilis among female prostitutes in Atlanta', *Journal of the Medical Association of Georgia* 77: 162–7.

Luthy, R., Ledergerber, B., Tauber, M., and Siegenthaler, W. (1987) 'Prevalence of HIV antibodies among prostitutes in Zurich, Switzerland', *Klinische Wochenschrift* 65: 287–8.

Mann, J. *et al.* (1987) 'Condom use and HIV infection among prostitutes in Zaire' (letter), *New England Journal of Medicine* 316: 345.

Mann, J. *et al.* (1988) 'HIV infection and associated risk factors in female prostitutes in Kinshasa, Zaire', *AIDS* 2 (4): 249–54.

Mintz, E., Peale, R., Mathur, S.K., Prince, A., and Brotman, B. (1988) 'A serologic study of HIV infection in Liberia', *Journal of Acquired Immune Deficiency Syndromes* 1 (1): 67–8.

Naucler, A., Andreasson, P.-A., Costa, C.M., Thorstensson, R., and Biberfeld, G. (1989) 'HIV-2-associated AIDS and HIV-2 seroprevalence in Bissau, Guinea-Bissau', *Journal of Acquired Immune Deficiency Syndromes* 2 (1): 88–93.

Nayyar, K.C., Noble, R.C., Michel, M.F., and Stolz, E. (1980) 'Gonorrhea in Rotterdam caused by penicillinase-producing gonococci', *British Journal of Venereal Disease* 56: 244–8.

Nayyar, K.C., Cummings, M., Weber, J., Benes, S., Stolz, E., Felman, Y., and McCormack, W.M. (1986) 'Prevalence of genital pathogens among female prostitutes in New York City and Rotterdam', *Sexually Transmitted Diseases* 13 (2): 105–7.

Neequaye, A.R., Neequaye, J., Mingle, J.A., and Adjei, D.O. (1986) 'Preponderance of females with AIDS in Ghana' (letter), *Lancet* 2: 978.

Ngugi, E.N., Plummer, F.A., Simonsen, J.N., Cameron, D.W., Bosire, M., Waiyaki, P., Ronald, A.R., and Ndinya-Achola, J.O. (1988) 'Prevention of transmission of human immunodeficiency virus in Africa: effectiveness of condom promotion and health education among prostitutes', *Lancet* 2: 887–90.

Nzilambi, N. *et al.* (1988) 'The prevalence of infection with human immunodeficiency virus over a 10-year period in rural Zaire', *New England Journal of Medicine* 318 (5): 276–9.

Ouattara, S.A., Meite, M., Cot, M.C., and de-The, G. (1989) 'Compared prevalence of infections by HIV-1 and HIV-2 during a 2-year period in suburban and rural areas of Ivory Coast', *Journal of Acquired Immune Deficiency Syndromes* 2 (1): 94–9.

Padian, N.S. (1987) 'Heterosexual transmission of acquired immunodeficiency syndrome: international perspectives and national projections', *Review of Infectious Diseases* 9: 947–59.

Padian, N.S. (1988) 'Prostitute women and AIDS: epidemiology', *AIDS* 2 (6): 413–19.

Papaevangelou, G. *et al.* (1988) 'Education in preventing HIV infection in Greek registered prostitutes', *Journal of Acquired Immune Deficiency Syndromes* 1 (4): 386–9.

Pepin, J., Plummer, F.A., Brunham, R.C., Piot, P., Cameron, D.W., and Ronald, A.R. (1989) 'The interaction of HIV infection and other sexually transmitted diseases: an opportunity for intervention', *AIDS* 3 (1): 3–9.

Peterman, T.A., Stoneburner, R.L., Allen, J.R., Jaffe, H.W., and Curran, J.W. (1986) 'Risk of human immunodeficiency virus transmission from heterosexual adults with transfusion-associated infections', *Journal of the American Medical Association* 259 (1): 55–8.

Philpot, C.R., Harcourt, C., Edwards, J., and Grealis, A. (1988) 'Human immunodeficiency virus and female prostitutes, Sydney 1985', *Genitourinary Medicine* 64: 193–7.

Piot, P. *et al.* (1987) 'Retrospective seroepidemiology of AIDS virus infection in Nairobi populations', *Journal of Infectious Diseases* 155 (6): 1108–12.

Rabkin, C.S., Thomas, P.A., Jaffe, H.W., and Schultz, S. (1987) 'Prevalence of antibody to HTLV-III/LAV in a population attending a sexually transmitted diseases clinic', *Sexually Transmitted Diseases* 14 (1): 48–51.

Reeves, W.C. and Quiroz, E. (1987) 'Prevalence of sexually transmitted diseases in high-risk women in the Republic of Panama', *Sexually Transmitted Diseases* 14: 69–74.

Reeves, W.C., Cuevas, M., Arosemena, J.R., Loo de Lao, S., Gomez, B., Ulloa, E., Quiroz, E., Canton-Dutary, A., Reyes, R., Saenz, R., Dormoi, G., Altafulla, M., de Bernal, J., Diaz-Isaacs, M., Rodriguez, J., Brenes, M.M., de Britton, R., and Wignall, F.S. (1988) 'Human immunodeficiency virus infection in the Republic of Panama', *American Journal of Tropical Medicine and Hygiene* 39 (4): 398–405.

Roumeliotou, A., Papautsakis, G., Kallinikos, G., and Papaevangelou, G. (1988) 'Effectiveness of condom use in preventing HIV infection in prostitutes' (letter), *Lancet* 2: 1249.

Ruijs, G.J., Schut, I.K., Schirm, J., and Schroeder, F.P. (1988) 'Prevalence, incidence, and risk of acquiring urogenital gonococcal or chlamydial infection in prostitutes working in brothels', *Genitourinary Medicine* 64: 49–51.

Schoub, B.D., Lyons, S.F., McGillivray, G.M., Smith, A.N., Johnson, S., and Fisher, E.L. (1987) 'Absence of HIV infection in prostitutes and women attending sexually-transmitted disease clinics in South Africa', *Transactions of the Royal Society of Tropical Medicine and Hygiene* 81: 874–5.

Schultz, S., Milberg, J.A., Kristal, A.R., and Stoneburner, R.L. (1986) 'Female-to-male transmission of HTLV-III' (letter), *Journal of the American Medical Association* 255 (13): 1703–4.

Seidlin, M., Krasinski, K., Bebenroth, D., Itri, V., Paolino, A.M., and Valentine, F. (1988) 'Prevalence of HIV infection in New York call girls', *Journal of Acquired Immune Deficiency Syndromes* 1 (2): 150–4.

Simonsen, J.N., Cameron, D.W., Gakinya, M.N., Ndinya-Achola, J.O., D'Costa, L.J., Karasira, P., Cheang, M., Ronald, A.R., Piot, P., and Plummer, F.A. (1988) 'HIV infection among men with sexually transmitted diseases: experience from a center in Africa', *New England Journal of Medicine* 319 (5): 274–8.

Smith, G.L. and Smith, K.F. (1986) 'Lack of HIV infection and condom use in licensed prostitutes' (letter), *Lancet* 2: 1392.

Tirelli, U., Vaccher, E., Carbone, A., DePaoli, P., Santini, G., and Monfardini, S. (1985) 'HTLV-III antibody in prostitutes' (letter), *Lancet* 2: 1424.

Traisupa, A., Wongba, C., and Taylor, D.N. (1987) 'AIDS and prevalence of antibody to human immunodeficiency virus (HIV) in high risk groups in Thailand', *Genitourinary Medicine* 63: 106–8.

Van de Perre, P., Clumeck, N., Careal, M., Nzabihimana, E., Robert-Guroff, M., De Mol, P., Freyens, P., Butzler, J.-P., Gallo, R.C., and Kanyamupira, J.-B. (1985) 'Female prostitutes: a risk group for infection with human T-cell lymphotropic virus type III', *Lancet* 2: 524–7.

Van den Hoek, J.A.R., Coutinho, R.A., van Haastrecht, H.J.A., van Zadelhoff, A.W., and Goudsmit, J. (1988) 'Prevalence and risk factors of HIV infections among drug users and drug-using prostitutes in Amsterdam', *AIDS* 2 (1): 55–60.

Vittecoq, D., May, T., Roue, R.T., Stern, M., Mayaud, C., Chavanet, P., Borsa, F., Jeantils, P., Armengaud, M., Modai, J., Autran, B., Rey, F., and Chermann, J.C. (1987) 'Acquired immunodeficiency syndrome after travelling in Africa: an epidemiological study in seventeen Caucasian patients', *Lancet* 1: 612–15.

Woolley, P.D., Bowman, C.A., and Kinghorn, G.R. (1988) 'Prostitution in Sheffield: differences between prostitutes', *Genitourinary Medicine* 64: 391–3.

Yoshida, S., Mizuguchi, Y., Mizue, K., Sakamoto, H., and Urabe, S. (1987) 'Prevalence of hepatitis B markers, antibodies to adult T cell leukemia/lymphoma virus and antibodies to human immune deficiency virus in prostitutes in Fukuoka, Japan', *Japanese Journal of Medical Science and Biology* 40: 171–4.

Chapter three

Safer prostitution: a new approach in Holland

Petrien Uniken Venema and Jan Visser

Introduction

The field of prostitution has undergone many changes in the past ten years. Change might be even more far-reaching in future. During 1989 the Dutch Government made preparations to change the laws on the exploitation of commercial sex. It is to be expected that houses of prostitution will be legalized and that existing law related to the regulation of labour and commerce will be applied to prostitution. The aim of these innovations is to improve the working conditions of prostitutes and to decriminalize prostitution in general.

This chapter sets out to provide an overview of prostitution in Holland with emphasis on the effects that a new system of legal regulation might have. The possible effects are considered in relation to the legal and social status of prostitutes and to the spread of sexually transmitted diseases. In order to provide this overview an introduction to the position of prostitution in Holland is offered. The Dutch orientation towards this subject has to be considered in relation to the social structure and cultural atmosphere of Holland. The new policy measures that are being considered are rooted in the Dutch way of living and thinking. Even so, the basic principles that underlie the suggested legalization are fundamental for any type of policy designed to minimize the problems associated with prostitution. These include drug use and the spread of HIV infection and other sexually transmitted diseases.

Prostitution in Holland

The Amsterdam red light district with its overt and provocative window prostitution is one of the major tourist attractions of the Dutch capital.

41

In other large cities and in cities that have a regional function one can easily find the streets where women sit 'on display'. Often their business is an integrated and accepted part of the inner city. In the vicinity of these areas women who solicit on the streets are met with less tolerance. This nightly activity, which is accompanied by the noise of kerb-crawling cars and drug dealing, is met with residential opposition. Some city councils have confined this type of prostitution to special zones.

Besides such overt prostitution, it is also possible to distinguish a covert prostitution that can be found all over the country. A 'sex club' is a closed brothel with a bar. These establishments vary from very modest to very luxurious. Sex clubs may be situated in the heart of a city or in a farm in the countryside. The same applies to agencies. These can mediate for call girls who sell their services to businessmen from out of town or for housewives who receive an occasional client in order to supplement the family income. Independent prostitutes may also advertise openly in newspapers and magazines.

Male prostitution exists largely in the major cities. Males solicit through newspapers or find their customers in bars and saunas. There are only a few sex clubs and agencies which cater for male prostitution.

The total number of professional prostitutes in Holland is estimated to be at least 20,000. This total could be at least doubled if part-time prostitutes were included.

During the 1960s, as a side effect of the so-called 'sexual revolution', prostitution became more visible and in some cities expanded together with peep shows, live shows, and porno shops. Since the later 1970s, heroin (and later other drugs) have been introduced among prostitutes, predominantly among street workers. Also, both males and females who had become drug dependent have turned to prostitution in order to finance their habits. This has weakened the social control of prostitution, as these drug users were not schooled in the codes of commercial sex. This enhanced an already existing trend towards individualization in the business. The distinctive subculture of prostitution has been slowly vanishing. This trend has been further reinforced by the immigration of foreign prostitutes. During the early 1980s European men went to southeast Asia, Africa, or South America to meet 'exotic' women. A few years later these women came to western Europe, either trafficked as innocent victims of international criminal organizations or on their own as a means of upward economic mobility. Such women are often very vulnerable. They are unfamiliar with Dutch society, often do not speak

Dutch, and frequently have an illegal and, therefore, precarious status. It is very difficult to estimate the numbers of such women because, like the Thai prostitutes described in Chapter 8, they are highly mobile.

The Dutch are well known (or perhaps one should say 'notorious') for their tolerant attitude towards 'deviant' behaviour. Prostitution itself is not prohibited, but the exploitation of someone else's prostitution and pimping are illegal. This law is based on the so-called 'abolitionist' view which aims at eradicating prostitution as such. This law is not actually enforced in the Netherlands for two reasons. First, it is difficult to prove exploitation and pimping in court. Testimonies and other evidence are hard to obtain. Second, it is firmly believed that prosecution will merely drive prostitution underground and opportunities for control and surveillance by police vice squads will be reduced. This has led to the above noted climate of tolerance. As long as this business takes place within certain geographical and social boundaries and is not accompanied by serious crimes, people engaged in prostitution are left alone. In this situation it is possible for a number of prostitutes to work independently in every sector of this industry. They do not need the 'protection' of pimps and exploiters as there is no daily threat of police 'harassment'. An enterprising woman can rent a window in a prostitution area and keep her earnings for herself. Prostitutes in brothels may accept or refuse clients. They can work out an agreement with the owners on the money they will pay for their services and quit whenever they choose to do so.

Even so, as in other sections of society, prostitute women are not always in a position to make their own choices. In spite of this, prostitutes in the Netherlands are markedly better off than most of those in other industrialized countries. They have a chance to work independently, but they still lack the safeguards which are taken for granted in other occupations. This exposes the prostitute to stigma, social isolation, and oppressive working conditions.

Prostitution and the law

Since 1911 the Penal Code has reflected the 'abolitionist' view of prostitution. In short, this ideology states that prostitution is a degrading and inhumane social 'cancer' that has to be cut out of society. The way to do that is to treat the prostitute as a victim and offer her help to leave prostitution and become a 'respectable' woman again. People are not penalized for engaging in prostitution. Even so, those (pimps) who live on the earnings of prostitutes and those who organize prostitution are regarded as criminals. This moralistic view is commonplace throughout much of the world.

Prostitution is hard, if not impossible, to eradicate. Everywhere men (and women) seek sexual gratification and are willing to pay for it. Accordingly, every society has to compromise, to find a way to contain this 'necessary evil'. In many cases this leads to the situation whereby prostitution is tolerated to a certain degree, the boundaries being defined by the nuisance it gives to public order. This has led to systems of open or covert tolerance of prostitution, in which police rather than politicians are the people to decide when the acceptable limits are exceeded. The effect of this pragmatic system of tolerance is often that pimps and exploiters are left alone while prostitutes are being criminalized and stigmatized in both their public and private lives. Prostitutes, in effect, receive the sole blame for the social phenomenon of prostitution. The role of pimps, exploiters, and, not least, clients is ignored. In Holland this way of dealing with prostitution has come under severe criticism from several directions.

First, prostitutes have claimed both their civil rights and the right to work as a prostitute. These claims have been set out in the following charter:

International Committee for Prostitutes' Rights World Charter and World Whores' Congress Statements

International Committee for Prostitutes' Rights

World Charter

Laws

Decriminalize all aspects of adult prostitution resulting from individual decision.

Decriminalize prostitution and regulate third parties according to standard business codes. It must be noted that existing standard business codes allow abuse of prostitutes. Therefore special clauses must be included to prevent the abuse and stigmatization of prostitutes (self-employed and others).

Enforce criminal laws against fraud, coercion, violence, child sexual abuse, child labour, rape, racism everywhere and across national boundaries, whether or not in the context of prostitution.

Eradicate laws that can be interpreted to deny freedom of

association, or freedom to travel, to prostitutes within and between countries. Prostitutes have rights to a private life.

Human rights

Guarantee prostitutes all human rights and civil liberties, including the freedom of speech, travel, immigration, work, marriage, and motherhood, and the right to unemployment insurance, health insurance, and housing.

Grant asylum to anyone denied human rights on the basis of a 'crime of status', be it prostitution or homosexuality.

Working conditions

There should be no law which implies systematic zoning of prostitution. Prostitutes should have the freedom to choose their place of work and residence. It is essential that prostitutes can provide their services under the conditions that are absolutely determined by themselves and no one else.

There should be a committee to ensure that protection of the rights of the prostitutes and to whom prostitutes can address their complaints. This committee must be comprised of prostitutes and other professionals like lawyers and supporters.

There should be no law discriminating against prostitutes associating and working collectively in order to acquire a high degree of personal security.

Health

All women and men should be educated to have periodic health screening for sexually transmitted diseases. Since health checks have historically been used to control and stigmatize prostitutes, and since adult prostitutes are generally even more aware of sexual health than others, mandatory checks for prostitutes are unacceptable unless they are mandatory for all sexually active people.

Services

Employment, counselling, legal, and housing services for runaway children should be funded in order to prevent child prostitution and to promote child well-being and opportunity.

Prostitutes must have the same social benefits as other citizens according to the different regulations in different countries.

Shelters and services for working prostitutes and re-training programmes for prostitutes wishing to leave the life should be funded.

Taxes

No special taxes should be levied on prostitutes or prostitute businesses.

Prostitutes should pay regular taxes on the same basis as other independent contractors and employees, and should receive the same benefits.

Public opinion

Support educational programmes to change social attitudes which stigmatize and discriminate against prostitutes and ex-prostitutes of any race, gender, or nationality.

Develop educational programmes which help the public to understand that the customer plays a crucial role in the prostitution phenomenon, this role being generally ignored. The customer, like the prostitute, should not, however, be criminalized or condemned on a moral basis.

We are in solidarity with all workers in the sex industry.

Organization

Organizations of prostitutes and ex-prostitutes should be supported to further implementation of the above charter.

(First World Whores' Congress 1985)

A detailed account of the recent history of the prostitutes' movement has been provided by Pheterson (1989).

Politicians and civil servants have criticized the existing policy towards prostitution on the grounds that it does not regulate or monitor activities efficiently. Women in the feminist movement have supported the rights of prostitutes to sell sexual services if they voluntarily deem this to be their best method to earn a living. An important element in this debate has been the 'Red Thread', a prostitutes' rights group. The Government has responded to their claims by proposing to change the law, to remove the exploitation of voluntary prostitution from the Penal Code, and to give municipal authorities the option of regulating prostitution through administrative law: a licensing system, including conditions regarding health, public order, and working facilities. The most important consequence of this new law will be a clear legal distinction between voluntary and involuntary prostitution. In this way it will be possible simultaneously to improve the protection and assistance of women and boys who are forced into prostitution and to strengthen the legal, social, and economic position of women and boys who choose to be prostitutes. The last group will be granted the rights and duties that every labourer or entrepreneur has in Holland as a vital element in a campaign to end discrimination against prostitutes. The aim is not to register and control prostitutes but to register and control prostitution businesses.

The law on trading in women will be redefined in the same way. Cases against traffickers will be dealt with more seriously and the women involved will be better cared for and safeguarded in future.

Another aspect of the new policy is to set up programmes to enable people to leave prostitution should they wish to do so. It is generally understood that this often means a difficult step and requires help in the fields of work, finance, housing, and counselling.

Preventing the spread of HIV infection and other sexually transmitted diseases

The contemporary Dutch policy towards sexually transmitted diseases (including HIV infection) has been based upon an appeal to personal responsibility and a pragmatic approach. Prevention, contact tracing, and cure have been integrated into a flexible and easily accessible system that is attuned to the range of types of open and covert prostitution: street and window prostitution, brothels, sex clubs, private houses, call girls, and gay prostitution.

The aim is to reach as many prostitutes as possible. Key words are: 'anonymous', 'voluntary', 'inexpensive'. The policy is to offer a variety of medical provisions to facilitate examination.

1. The family doctor: the cost will be covered by health insurances.
2. Free clinics for sexually transmitted diseases. These are run by health departments.
3. Specialist doctors visit brothels and sex clubs. These work with health departments.
4. Private doctors are also sometimes hired by brothel owners. In such cases the costs are often shared between the prostitute and the brothel owner.

An independent working prostitute may decide to consult a doctor of her or his own choice for reasons of anonymity.

Prostitutes are not obliged to register with the police vice squad or to have regular medical examinations. The Dutch constitution gives everybody the right of respect of one's personal life-sphere (article 10) and protects the right of inviolability of the human body (article 11). Only special laws can change this. Sexually transmitted diseases are not spread by 'casual' contact and there is no legal basis for mandatory examinations for such conditions. The majority of Dutch clinicians and policy makers believe that such compulsory examinations would be counter-productive. The nineteenth century, with its regimented, repressive approach to prostitution, showed that draconian policies neither eliminate prostitution nor contain the spread of sexually transmitted diseases. A policy which harasses and persecutes prostitutes, while at the same time ignoring their clients, simply drives activities underground and undermines medical provision. The criminalization of prostitution curtails the prevention of sexually transmitted diseases. Such a policy further involves repression and stigmatizes prostitutes as being dishonourable and dirty.

The Dutch health authorities firmly believe in their voluntary system. A prostitute can choose to use the facility which suits his or her personal circumstances best. The tolerant attitude of the Government towards the sex industry and prostitutes makes it possible for many women and men to determine their own work conditions to a considerable extent.

AIDS policy

AIDS was first diagnosed in the Netherlands in 1982. By the end of May 1989 the total number of reported AIDS cases had grown to 852. About 85 per cent were homosexual or bisexual men. The number of people in Holland who are HIV seropositive has been estimated as being between 15,000 and 30,000 (National Committee on AIDS Control 1988).

Initially AIDS prevention was specifically directed at 'high-risk' groups, in particular homosexual men and intravenous drug users. Preventive and educational initiatives were undertaken by gay organizations and bloodbanks sponsored by the Government. A campaign was mounted to deter people from high-risk groups from donating blood. AIDS information was also circulated among gay men.

A national co-ordinating team was formed to co-ordinate preventive actions and to arrange for care for AIDS patients. It was realized that

AIDS was not a problem only for 'high-risk groups' and that AIDS was not only a health issue. Accordingly, a broad view of AIDS policy was accepted. The National Committee on AIDS Control took the place of the former national co-ordinating team. The new body included representatives of relevant agencies as well as specialists in the fields of ethics and law. The Committee's work is based upon the following assumptions:

- Organizations of high-risk groups have an important say in policy formation.
- Avoidance of HIV-infection is primarily seen as an individual responsibility. Therefore coercive measures aimed at identifying HIV seropositive people or imposing restrictions on such people is considered undesirable.
- In the absence of a cure for AIDS, caution should be exercised in advising people to be tested for HIV antibodies. However, if individuals want to be tested facilities must be easily accessible.
- Health care for AIDS patients has to be incorporated in existing health care institutions.

The National Committee on AIDS Control has concluded that, currently, prostitution poses no major threat in the spread of HIV infection. Even so, education and prevention should be greatly extended. The message for prostitutes and their clients is the same as that for the general public: masturbation, vaginal intercourse and fellatio with a condom may be regarded as 'safer sex'. Unprotected penetrative sex, especially anal sex, is 'unsafe'.

In line with established policy related to sexually transmitted diseases, repressive measures are not advised. These would lead to an increase in 'hidden' prostitution. In addition, as elaborated elsewhere in this book, such policies would deter prostitutes from seeking medical care and would also be very expensive. Mandatory HIV testing is not a government policy and testing is not encouraged. This might give clients a false sense of security and discourage condom use. The time between HIV infection and detection of seropositivity may be several months, or even longer, so nobody can be guaranteed to be 'AIDS free'.

It is believed that low-key and clear information campaigns are a far more worthwhile approach. These need to emphasize that both sexual partners share the responsibility for 'safer sex'. One does not receive AIDS. One 'takes' it.

Because of the stigmatization of prostitution and the variety within the sex industry a special effort and a considerable amount of ingenuity are required to contact prostitutes. A number of approaches have been adopted in Holland. Health workers have run group educational sessions in brothels, brochures have been distributed in the waiting-rooms of clinics for sexually transmitted diseases. Commercial sex has been mentioned explicitly in public information campaigns. It has been difficult to contact foreign prostitutes, who constitute half the target group in some areas. Some of them come from developing countries and are illiterate or have low levels of literacy or do not understand Dutch well. Some live in social and physical isolation.

AIDS prevention and education have to be continuing processes. This is because people constantly enter and leave the sex industry and because the social structure of prostitution has been weakened. A clear subculture with a firm set of rules no longer exists. Prostitutes are now a far less cohesive group and have more varied working styles than before.

The prostitutes' rights group the Red Thread has claimed that the majority of professional prostitutes have always worked with 'safer sex' procedures ('my body is my capital'). They further contend that, instead of scapegoating prostitutes for the spread of sexually transmitted diseases, it would be far more productive for authorities to co-operate with those in the sex industry. Prostitutes could be valuable educators in relation to AIDS prevention.

The circumstances under which the prostitute works vary with the type of prostitution. For instance, when a woman rents a window in the red light district of a major city she can refuse customers or their sexual wishes; when she works in a sex club the manager may put pressure on her to accept every customer and acquiesce to all of their demands. In addition to prostitutes themselves three target groups are distinguished: management (brothel owners), clients, and partners/lovers.

All of these groups have to be made aware of the importance of 'safer sex'. The managers must understand that a sound business requires safer sex and that a reputation for sexually transmitted diseases will cost them money in the long run.

More and more, clients of prostitutes are being regarded as playing the key role in the decision as to whether a commercial sexual contact is safe or not. Many clients request sex without a condom, even though they know that this may be dangerous and sometimes even when they know that the prostitute is an intravenous drug user. Research has shown that such clients invent irrational arguments like 'I can see if a prostitute is seropositive' or 'I am her regular customer' or 'it cannot happen to me'. It appears that sexual arousal, possibly accompanied by the effects of alcohol or other drugs, may lead a man to engage in totally irresponsible behaviour.

In association with the health authorities the KLEP ('association of clients'), an organization which aims to destigmatize prostitution, has embarked upon outreach work. Members have visited red light districts to hand out condoms to fellow clients and to persuade them to adopt 'safer sex' practices. Both prostitutes and clients have been positive in their response to this initiative.

It is important that the target groups (e.g. prostitutes, clients) participate in such initiatives. They are, after all, experts on their own behaviour.

Street prostitution

In Holland most street prostitutes use drugs and some are intravenous users. As emphasized throughout this book, one of the major methods whereby HIV infection has been spread is the sharing of infected injecting equipment by drug users. Public debate about the drug-using prostitute has emphasized concern that commercial sex may transmit HIV infection to the 'general population'. At the time of writing there was little evidence of such spread having occurred in Holland.

Even before the advent of the AIDS epidemic Holland had a system to regulate street prostitution which was also designed to improve the working and living conditions of prostitutes. In the larger cities a street or streets are designated as areas in which prostitutes may solicit. This enables health and social agencies to make contact and establishes a degree of social control among otherwise isolated women. Facilities may be provided to enable women to meet, rest, shower, and eat during the night. In addition, they may participate in methadone maintenance programmes and use the widespread injecting equipment exchange facilities. In Amsterdam the clinic for sexually transmitted diseases is opened one evening each week specially for drug-dependent prostitutes.

Research findings

During recent years several studies have been conducted which provide information about AIDS risks and prostitution. Some studies were set up for this purpose. In others, primarily initiated for other reasons, relevant information has been produced as a 'spin-off'. Two primary issues are considered here. These are the spread of HIV infection among prostitutes and their clients and the risk of more general transmission of HIV infection through prostitution.

Unfortunately, information has not been collected evenly from the different sectors of the sex industry. Most studies have been conducted among street prostitutes, most of whom were intravenous drug users. Far less is known about the situation in clubs or behind the windows in red light areas. Virtually nothing is known about the women who run their own businesses or who work for escort agencies. The latter are featured in Chapter 4.

Prevalence of sexually transmitted diseases and AIDS

Since 1980 the incidence of gonorrhoea among prostitutes has been declining. In 1987, 43 per cent of female prostitutes examined in clinics had this condition. There has been a fall in the incidence of syphilis. Data from Amsterdam free clinics indicate that this decline reflects changed behaviours among homosexual men. In 1984 there were 208 cases and in 1987 there were only thirty-three. Among heterosexual males there has been an increase (1986: twenty-three cases; 1987: fifty-three). There was also a rise among women (1986: fifteen cases; 1987: twenty-six). Among female prostitutes there were nine cases of syphilis in 1986 and sixteen in 1987.

Non-specific urethritis has also increased. This is consistent with findings in the USA (Centers for Disease Control 1988). The reasons for this increase are unclear. The obvious inference is that heterosexuals have not increasingly adopted 'safer sex' procedures. It is possible that such failure to take precautions has been exacerbated by the use of such disinhibiting drugs as Ecstasy and cocaine. In the light of the AIDS epidemic these trends are alarming.

In 1985 the municipal health service of Amsterdam tested eighty-four Dutch non-drug-using prostitutes (who were selected on a voluntary basis) for HIV antibody (Coutinho and Van der Helm 1986). None of them turned out to be HIV seropositive. The women worked in different sectors of the sex industry (clubs, behind windows, on the streets, and elsewhere).

This investigation was followed by a pilot study on a larger scale. This involved eighty people with frequent heterosexual contacts but who did not belong to a known high-risk group. The participants had each had five or more different sexual partners of the opposite sex and/or were the partner of someone belonging to a high-risk group. Seventy per cent of the women involved were prostitutes (mostly working in clubs). Sixty-four per cent of the men were clients of prostitutes.

Antibody testing showed that one man (a client) was HIV seropositive. This man had reportedly had sexual contact with an intravenous drug user five years earlier (Hooykaas 1988).

At the time of writing HIV infection had not been detected in Dutch prostitutes who were not intravenous drug users. Thirty-one per cent of a study group of 110 drug-using prostitutes were found to be HIV seropositive (Van den Hoek *et al.* 1987). Four out of a group of thirty-two male prostitutes who were tested were found to be HIV seropositive. One of these had injected drugs (Van Andel 1987).

Barriers to safer sex

The evidence cited above was all quantitative. The studies referred to were all small-scale investigations. It is therefore difficult to draw any conclusions about the general prevalence of HIV infection among Dutch prostitutes or their clients. This limits attempts to assess the risks that HIV infection will be spread to the general population through commercial sex.

Some qualitative studies provide a different perspective on AIDS-related risks and prostitution. Through observation and interviews with prostitutes and clients information has been elicited about attitudes to safer sex and the prostitute–client negotiation process. Several factors have been identified which obstruct the adoption of safer sex practices (Van de Raadt *et al.* 1988; Van Gelder and Van Roekel 1989).

Evidence suggests, as emphasized by other contributors to this book, that unsafe sex occurs in the context of all types of prostitution. Attempts to use a variety of social characteristics to distinguish between prostitutes and clients who engage in unsafe sexual practices and those who do not have failed (Van Gelder and Van Roekel 1989). It would appear to depend more upon circumstances than upon social characteristics whether or not prostitutes and clients insist upon safer sex.

The initial publicity about AIDS had little impact on the lives of female street prostitutes. AIDS was largely perceived as a disease of homosexual men. When it became known that intravenous drug users were also vulnerable to HIV infection and that any form of unprotected penetrative sex was a risk factor, more signs of concern became evident among prostitutes. Even so, denial of the risks and refusal to discuss them were also noted frequently. A study that assessed the impact of AIDS information leaflets for prostitutes indicated that these did succeed in increasing levels of knowledge. Television, magazines, and verbal information appeared to be the main sources of information about HIV infection and AIDS (Van den Putte 1987).

Most street prostitutes appear to be reasonably well informed about AIDS. However, some false beliefs about HIV transmission have been in circulation. Many prostitutes believe that kissing or sharing a glass with an infected person is dangerous. It has also commonly been reported that washing after sexual contact with an infected person can prevent infection. Accordingly, some women perceive unsafe sex to be safer if conducted in a setting, such as a hotel, where they can wash themselves.

Ideas about the need for safer sex also depend upon the prostitute's perception of each client. If a client appears to be 'clean' or looks like 'a real family man' some women believe there is less need to insist upon safer sex.

All prostitutes appear to believe that, in general, safer sex is preferable to unsafe sex. Prostitutes often watch one another's behaviour. If one turns away a client who refuses to engage in safer sex and another woman leaves the area with this man, it is inferred that the second woman 'does it without'.

All clients have also heard about AIDS risks. Many believe that they are not at greater risk through commercial sex. Such men are commonly ill informed on the methods of infection and often do not know the difference between HIV infection and AIDS. Many clients believe that they can avoid infection by carefully selecting a prostitute who looks healthy. Some state that they prefer women who resemble 'housewives' for the same reason. It is common for both prostitutes and clients to report that condoms are 'uncomfortable' for clients. Many clients prefer to have sex without condoms. This is a recurrent theme throughout this book. Reluctance to use condoms is more evident among men from some cultures and countries than others. For example, males from Mediterranean countries appear to be more averse to using condoms than do those from northern Europe.

Some clients claim not to be concerned whether or not they do contract AIDS. Such people state that they place little value on life and are not deterred by the prospect of an incurable, fatal disease.

Both prostitutes and clients have reported a general increase in the level of willingness or preference for safer sex. Some prostitutes have reported that old established clients who were scrupulous about condom use have not frequented their zones since the dangers of AIDS became known.

The need for drugs

Drug-dependent prostitutes have a constant and pressing need for money. Many such prostitutes work not only to buy drugs for themselves but also to purchase supplies for their partners. In general, drug-dependent prostitutes prefer to restrict their client encounters to safer sex. Even so, it is widely reported that, as their need for a new fix grows, they become much more vulnerable if clients insist upon unsafe sex. Some clients appear to be aware of this vulnerability and to seek women in this situation. It is sometimes reported, as in Chapter 6, that some clients pay more for unsafe sex.

'Work'/private sexual contacts

The study of heterosexual non-drug users included several questions about safer sex (Hooykaas 1988). The prostitutes included in this investigation reported having, on average, approximately two non-paying sexual partners. These women reported that they were far more likely to use condoms with clients than with non-paying partners. This is indicated in Table 3.1. This is consistent with evidence from more qualitative studies of street prostitution. Sex workers distinguish between sex 'at work' and sex 'in private'. At work they are more likely to use condoms. The condom is often used as a symbol, to maintain a psychological as well as a physical barrier. With a non-paying partner or lover sex means making love. Accordingly, some prostitutes may be more at risk from HIV infection through their non-paying partners than through client contacts.

Qualitative studies further indicate that the distinction between 'work' and 'private' sex may sometimes be blurred. Most prostitutes are less likely to insist upon condom use as clients become better known to them or become 'regulars'. There are men who often 'hang around' street prostitutes and who provide them with special services. The latter include material help, protection, and transport. Sometimes such men take prostitutes to their homes and offer them food and accommodation. Unsafe sex is easily enacted during such contacts. In addition, clients appear to be far less concerned about safety if they do not have a wife or other regular sexual partner.

Table 3.1 Use of condoms in sexual contacts

Condom use	Males		Females	
	With clients	With non-paying partners	With clients	With non-paying partners
	(n = 18)	(n = 28)	(n = 36)	(n = 52)
	%	%	%	%
Oral contacts				
Never	17	65	–	74
Always	25	6	55	11
Vaginal contacts				
Never	22	43	–	57
Always	33	10	49	11

Source: Hooykaas 1988.

Sexual techniques

As indicated in Table 3.1 it appears that there may be little difference in the extent of condom use during oral and vaginal contacts. Field research in areas of street prostitution indicates a rather different picture. Prostitutes are less likely to use condoms for oral sex, when a client asks for it, than they are for vaginal intercourse. It is generally believed that oral contact is far less risky than vaginal contact. Nevertheless, many street prostitutes are drug dependent and have poor dental health and often have cut or bleeding gums.

Varying results have been obtained in relation to anal sex. Some researchers have found that prostitutes do not engage in this practice. One recent study reported that this technique was becoming more popular (Van de Raadt *et al.* 1988). It appears that condoms are invariably used for anal sex, but not always the special, stronger types that are needed to minimize risks.

Force

It is possible that even after a prostitute and client have agreed to use a condom the client will enforce unsafe sex. It has regularly been reported that some clients remove condoms and, in effect, commit rape by enforcing unprotected sex.

Other barriers to condom use

Condoms may be purchased relatively cheaply in prostitution zones. However, prostitutes may not always have the correct coins to facilitate purchases. This may be because they pay drug dealers with the same amounts that they receive from clients.

Before the advent of the contraceptive pill, condoms were widely used. Condom use was, in effect, part of the ritual of visiting a prostitute. During the past fifteen years or so condoms have become regarded as obsolete. Many men claim to be unable to attain orgasm when they use a condom. Apart from this psychological barrier, new generations of prostitutes have had no training in the use of condoms. Accordingly, the act of using a condom may be viewed as de-eroticizing. Another problem is that most condom retailers only sell a standard size. Some men require different sizes. In addition, men from Islamic backgrounds claim that they cannot use condoms for religious reasons. In general men tend to ascribe responsibility to the state, the doctor, or the prostitute. The preceding factors all foster unsafe sex.

One important fact may lead a woman to insist upon confining client contacts to safe sex: those who know that they are HIV seropositive appear to be very careful about this.

The possibility of legalized prostitution

In Holland prostitution is accepted pragmatically as a social fact. In spite of this, the 'whore stigma' can be as real and as devastating for individual prostitutes as in other countries. Nevertheless, it is possible to discuss prostitution. It is a public issue. The improvement of the working conditions of prostitutes by controlling (and not simply tolerating) its management has widespread support, including that of the feminist movement.

Licensing

By decriminalizing prostitution and treating it as a legitimate form of work, it is proposed, social isolation and denial of human rights will be countered. Dutch society appears to be prepared to accept the reality of prostitution and to accord to prostitutes the same rights and duties that are enjoyed by and expected of other workers.

The new article in the Dutch Penal Code explicitly defines what is punishable: enforced prostitution. When a woman agrees to work in a brothel she is entitled to be protected by common employment laws. The city council may specify standards related to safety, hygiene, and working conditions. Managers who fail to comply with such regulations may lose their licences. Legal prostitution will take time to become part of the social scene. A basic rule is that, as long as prostitution is stigmatized, nobody should be forced to register. This would simply drive prostitution underground. To summarize, management will be regulated but prostitutes will remain anonymous.

Starting from 1990 every Dutch city may devise a licensing system to regulate prostitution. It is important to avoid the pitfalls encountered in the nineteenth century's system of regulation. These involved state-approved brothels in which an under-caste of 'fallen women' were held in captivity for the pleasure of males. Even so, there is little merit in a system which, in theory, criminalizes pimps and exploiters yet in practice ignores them and harasses prostitutes.

Regulation and the control of AIDS and other sexually transmitted diseases

What will the new system mean for sexually transmitted diseases and for health in general? The authors believe that, if cities ensure that individual prostitutes are not forced to register, the general health of those in the sex industry will be enhanced. The decriminalization of prostitution and the involvement of those in the sex industry in the political process can improve health care for prostitutes. Such recognition will enhance prostitutes' self-image and independence.

Even at the time of writing, brothel owners in Amsterdam have joined forces and have proposed that they finance a general practitioner who would offer a complete range of medical services for prostitutes. A report by the municipal health authorities has emphasized that prostitutes risk not only sexually transmitted diseases, but also stress, violence, poor diet, night-work, long working hours, inferior housing, bronchitis, and skin diseases. Clearly a doctor with a specialist responsibility for prostitutes and authorized to consider and to advise on such matters can make a considerable contribution. In this context it is relevant to cite Dr Peter Greenhouse of London. Greenhouse (1986) stated that sexually transmitted disease doctors who have no gynaecological knowledge often fail to detect pelvic infections and early signs of cervical cancer among their prostitute clients.

Conclusion

This chapter reflects the situation in Holland, with its unique socio-cultural circumstances. The authors do not propose the complete or uncritical adoption of Dutch policy in other countries. What they do advocate, however, is a fair and open debate on prostitution. Prostitutes themselves should have a voice and their views, both on prostitution in general and on AIDS-related issues, warrant serious consideration. Prostitutes deserve respect not only as human beings but also as prostitutes.

References

Alexander, P. (1988) *Prostitutes Prevent AIDS: A Manual for Health Education*, California: California Prostitutes' Education Project.

Centers for Disease Control (1988) *Morbidity and Mortality Monthly Report*, 29 January.

Coutinho, R.A. and Van der Helm, T. (1986) 'Geen aanwijzingen voor LAV/HTLV III onder prostituees in Amsterdam die geen drugs gebruiken', *Nederlands Tijdschrift Voor Geneeskunde* 13: 508.

First World Whores' Congress (1985), Amsterdam.

Greenhouse, P. (1986) Verbal contribution at Second World Whores' Congress, Brussels.

Hooykaas, C. (1988) *AIDS: een Bedreigende Situatie*, MD thesis, University of Amsterdam.

National Committee on AIDS Control (1988) *AIDS and Prostitution*, Amsterdam: Working Group on AIDS and Prostitution.

Pheterson, G. (ed.) (1989) *A Vindication of the Rights of Whores*, Seattle: Seal.

Van Andel, R. (1987) 'Eindrapport onderzoek onder homo-prostituees in Amsterdam', G.G. and E.D.

Van den Berg, T. and Blom, M. (1987) *Tippelen Voor Dope*, Amsterdam: S.U.A.

Van Gelder, P. and Van Roekel, A. (1989) *Baltsen en Banen*, Rotterdam: Public Health Department and the A. de Graaf Foundation, Amsterdam.

Van den Hoek, J.A.R., Coutinho, R.A., Van Haastrecht, H.J.A., Van Zadelhoff, A.W., and Goudsmit, J. (1987) 'Prevalence and risk factors of

HIV infections among drug users and drug using prostitutes in Amsterdam', *AIDS* 2: 55–60.

Van den Putte, B. (1987) 'Harddruggebruikerde straat prostituees en AIDS', in J. Blans (ed.) *AIDS: Voorlichting en Gedragsverandering*, Meppel: Boom.

Van de Raadt, S., Van Namen-Malkus, D.M., and de Lang, J. (1988) *Aids problematiek en Straat prostitutie*, Rotterdam: BOOG.

Chapter four

The Praed Street Project: a cohort of prostitute women in London

Sophie Day and Helen Ward

Introduction

Prostitute women have long attended the Praed Street Clinic, St Mary's Hospital, London, for screening and treatment of sexually transmitted diseases. It became apparent that the women were attending with particular needs, including, by 1985, concern about AIDS. An initial study by a physician in the clinic revealed that one out of fifty women who were tested were HIV seropositive (Barton *et al.* 1985). In 1986, a research project was established by the authors (a social anthropologist and a clinical epidemiologist) to explore the relationship between life-style and sexually transmitted diseases. This investigation was initiated in the context of emerging epidemiological evidence concerning HIV infection, which related to certain so-called 'risk groups' and activities (Curran *et al.* 1985). These data were proving difficult to interpret in the absence of knowledge about relevant social and sexual practices. The authors suggested that work with prostitutes in the clinic should combine clinical and epidemiological research with an anthropological study of life-style to try to fill this gap. This chapter attempts to demonstrate the importance of this approach by means of a review of condom use by a cohort of female prostitutes.

Methods

This study was related to a cohort of women who exchanged sex for money (or materials of monetary value). Past research on prostitution has also focused largely upon those who 'sell' sex. In so far as 'prostitution' refers equally to those who 'buy' sex and those who manage the exchange as middlemen or agents, this is clearly a partial perspective. It is anticipated that the Praed Street Project will, in the future, contact some of the sexual partners of prostitutes. The present report concerns only one subgroup of those involved with prostitution, namely, women who sell sex.

A cohort study was designed to recruit a hundred female prostitutes who would be seen regularly at the clinic over a period of two years. Because this study was based in a Genito-Urinary Medicine Clinic, it has been possible to include prostitutes working in a variety of ways in the study. Previous research has often been concerned with particular categories of prostitutes; for example, those who work on the streets or in saunas (Cohen 1980; Velarde and Warlick 1973). Diversity in the cohort made it possible to explore different dimensions of life-style and the incidence of sexually transmitted diseases in relation to parameters such as age, work-place, and use of drugs.

Two central research aims are facilitated by prospective research with prostitute women. First, a cohort study enables information on social and sexual practices to be related to the incidence of sexually transmitted diseases over time. Second, appropriate interview schedules may be developed and refined. Past research with prostitutes has frequently been based upon single interviews in contexts that are likely to bias answers, such as police custody (e.g. Jackman *et al.* 1967). Unless the researcher has already worked with prostitutes, this approach makes it difficult to gather appropriate data which reflect the ways in which prostitutes organize their lives. It is also difficult to evaluate the reliability (consistency) of the method and results. In other words, the results may reflect simply the structure of the interview situation and schedule. A cohort study makes it possible to check the reliability of the methodology and results over time. The Praed Street Project involved both a structured questionnaire that was administered formally and a series of informal, unstructured interviews on subsequent visits to the clinic. The structured questionnaire included questions on a number of topics relating to work history, life history, medical history, possible risks of infection, and perceptions about HIV. This questionnaire included some internal consistency checks through the repetition of questions. These same questions were repeated informally on subsequent meetings. Later interviews included a seven-day recall of sexual history. The latter were based largely on informal conversations organized in terms of what prostitutes wanted to discuss and what they considered important to their lives. Input from prostitutes offered a corrective to the formal questionnaire which was necessarily structured largely in terms of researchers' perceptions. It also ensured flexibility in the collection of information over time, since life-styles and perceptions may change. Notes were made from all interviews. Ten per cent were taped and transcribed. The tapes were then destroyed. As prostitutes began to re-attend the clinic, familiarity between the interviewer and the subject made it possible to interpret questions and answers more fully.

Three aspects of the cohort study are thus methodologically central: first, to include a wide range of prostitute women; second, to relate information to life-style and the incidence of sexually transmitted diseases over time; third, to evaluate interview methodologies and develop appropriate schedules. A fourth feature of the methodology is discussed separately as it is felt to be essential to the success of research. Service provision was included as a central aspect of the project, thereby minimizing exploitation of an already stigmatized population and making available resources that are not readily accessible elsewhere. Prostitutes attending the Praed Street Project are offered medical examinations, screening for sexually transmitted diseases, serology, medical treatment, referrals within the National Health Service when appropriate, counselling, health information, and free condoms. These services have been developed with the help of prostitutes who have joined the study and they appear to have encouraged re-attendance. Prostitutes making use of these resources were asked if they would take part in interviews. People may, however, use services without participating in the study.

These methods combine anthropological, epidemiological, and clinical approaches to the study of prostitute women in the cohort. Limitations on one particular perspective were hopefully balanced by the gains to the cohort study as a whole.

Results

One hundred and forty-eight women were recruited to the study by December 1988, of whom 106 had been seen on two or more occasions. These women each made between one and forty-four visits to the study location. Initially (1986–87) women were referred primarily through the general clinic but latterly (1987–88) most prostitutes were referred by their friends and colleagues.

Tables 4.1 and 4.2 illustrate the diversity within the cohort which includes a wide age range, variable amounts of time spent working as a prostitute, and a variable number of clients seen in the week prior to the first visit.

Table 4.1 Profile of cohort at first visit (n = 48)

Variable	
Age range	16 – 55 years
Intravenous drug users	7.4%
Length of time spent working as a prostitute	1 month – 27 years
Number of clients in previous week	0 – 70 clients

Table 4.2 Main work method at first visit

	%
Escort agency	31.5
Street	19.0
Flat/brothel	15.0
Privately	13.0
Club/sauna	9.5
Madame	9.0
Other	3.0

Women participating in the study worked in all the main ways used by London prostitutes, though the cohort was biased towards those meeting clients through escort agencies. This contrasts with the Edinburgh study group described in Chapter 6. Most of the prostitutes were white. The cohort included eight non-British nationals working in London. Three women of a total of 187 screened with consent (including approximately 80 per cent of the cohort and a number of other prostitutes attending the Praed Street Clinic) were seropositive for HIV-1. Two had shared equipment for injecting drugs in the past and one seemed to have been infected by her one seropositive boy-friend.

Since the project began in August 1986, the structured questionnaire has been modified substantially in the light of experience and suggestions made by women associated with the study. None the less, the data gathered in this way are treated with some caution, partly because of the results of an evaluation in the last three months of 1987. During this period, the authors both asked each woman standard questions about their previous week's sexual history on the same day. Interviews with thirty-six women were compared. Answers agreed exactly in only twenty of the thirty-six cases. These results indicated the limitations of formal structured questionnaires, at least in relation to certain areas of life such as sexuality. For prostitutes specifically, it may be difficult to remember contacts with clients and few women kept diaries. Accordingly, reliance is placed as much on qualitative as on quantitative data.

Condom use

Data on condom use reported in the cohort illustrate the relevance of the combined methodology. This illustration does not deal with differences in the cohort, which might be presented in terms of age, work-place, or injecting practices. The focus is rather upon a very general feature of prostitution in London, as reflected in the cohort, which concerns the way that women separate their work from their private lives. The description is based upon women who had sexual intercourse both with male clients at work and with private male sexual partners outside work. It does not, therefore, include a discussion of women who had no private sexual partners or those who had female sexual partners at home.

Many women reported condom use at work when they first attended the clinic. Indeed, many reported condom use long before they had heard of AIDS. Figures at first visit and during follow-up are illustrative. Three groups of women recruited approximately a year apart and similar in terms of age, work-place, and injecting practices are compared at their first visit to the project in Table 4.3. These details are based upon the previous week's sexual history and show the proportion of women reporting condom use with all clients for vaginal intercourse during that week.

Table 4.3 Proportions of respondents who reported always using condoms for penetrative sex with clients (1986–87/88)

	Group 1 (1986) n=25	Group 2 (1987) n=25	Group 3 (end 1987–beg. 1988) n=25
	%	%	%
Proportion using condoms with all clients	48	88	96

Reports over time during follow-up provide a more general impression of patterns of condom use. One hundred and six women reported, on two or more visits to the clinic, engaging in vaginal sex with clients. Their reported changes in condom use are shown in Table 4.4.

Table 4.4 Condom use with clients over time

Patterns of condom use for vaginal sex									
Always used condoms		Increased use over time		Variable		None		Total	
N	%	N	%	N	%	N	%	N	%
66	(62)	12	(11)	26	(25)	2	(2)	106	(100)

Two points about these reports are important. First, prostitutes reported high levels of condom use before the advent of AIDS. Second, worries about HIV infection have promoted increased condom use. Interview data suggested that peer pressure from other prostitutes provided the major impetus for change, although the project, media coverage, and government health campaigns are likely to have played some role. Since the middle of 1987, prostitutes have also reported that some clients are more willing to use condoms. These points raise the question of why prostitutes were using condoms at work before the advent of AIDS. Information on this subject is not readily collected in quantitative form and data were elicited on the basis of conversations in the clinic.

Prostitutes who attended this project described themselves as 'business girls' or 'working girls' and invariably stressed that the exchange of sex for money was 'work'. This attitude is illustrated by the following conversation. Pseudonyms and literal quotations are used:

Julia: 'I hate that word' (the interviewer had just used the word prostitute).
SD (Sophie Day): 'Some people say business girls.'
Julia: 'That's even worse. I'm a worker.'
SD: 'Yes, lots of people describe themselves as working girls.'
Julia: 'No. I'm just a worker. You hear "hooker" sometimes. Some of the older ones, who've been around for a while, they call themselves hookers. I'm not working. I'm a worker.'

Many prostitutes stressed the service aspect of their work, suggesting that they stopped men from raping other women or that prostitutes kept marriages intact. Some, usually those who worked as escorts, described themselves primarily as companions or hostesses. Others presented themselves as counsellors, social workers, sex therapists. Such arguments do not seek only to establish prostitution as work but as an *essential* work or service.

As already noted, the prostitutes who visited the clinic were very varied. They originated from eleven different countries and a wide range of work-places and socio-economic backgrounds. They rarely worked together; indeed, one of the more important aspects of prostitution in London is an enforced isolation at the work-place (Sion 1977). The women's universal concern to stress that prostitution was a form of work carried all the more significance against this background. This has been elaborated elsewhere (Day 1989).

It is clear from conversations in the clinic that condoms were associated with 'work' among this study group. Certain sexual activities were distinguished by means of condom use and turned into 'work' that had no relationship with a personal or private sex life. One young woman's comments about her work on the street were typical: 'I always use a sheath. I'd commit suicide if I didn't. But I don't use anything else, I couldn't prevent nature.' Other women mentioned a range of protective devices including, at times, a diaphragm, a spermicidal pessary, spermicide, and the oral contraceptive pill as well as a condom. One woman reported that she always put two condoms on her clients, and she stated that they 'never noticed'. She reported that she was currently seriously considering using three condoms during each client contact in order to protect herself from AIDS.

Women often stated that they regarded semen as 'dirty'. Both semen as well as any organisms it might carry were rejected. However, they appeared to take the view that it was only clients who had 'dirty semen' and that it was substances associated with work that must be kept outside their bodies.

Extracts from conversations and interviews in the clinic make it easier to understand why prostitutes use condoms and have always used condoms for many of their working contacts. A number of women said that condoms protected them from sexually transmitted diseases in general and not just HIV infection. They were particularly worried about infections that might cause infertility. More generally, however, condoms provide a means of keeping clients at distance and making sex at work distinct from sex outside work.

If condom use with clients makes sex into work, it is the absence of condom use with boy-friends that makes this kind of sex a private affair. The contrast can be illustrated initially by details of reported condom use at first visit and during follow-up (Tables 4.5 and 4.6). These figures were also based upon weekly sexual histories taken at first visit and subsequently. These tables relate to women who had boy-friends or husbands.

Table 4.5 Proportions of respondents who at first clinic visit reported always using condoms for vaginal sex with their non-paying partners (1986–87/88)

	Group 1 (1986) N=19	Group 2 (1987) N=19	Group 3 (end 1987–beg. 1988) N=19
	%	%	%
Proportion always using condoms with non-paying partners	10	10	17.6

Eighty-four women reported vaginal sex with private, male sexual partners ('boy-friends') at two or more visits to the project. Their reports of condom use are shown in Table 4.6

Table 4.6 Condom use for vaginal sex with non-paying partners over time

Always used condoms		Increased over time		Variable		None		Total	
N	%	N	%	N	%	N	%	N	%
6	(7)	5	(6)	4	(5)	69	(82)	84	(100)

As the preceding tables show, little condom use was reported with boy-friends, though a slight increase appears to have occurred. Interviews suggested that increased condom use in the cohort was related to changes of partner and concerns about possible infections. Condoms were also used for contraception. High and increasing rates of condom use at work contrast with little or no use outside work. Eighty-two per cent of the cohort reported no condom use at all in their private lives. These figures can also be understood better in the context of conversations and interviews at the clinic when most women distinguished sex at work from love at home.

Many women were horrified at the thought of using condoms with their private (non-paying) partners. Most said that their relationship would be finished, as illustrated by the following comments from three different women:

'We have a very good sex life. It would be spoilt if he wore a sheath. We would be finished.'

'I don't want strangers' semen inside. I only drop the barrier with someone I really love.'

'How could I? He would be like a client. It's different for people who don't work' (i.e. sell sex).

Much research with female prostitutes has focused only on the domain of work. However, it should be emphasized that women's private lives are equally important. First, what counts as work is established partly through a contrast with the rest of life. Therefore, an exclusive focus upon work provides only a partial perspective on prostitution. Second, reports of high and increasing rates of condom use at work suggest that both women and their clients may be increasingly better protected from HIV infection and other sexually transmitted diseases. It has been suggested that the high rates of partner change associated with work would be related to increased transmission of sexually transmitted diseases. This hypothesis may not be relevant if sex at work is effectively protected through condom use. It may be more relevant to consider prostitutes' non-working lives, which are not associated with high rates of partner change or directly with the sale of sex but which commonly involve unprotected sex (Day *et al.* 1988). Prostitutes in this cohort were well aware of this possibility. Many women attending the clinic with infections immediately attributed them to their private partners. Approximately half of the women with boy-friends reported that they knew these men had other sexual partners with whom, it was suspected, condoms were not used. Few of these men currently attended the clinic and research is necessary to establish whether their activities are associated with specific risks for acquiring sexually transmitted diseases. Campaigns to prevent the transmission of such diseases will need to be sensitive to the issues noted above. It is important to establish whether findings from this study can be generalized. If they can be, then preventive strategies will need to be directed as much at prostitutes' private lives as their work. This has been neatly summarized by a woman who revisited the clinic. She had moved from soliciting on streets to advertising and working in a flat because, she said, it was safer. She currently used two condoms each time for penetrative sex and one for 'hand relief' (masturbation). She engaged only in 'safer sex' with her clients. She commented:

> It's all right for you [Sophie Day]. You don't work with a gross of condoms by the bed, six days a week. How could I use condoms outside work? ... The mere thought of putting a condom on a boy-friend or watching him put it on just leaves me cold. I'd rather not have sex.

In fact, this woman later left her boy-friend in November 1988 partly because he had other sexual partners. She had not had a sexual relationship outside work in the previous four months. 'Celibacy' provided a more palatable alternative to the use of condoms outside work.

It is possible that the development of alternative distinctions between different types of sexual activity might make it easier for women to introduce condoms into non-working relationships. Some women did not sell penetrative sex but instead catered for a variety of fantasies, domination, and masturbation. Most women restricted the types of sex which they sold at work. Thus, no one in the cohort was currently selling passive anal sex at the end of 1988. If these other distinctions were developed, condoms might become less central to the demarcation between work and the rest of life. It is possible also that different types of condoms might come to stand for different relationships.

The picture that has been sketched makes it easier to understand why condoms are used at work but also makes it difficult to understand why condoms are not always used at work. A discussion of a third type of sexual partner, in between the casual or new client and the private partner, offers a partial answer to this question. This type of partner is the 'regular client' who pays to see the same woman repeatedly. Regular clients play a central role in a prostitute's career. With 'regulars', women are assured of an income; moreover, they can begin to establish themselves as self-employed businesswomen rather than employees

(Walkowitz 1980: 197). Money is frequently evaluated in a very different way from the transactions that occur with casual or new clients. Sometimes, regulars do not pay. On other occasions, they agree to meet expenses such as rent, private medical bills, or school fees. An example from the context of AIDS research is illustrative. A member of the International Committee of Prostitutes' Rights was invited to the Fourth International Conference on AIDS in Stockholm during 1988, initially unfunded. She tried to persuade a regular client to pay for her travelling expenses and one of the authors (Sophie Day) was involved in lengthy telephone conversations with this man to explain the purpose of the trip.

Regular clients may also be involved in women's personal lives. Indeed, a small number of women in the study cohort have turned regular clients into private partners. One is now married to an ex-client. In such relationships, women do not see themselves as prostitutes. One woman, for example, gave up work after her boy-friend had, yet again, turned out to be a pimp. She ran away and, later, began a college course. She has reported that she was no longer working even though all her fees were being paid by an ex-customer. Another woman, Tricia, reported that she had stopped work six to eight months previously. After a while it transpired that this meant she no longer worked for an agency. Tricia said:

> I couldn't afford not to work and I couldn't come off the methadone [which she had been using for ten years] because then I wouldn't be able to work. Withdrawing, the punters [clients] would think I was a junkie. I have this friend and he's agreed to support me for a year so now I can afford not to work and to come off the drugs.

This friend turned out to have been a customer who was so worried about AIDS that he agreed to keep Tricia and her son. She also saw another 'client'. This second man was not seen as a client; first, because they did not have 'sex' – 'I just masturbate him' – second, because he did not 'pay' her – 'he just sends me on holidays and things'.

Women in the cohort had different types of sex with regular clients and they did not always use condoms. An analysis was conducted of fifty-seven weeks' sexual history reported by thirty-four women in the last three months of 1987. Only one out of 161 contacts with new or casual clients was unprotected (by condoms) in comparison with twenty-eight out of 134 contacts with regular clients. This contrast was less apparent in data collected during 1988, since more women had begun to insist on condom use with their regular clients.

Patterns of condom use with regular clients provide a partial explanation of the failure to use condoms all the time at work.

The relevance of patterns of condom use in relation to the potential spread of sexually transmitted diseases, including HIV, clearly depends on how effective condoms are as a physical as well as a symbolic barrier. In vitro studies suggest that the latex of condoms is impermeable to HIV and other genital pathogens (Van de Perre *et al.* 1987). Studies demonstrating the protective effect of condoms in vivo are less clear. The incidence of common sexually transmitted diseases in two groups of women was compared. The first group included those who had reported condom use for all vaginal sex with every male partner, paying or non-paying. The second group included those who had ever reported unprotected vaginal sex. Ninety-one women were examined, with a total follow-up period of 693 months. The average number of visits per woman was 6.4 (range 2–27). The mean duration of follow-up was 7.6 months (range 1–18 months). A total of sixty-seven episodes of genital infection with *Neisseria gonorrhoeae* (GC), *Chlamydia trachomatis* (CT), and *Trichomonas vaginalis* (TV) were recorded in thirty-seven women. Table 4.7 records the differences between the consistent condom users and women who had ever reported unprotected vaginal sex. The first group had significantly fewer infections in relation to their follow-up time than had the second group.

Table 4.7 Genital infection in relation to condom use for vaginal sex

Subgroup	Months' follow-up	Episodes of infection	Type of infection	Episodes of each type of infection
Condom use with all partners (N=15)	105	4[1]	CT	4
Inconsistent condom users (N=76)	588	63	GC	24
			CT	21
			TV	18

[1] There were significantly fewer episodes of infection (based on follow-up time).

These results, using information collected over repeated interviews, give a clearer indication of the usefulness of condoms in the prevention of sexually transmitted diseases than do data based on information gained at only one visit.

In summary, an illustration of the importance of a combined methodology has been given with reference to patterns of condom use in the cohort. Three categories of sexual partner have been distinguished in relation to a general feature of this study group of prostitutes, which concerns the division created between work and private life. Possible implications for the transmission of HIV and other infections have been outlined. It should be reiterated that no case of HIV infection in the cohort was associated with work. Two HIV seropositive women had shared injecting equipment in the past and one appeared to have been infected by her seropositive boy-friend. The discussion elaborates this one case of sexually transmitted infection. It also provides important background for preventive initiatives. It may prove important to the prediction of future trends. In this context, it might be noted that research in the USA with prostitutes who do not inject drugs associates risk of HIV infection with large (fifty or more) numbers of non-paying partners (Darrow *et al.* 1988). The data on sexual and social practices which have been reported are not evident solely from a structured questionnaire. They were indicated by prostitutes in the study who suggested that they were most at risk of sexually transmitted diseases from their private lives. A picture has been built up through unstructured, informal interviews, over time. It is suggested that prostitutes cannot be divided into two parts, one of which is associated with work and which is an appropriate subject for research, and one of which is not associated with work and which is not a subject for research. Sexually transmitted diseases affect people in the course of their lives and transmission can only be understood when it is also known why, for example, women insist on prophylaxis in the first place and why they have their clients and private partners wear condoms on some occasions and not others. In sum, how do they organize their lives?

Conclusions: methods

It has been noted that this cohort study raises problems for purely anthropological or epidemiological research. For epidemiological purposes, the number of women is too small. One author, Helen Ward, has begun a cross-sectional survey of prostitutes working in London and hopes to recruit 600 women through collaborative research. Interview data through structured questionnaire will be assessed by means of comparisons with the cohort data and a measure of reliability will be produced. For anthropological purposes, interviews in a clinic setting are limiting. Outreach work and research have been established in the Paddington area since February 1989 which will enable data to be collected in other ways.

These new aspects of the Praed Street Project are partly designed to enable a fuller description of the study group. As noted, the cohort was biased towards women who worked in escort agencies and, obviously, towards clinic attenders. The authors have probably seen more women who work full-time as they are more likely to visit clinics regularly. It is hoped in future to compare participants with non-participants and to compare the relationships they have with other prostitutes, clients, and non-paying partners. A local enumeration will be made of those involved in prostitution and possible routes for the sexual transmission of infections will be delineated. It is hoped that the project will then be better able to specify risk associated with sexually transmitted diseases which, it must be emphasized in conclusion, derives as much from the wider social and legal context as from shared body fluids.

Acknowledgements

Dr J.R.W. Harris, Senior Consultant, and Catrina Donegan, Research Nurse, of the Praed Street Clinic, Professor D. Miller of the Academic Department of Community Medicine and the Jefferiss Research Trust are thanked for their help with this project. The authors thank the participants for their support. Sophie Day thanks AVERT for funding her research between 1986 and 1989. Helen Ward thanks the Medical Research Council for providing support since 1987.

References

Barton, S.E., Underhill, G.S., Gilchrist, C., Jeffries, D.H., and Harris, J.R.W. (1985) 'HTLV-III antibody in prostitutes', *Lancet* ii: 1424.
Cohen, B. (1980) *Deviant Street Networks: Prostitution in New York City*, Lexington: Lexington Books.
Curran, W.J., Morgan, W.M., Hardy, A.M., Jaffe, H.W., Darrow, W.W., and Dowdle, W.R. (1985) 'The epidemiology of AIDS: current status and future prospects', *Science* 229: 1352–7.
Darrow, W.W., Bigler, W., Deppe, D., French, J., Gill, P., Potterat, J., Ravenholt, O., Schable, C., Sikes, R.K., and Wofsy, C. (1988) 'HIV antibody in 640 US prostitutes with no evidence of intravenous (IV)-drug abuse', Fourth International Conference on AIDS, Stockholm, 1 June (abstract 4054).

Day, S. (1989) 'Prostitute women and the ideology of work in London', in D.A. Feldman (ed.) *AIDS and Culture: The Global Pandemic*, New York: Praeger (in press).

Day, S., Ward, H., and Harris, J.R.W. (1988) 'Prostitute women and public health', *British Medical Journal* 297: 1585.

Jackman, N.R., O'Toole, R., and Geis, G. (1967) 'The self-image of the prostitute', in J. Gagnon and W. Simon (eds) *Sexual Deviance*, New York: Harper & Row, pp. 133–46.

Sion, A.A. (1977) *Prostitution and the Law*, London: Faber.

Van de Perre, P., Jacobs, D., and Sprecher-Goldberger, S. (1987) 'The latex condom, an efficient barrier against sexual transmission of AIDS-related viruses', *AIDS* 1: 49–52.

Velarde, A.J. and Warlick, M. (1973) 'Massage parlors: the sensuality business', *Society* 11: 63–74.

Walkowitz, J. (1980) *Prostitution and Victorian Society: Women, Class and the State*, Cambridge: Cambridge University Press.

Chapter five

Outreach work with female prostitutes in Liverpool

Lyn Matthews

In October 1986 the Mersey Regional Drugs Information Centre started an injecting equipment exchange scheme in Liverpool as an attempt to prevent the spread of HIV through the sharing of used needles and syringes by local drug users. Despite minimal advertising of this service, word of this initiative travelled quickly among drug injectors and the scheme began attracting clients from the city and outlying areas. The scheme has currently attracted almost 1500 drug injectors. The service has developed into a comprehensive health care and AIDS prevention programme and new clients have been contacting the service at an average rate of two or three per day.

As well as supplying clean injection equipment, staff at the centre also provide free condoms and advice on 'safer sex'. Among the females attending the scheme were a number of prostitutes who also injected drugs. Initial discussions with these women revealed that prostitutes working a particular area, near to the city centre, were experiencing difficulties in obtaining sufficient supplies of condoms for their needs. Consequently, it was decided to supply these women with enough condoms to last them a week or more, free of charge. However, these women told their non-injecting colleagues of the scheme and soon they too requested supplies of free condoms.

Initial work with this group led to the realization that a number of strategies needed to be adopted in order to develop a coherent approach to the prevention of HIV infection among these women. These included problem definition, information gathering, and the identification of specific practical policies.

The first step was to clarify the problem and define the target population. From informal discussions with the women calling in for free condoms, it became clear that many of their clients were insisting on oral, vaginal, and anal sex without barrier protection. In fact, if a woman refused to have sex without a condom, many men (or 'mushes' as they are called by the women) would simply drive on until they found another woman who would consent. Since people engage in prostitution to make money, many women reported to acquiescing in such requests. Furthermore, their knowledge of HIV/AIDS and other infections was poor and largely based on information gleaned from the mass media, much of which was confused, contradictory, or inaccurate.

From this early feedback it was becoming clear that some form of immediate intervention was needed and that more detailed information was required in order to formulate and develop constructive prevention programmes. To this end, it was decided that condoms should be made more readily available and that information about infection should be disseminated. It was also decided to establish contact with more women who were working as prostitutes. It was initially unclear how this goal could be achieved.

Because of the stigma attached to prostitution there is a long, and not wholly unwarranted, suspicion of statutory services of all kinds among female sex workers. An early attempt to invite a group of women to a meeting to discuss AIDS prevention was a complete failure. No one attended. One of the women explained that they were afraid 'it would be full of social worker types'. In order to gain the confidence and co-operation of prostitutes it was obvious that different methods were needed.

The Mersey Regional Health Authority was beginning to develop AIDS prevention strategies aimed at those (such as drug injectors and sex workers) who were involved in high-risk activities. In April 1988 the injecting equipment exchange scheme moved into a larger building on the same site, which incorporated the Mersey AIDS Prevention Unit. The Maryland Centre, as it is now known, runs an injecting equipment exchange and distributes condoms. In addition, the Centre also provides HIV testing and counselling, health care facilities, advice, information, training, and conducts research. Each service is run by qualified staff. However, despite the 'user-friendly', open-door atmosphere of the Maryland Centre, detailed information about the prostitution scene in Liverpool was still sparse.

In October 1987, the author was asked by the Regional Drugs and AIDS co-ordinator of the Mersey Regional Health Authority to take part in a small exploratory survey of certain aspects of the prostitution scene in Liverpool. This request was initially rather intimidating. Preliminary discussions indicated that there was professional support for the proposed venture from workers at the Maryland Centre, the genito-urinary medicine clinic, and welfare agencies. Accordingly, a pilot initiative was launched. It was thought that an informal 'outreach' approach would be more productive and appropriate than the use of conventional health or social services. 'Outreach', as the name suggests, involves initiating friendly contacts with female sex workers on the streets or wherever they meet their clients.

The main purpose of this project was to assess the knowledge and attitudes of female sex workers related to HIV/AIDS and to design possible strategies for education and intervention into some of the more high-risk activities in which they might be involved. Field-work was undertaken without delay. Quite simply, the author approached the first woman she saw and could identify quite easily as a prostitute (by observing a particular area, her dress, her actions, etc.) and asked for her help. This individual was understandably very suspicious at first. However, a full explanation of the outreach project allayed her fears and she agreed to assist this initiative.

As initial contacts with this group developed, a clearer picture emerged of the size and nature of the prostitution scene in Liverpool. Although much of the prostitution in the city is difficult to discover and is covert (involving call girls, massage parlours, hostess clubs, etc.), it was possible to identify certain areas where high-profile, street work takes place. The main study areas are a residential area near the city centre, known by the women as 'The Block', and some public bars and clubs adjacent to the docks.

A hard core of between fifty and sixty women work the Block, supplemented by a peripheral, transient population who work the area as fortunes dictate. Many of this secondary group may work only two or three weeks a year (when the electricity or gas bills need to be paid, to buy Christmas presents, or because of other financial pressures). They lead 'normal' lives the rest of the time. The women work the street corners in pairs, with most clients picking them up in cars. This method serves as a form of protection as well as providing company. When a woman is picked up the other will note the car registration number in case of assault or robbery – not infrequent occurrences. In this way, the description of dubious or violent clients can be obtained, not necessarily for reporting to the police, but for circulation to other prostitutes.

Business conducted by the women operating the dockland area in the north end of the city differs considerably from that on the Block. There appears to be a hard core of thirty to forty women regularly working this area, but that can vary depending on how busy the docks are. These women are generally older and better established than those who work the Block. Clients are contacted in the bars or clubs facing the docks. Although Liverpool as a port has declined over the past twenty years, there is still a regular trade with West Africa, the Far East, South and North America. The women typically spend the evening drinking and dancing with the same client, before accompanying him back to the ship for the rest of the night. On occasions when the port is busy, with several large ships tied up, it is not uncommon for a woman to spend up to several weeks without leaving the docks at all, working, eating, and sleeping on board then moving on to the next ship. For some, it is like a holiday, free food and drink, plenty of money, and parties on board every night. The only things that usually go overboard are 'safer sex' and condom use.

Within a short time the author was introduced to many women who were pleased to meet someone who was not judgemental about what they were doing and was attempting to provide a useful service for them. Many of these women experience violence or theft at the hands of clients. In addition, many are frequently arrested, make numerous court appearances, and some spend short periods in prison. There was little evidence of pimps. Many of the women lived with husbands or boy-friends, for whom under present law that constitutes 'living on immoral earnings', but among this group there was no evidence of men forcing women on to the streets and confiscating their earnings.

Apart from gathering anecdotal information which would give only a very generalized picture of the scene, it soon became apparent that some hard evidence was required to support and direct any future initiatives. To this end, a simple, anonymous questionnaire was designed by a researcher from Liverpool University. This instrument was designed to provide uniform data related to specific aspects of the project. The questionnaire was self-completed by respondents. It examined approximately forty variables. These included details of condom use with clients, average daily number of clients, use of health care facilities, alcohol, tobacco, and illicit drug use, condom use with lovers/ non-paying partners, and HIV status (if known). This instrument was generally completed in ten to twenty minutes. Names and addresses of respondents were not recorded. At first, the author was concerned that this type of data collection might appear to be intrusive and threatening.

Luckily, a good relationship had been made with one of the women, 'Mary', whose assistance was invaluable. She knew most of the women working in this particular area and was able to explain the background to the outreach project and introduce the author to people who would otherwise have been hard to contact.

In background and experience, Mary was fairly typical of many of the women encountered. Aged 23, she had been working as a prostitute for the past eight years. Though she bore the scars of years on the street (knife wounds, missing teeth, etc.), her personality and sense of humour were surprisingly undiminished – a testament to her spirit and ability to survive awful hardships. She began working as a prostitute at the age of 15, after a bureaucratic error released her from social services care prematurely. She was one of the first women interviewed for a case study:

Q. How old were you when you were taken into care?
A. Ten months old.
Q. How long were you in care for?
A. Until I was fifteen and a half.
Q. Would you say that being in care had any effect on you going into prostitution?
A. Well, I got kicked out and had nowhere to go. I only had £20, so I had to go on the game. When I left, for about a year and a half I got visits from a social worker who was all apologetic because they thought I was a year older than I was. That's why they kicked me out. They thought I was sixteen and a half.
Q. So when you left, you had no money and no one to help?
A. They had a case conference and they decided they couldn't control me and it was up to me what I did. So I wanted to leave and they gave me £20.
Q. Did you go to the Social Security?
A. No. I couldn't get any Social. I wasn't eligible. I had nowhere to live. I booked into a bedsit and told her that I had a job and wasn't on Social and I used to go out in the morning. I had to pay her £13 a week rent.
Q. How long did you have to wait before you got money from the Social?
A. About a year.
Q. Do you know if any other girls have had similar experiences and felt they had no other option but to go into prostitution?

A. I know loads. But if they don't go into prostitution or robbing there is no way you could survive. You just walk the streets and that's terrible.

Mary's experience was typical of that of many of the women encountered during this project. A disrupted family life, periods (often years) in institutions, limited education, and a stifled upbringing all leading to self-reliance and sense of survival. A good rapport was developed with these women and it was possible to interview a study group quite quickly.

The survey

The study group for this initial pilot survey consisted of twenty-five women aged between 16 and 39. Of these, seventeen worked the street, six worked the docks, and two claimed to work in other locations. This survey was carried out between September and November 1987. Although no questions related to socio-economic status were asked, these girls were mainly lower working class. They were under-educated and lacked resources such as clothes, child care facilities, stable accommodation, and a polished manner that might have enabled them to move into physically and legally safer areas, such as hotels, massage parlours, and call girl work.

Sexual behaviours

The women claimed to have between one and thirty clients per day. Almost all used fewer condoms than they had client contacts. This discrepancy is, in part, due to the fact that full penetrative intercourse does not always occur. Even so, part of this discrepancy certainly also represents unprotected intercourse. The most common service provided by the women was masturbation (a 'play around' £5), but oral sex (a 'gam' £10), and vaginal sex (outdoors £15, indoors £25) were popular with the 'mushes' (clients). Anal penetration and other activities were less common, but prices were negotiable.

Although the majority of the women claimed to be scrupulous about using condoms, it was difficult to ascertain whether these replies were shaped by their expectations of what the author wanted to hear. One 16-year-old, however, admitted she never used them because 'seamen don't like them, and anyway, I use the sponge, so I'm OK'.

Unfortunately, the belief that contraceptive devices, in any form, act as a prophylactic and prevent sexually transmitted diseases was not uncommon. Despite the insistence of many women that they almost always use condoms while 'doing business', the majority also had sexual partners outside work. Almost all stated that they never used a condom for sex with their husbands or other lovers.

Alcohol and drugs

The use of various drugs, both legal and illegal, was far higher for the women in this study group than could be expected for the population as a whole. Twenty-two of the twenty-five questioned smoked between ten and sixty cigarettes a day and over half reported drinking heavily on a regular basis. However, of those who never or seldom consumed alcohol almost all used illicit drugs. For more than half of these women the drug of choice was an opiate, usually heroin, although five reported using cannabis (marijuana), one had used amphetamines, and one was a non-opiate poly-drug user. Six of the opiate users injected and three of these admitted to sharing needles and syringes. Despite a range of helping agencies in the area, more than half of the study group said they did not know where to find a service dealing with drug problems.

Action taken

As a result of this information it was decided that a number of objectives should be met, both long and short term. It was felt that, in the long term, a specific health response was needed, aimed at providing a service to this group who were traditionally apprehensive of interference from health and social agencies. This would need to be designed to meet the special requirements of this group. This required a confidential, non-judgemental, friendly approach and easy access. It would take time to mount a proper service. Accordingly, it was decided to proceed without delay to raise awareness of the danger of HIV transmission and to encourage women who needed immediate help in the direction of appropriate services. The most obvious course of action was to make condoms and educational materials readily available.

So, since early in 1988, the author, supplied with condoms and leaflets, has gone out two or three evenings each week to meet working prostitutes. She quickly became established as 'the health worker' and whenever she appeared in their area women sex workers would flock round her car for free condoms. The most visible sign that changes in the women's behaviour have taken place is the fact that condoms have been in far greater demand than before. Complaints about the taste or strength of certain brands make it clear that they have been used. One woman, when offered ribbed condoms, replied, 'Oh, I don't want them, the mushes [clients] might think I'm enjoying myself.' Certain sexual practices are being discouraged by the women who have visited or who continue to attend the Maryland Centre for both condoms and advice.

One of the most important factors in attempting to influence behaviour is raising self-esteem. Safer sex messages may mean little to many of the women encountered over this period since they have a very low opinion of themselves and consequently show scant regard for their health and general well-being. Support and trust are vital factors here. Advocacy and befriending are things that many of these women are unfamiliar with. Attempts to make contact with a group such as this may stand or fall on the way the worker is perceived. In the initial stages, the author was concerned that asking too many questions may have seemed intrusive or insensitive. Little things, such as not being intimidated by the police or not believing everything the sex workers say, go a long way to establishing a good rapport and enhancing one's credibility. In time, helping women with other problems (such as housing, child care, and legal issues) allowed the project to develop into a more comprehensive service.

Drugs and risks of HIV infection

Since this pilot survey was undertaken, a dramatic change has taken place in the drug-using behaviour of many of the women encountered. A fall in purity and availability of street heroin has led to the majority of users switching from smoking to injecting, adding further importance to the use of clean equipment, condoms, and knowledge of HIV transmission. Furthermore, the appearance and rapid uptake of crack (smokable cocaine) in the latter months of 1988 changed not only their drug use, but also their work. Some of the women, however, admit that they did not particularly like this drug – 'I don't rate it that much, it makes my eyes water. But if it's there . . . I'll take it.'

One of the more worrying side-effects of crack use that has been witnessed is the associated change in demeanour of some of the women. Many who were generally cheerful by nature became surly and depressed. There was a marked increase in aggression and outbursts of violence, which had previously been rare. Fighting would break out over the smallest thing – a glance here, a word there – but more often fighting would break out in competition for clients. Money was becoming more and more important. Increasingly, the author has been confronted with women who are desperate to raise the £60 for a small 'rock' and who are in such a state of distress that they will engage in high-risk sex to raise the money quickly. As one woman stated: 'I'll do anything to make my money when I'm turkeying . . . you have to take that risk when you need the money.'

Another group who have been contacted through the female sex workers are the local drug dealers. As already noted, prostitutes in the study area generally do not work for pimps. Even so, some of them do have a close relationship with dealers. Some dealers are known to exchange drugs for sex, and many of the women use dealers' flats as a base in the area. The author gained access to several drug dealers through introductions by the women. One house visited was occupied by a well-known local dealer. This was a good place to meet the women since they used it as a resting place for short periods, to adjust their make-up and to buy and take drugs. On every occasion when the author visited this house there were always at least eight or ten women there. The dealer himself was quite open, even boastful, about his relationship with the women. He readily admitted having sex with them and professed never to use a condom – 'No, I don't like rubbers, and anyway, you can't catch AIDS through heterosexual sex.'

The women themselves confirmed this and other females who used different dealers also claimed that this was common practice. Many women admitted that although they did not like working in this manner, they felt they had little option – 'I only do it with him 'cos he gives me gear. I hate the bastard, but the gear's good at least.'

Some women further reported that clients sometimes waved bags of heroin around to entice them into engaging in unprotected sex.

You've got smackheads [heroin users] out there who'd do anything for a flim [£5] bag. Go up the arse and everything. There was a guy who used to hang around and he used to buy a £10 bag of smack and he would know he could pick a junkie up. He knew he could get anything he wanted with that £10 bag. He would say you could have half now and half later. That was bad 'cos he was playing on them.

Despite the encouraging signs that attitudes and behaviour are changing among the majority of the women, there are a number of other groups that require far more work if major gains are to be made. First, the greatest inconvenience of working as a street prostitute is the policing of the area. It is plain that the law, as it stands, forces women further and further into the shadows and also into more dangerous situations. The women themselves view arrest and prosecution as simply an occupational hazard. In fact, the police appear to arrest the women on a rota basis to comply with the letter of the law. However, it is obvious that some changes, either in the law or in punishment, need to be made. It is ironic that punishment by fining merely increases the women's work-load. As well as having to raise money for rent/food/child care/drugs, etc., they are also expected to pay a fine and may have sex with additional clients to obtain extra money. Obviously, fines often do not get paid and consequently some prostitutes spend short periods in prison. As one woman stated: 'I just think of it like paying my taxes.'

The advent of AIDS must surely now force a reappraisal of how society deals with commercial sex. The behaviour of the police is often over-zealous. In some respects the law is now at odds with the requirements of public health.

The most obvious problem is the fact that when a woman is fined for prostitution, she has to work harder to raise money to pay the fines. One woman, 'April', had decided to give up prostitution because the police were having one of their periodic purges and arresting local prostitutes. Unable to manage solely on Social Security, she resorted to shoplifting, was arrested, and returned to prostitution.

Many of the women do not have a permanent address and are not entitled to Social Security benefits. It must be obvious to the courts, therefore, that these women have few means of paying fines apart from prostitution. One woman, after appearing in court in the morning, was back on the Block the same afternoon to raise money for the fine. After being moved on several times by the police, she said indignantly: 'They know I can't pay the fine any other way than doing business. I wish they'd just piss off and leave me to work in peace. If I don't pay the fine they'll lock me up for a week.'

Second, the group that has the most influence on a prostitute's behaviour is the paying customer. It is obviously sensible to educate these women about high-risk activities. Even so, this does not deter many clients from offering more money for sex without a condom. No contact has been made with the clients in Liverpool, so it is difficult to know what the best approach to educating them could be. Clients are numerous. Some of them could spread HIV infection to their wives and other partners and eventually into the rest of the community. Clients are a key group for future HIV prevention strategies.

Last, but not least, is the problem of the prostitutes who also inject drugs. This group is obviously at risk not only from their sexual behaviour but also from drug taking if they share injecting equipment. This project is to continue with the priority objective of contacting drug-using prostitutes, since these may be likely to engage in high-risk behaviour due to the added pressure of financing drug use. It is also planned to conduct a second survey with this particular group. It is hoped that this will identify specific interventions into their behaviour and facilitate the design of educational and health care strategies to minimize the risks of HIV infection.

Despite what must seem a very depressing and disheartening job, this project has been both enjoyable and rewarding. Occasional 'successes', when practical interventions improve the situation for some women, make the time and effort worthwhile. 'Miriam', for example, had expressed a wish on several occasions to come off drugs and quit the work. However, as she explained, 'I can't get to see anyone. By the time I get up, come out here to make my money, go and score and stop the turkey, everywhere's closed. We don't live office hours.' The author repeatedly offered to accompany her to the Maryland Centre on one of the nights that it was open late, to discuss the problem with one of the nurses there. After weeks of encouragement, she finally agreed to such a visit. As a result of this, she was given a course of methadone by her family doctor, moved back home to her mother's house, and was awaiting a place at a residential rehabilitation project. She has not returned to the Block since.

While methadone programmes do not automatically stop opiate-using women from engaging in prostitution, they do relieve them from the pressure of work and may cut down the likelihood of prostitutes engaging in dangerous practices. Those women who received methadone on prescription did not appear as often on the Block as did drug users who lacked such prescriptions. Shirley was a typical example of this. She had a particularly expensive drug habit and had been waiting some considerable time for an appointment at the local drug-dependence clinic. In addition, the number of clients she had to have to maintain her habit was making her very depressed – 'It's awful. I feel like one of them fuckin' mice runnin' round a wheel all the time and gettin' nowhere.'

It emerged that there had been a clerical error related to her appointment at the clinic. This was corrected and she was seen fairly quickly. Her prescription for methadone has stabilized her and, despite the fact that she still works on the Block, she has had contacts only with two regular clients since the pressure to pay for drugs has been removed.

In some cases, interventions into health problems are more urgent and not drug-related. Denise was one such case. One evening, while waiting for her friend who was with a client, Denise stated that she was concerned about her psoriasis, which she thought had worsened over the months. She explained that she had had no treatment for this condition for several years and wanted the author's opinion. She removed the thick tights that she always wore to reveal a rash that covered most of her legs. It appeared to be badly infected, with open, weeping sores. It was obvious that she could be in greater danger of HIV infection through contact with seminal fluid if she continued to work with this condition. She was advised to see her doctor as soon as possible or to contact a nurse at the Maryland Centre. One afternoon, about a week later, the author met her again. She had not done anything about the rash. The author took her to the Centre, where a nurse was able to see her immediately. A telephone call to a local health centre obtained an immediate appointment to see a doctor. Within half an hour she was receiving medical treatment. Luckily, the author was able to stay with her through the appointment, discuss the problem with the doctor, and give her support and reassurance.

So far, this project has only scratched the surface of the prostitution scene in Liverpool. Contact has been established with only one group of women, those who work particular streets. There are a number of other groups of women and, of course, male prostitutes that remain to be contacted. These are in other localities and represent different branches of the sex industry. Contacting such workers and their numerous clients will require different strategies.

Chapter six

AIDS risks, alcohol, drugs, and the sex industry: a Scottish study

Ruth Morgan Thomas

Introduction

Edinburgh, the capital of Scotland, is in the unenviable position of having the highest proportion of intravenous drug users who are known to be HIV seropositive in any British city. Over half of those who have been tested have been exposed to HIV infection (Robertson 1986; Robertson *et al.* 1986). By the end of March 1989, 969 people had been tested as HIV seropositive in Edinburgh. Fifty-five per cent of those were intravenous drug users and it was known that some of these were working in the sex industry (Morrison 1988a; Robertson 1988; Goldberg 1989). As described in Chapter 1, growing evidence indicates that prostitutes and their clients are at risk of HIV infection. In addition, such infection is clearly related in some localities to intravenous drug use and may also be connected with the disinhibiting effects of alcohol and other drugs. Accordingly, a research project was initiated in May 1988 in Edinburgh to examine the behavioural aspects of AIDS-related risks, alcohol, and drug use in relation to the sex industry with regard to both workers and clients.

The study was designed to achieve the following aims:

1. To ascertain to what extent sex workers and their clients engage in sexual activities which involve a high risk of HIV infection and whether they adopt measures (e.g. condom use or refraining from 'high-risk' activities) which reduce these risks.
2. To examine self-reported levels of tobacco, alcohol, and illicit drug use and related problems among sex workers and their clients.
3. To examine whether patterns of alcohol and illicit drug use are

associated with sexual activities which involve a 'high risk' of HIV infection.

4. To determine levels of knowledge about 'high-risk' behaviours among sex workers and their clients.

Method

For the purposes of this study a 'prostitute' or 'sex worker' was defined as a male or female who provides sexual services in exchange for some form of payment such as money, drugs, or other items of value. The client was, therefore, defined as a male or female who provides some form of payment in exchange for sexual services.

The size and location of the study groups of sex workers and their clients were unknown. Accordingly, it was not possible to conduct random or representative sample surveys. Instead, a non-random procedure known as 'snowballing' was employed as a method of contacting potential respondents. This is a standard means of locating specific subgroups for social/epidemiological research. 'Snowballing' involves the researcher or researchers establishing contact with initial members of the intended study group (e.g. sex workers, clients) who in turn provide introductions to others (Polsky 1969; Plant 1975; Morrison 1988b).

Information was elicited by standardized interviews conducted by twelve trained field-workers. An interview schedule was used for sex workers and a second, similar, instrument was used for clients. These interviews took between an hour and an hour and a half to complete. Respondents were not paid for their co-operation, which is standard procedure in British epidemiological research. The interview schedules contained questions on approximately 330 variables. These related to the following topics:

1. Biographical characteristics.
2. 'Commercial' sexual behaviour, including details of length of time involved in sex industry, methods of contacting clients, hours worked, localities used, activities engaged in, activities NOT engaged in, condom use, contraception, extent to which clients discuss or request safer/unsafe sexual practices, and response to AIDS risks.
3. 'Personal' sexual behaviour. This related to sex with lovers or non-paying long-term or casual partners.

4. Health care, including history of sexually transmitted diseases, use of health services, and HIV status.
5. Alcohol, tobacco, and illicit drug use and their related social, medical, and legal consequences.
6. AIDS-related attitudes, knowledge, and beliefs.

Results

At the time of writing, information is not yet available on a study group of approximately 200 clients of prostitutes. These will be described in other publications. The results that are presented here relate to the first 205 sex workers from whom data were obtained. These were interviewed between July and December 1988. This initial study group consisted of 102 males and 103 females. The even balance between males and females should not be seen as representative of those working in Edinburgh's sex industry. It reflects the fact that some of the interviewers had more contacts with male sex workers than with female workers. The former are frequently referred to in Britain as 'rent boys'.

There was limited non-response to some of the questions included in the interview. Accordingly, the totals presented below vary from item to item.

The marital status of the study group is shown in Table 6.1.

Table 6.1 Marital status of the study group

Marital status	Males N	Females N
Single	84	47
Married	2	3
Separated	7	19
Widowed	1	–
Divorced	1	14
Cohabiting/single	6	13
Cohabiting/separated	–	1
Cohabiting/widowed	–	1
Cohabiting/divorced	1	5
Total	102	103

Biographical characteristics

The mean age of the male respondents was 23 and that of the females was 26. Only six males and two females (i.e. 4 per cent of the study group) had left school when they were over 16 years of age. Two respondents, one male and one female, were still attending school. During the latter half of the 1970s approximately 39 per cent of Scottish school pupils stayed at school beyond 16 (Scottish Office 1984). These respondents were a highly atypical group of people in comparison with the general population.

Nine of the males reported having one or two children. Seven of these stated that their children never lived with them. In contrast, forty-four of the females had children. Twenty of these stated that their children never lived with them. Only 17 per cent of the males and 37 per cent of the females described themselves primarily as sex workers. The self-identified employment status of the study group is shown in Table 6.2. Overall, half of the males and 70 per cent of the females stated that they regarded prostitution as 'work'.

Table 6.2 Employment status of the study group

Employment status	Males N	Females N
Sex industry worker	17	38
Government training scheme	9	–
Full-time work	5	5
Part-time work	8	9
Unemployed, seeking work	55	19
Unemployed, not seeking work	5	14
Mother/housewife	–	3
Part-time education	–	2
Temporary job	1	–
Out of work through illness	–	2
Temporarily out of work through illness	1	1
Other	–	8
Total	102	101

Methods of contacting clients

Edinburgh, a city with a population of approximately 500,000, does not have a 'red light' district. This is reflected by the methods of contacting clients which were reported by the study group. These are shown in Table 6.3.

Table 6.3 Methods of client contact

Point of contact	Males	Females
	N	N
Bar	57	54
Disco	71	39
Street	35	43
Clients	36	37
Through sex workers/pimps	24	41
Massage parlour/sauna	3	29
Escort agency	1	19
Advertising	3	12
Brothel/private flat	3	5
Club/hostess work	–	1
Other	19	10

Note Some respondents reported two or more methods of contacting clients.

The male sex workers fell into two categories. First, some worked the streets, bars, discos, and actively sought clients. Second, others worked from private flats, saunas, escort agencies, and through advertising. The latter relied on clients to seek them out. The females, on the other hand, could be divided into three groups. First, some worked around the streets, bars, and discos, and sought out clients. Second, some worked primarily from saunas, private flats, and brothels. Third, others worked through escort agencies, visiting massage agencies, and through advertising. The last group were normally contacted by telephone and often visited the clients at their hotels, homes, or other locales. The last two groups relied on clients to seek them out.

A substantial minority of both males and females reported sometimes working outside Edinburgh. This is shown in Table 6.4. As this table shows, a third of the males and approximately 40 per cent of the females had at some time engaged in prostitution outside Edinburgh. Almost a fifth of the males and a quarter of the females had worked in London.

Ninety-eight per cent of the study group accepted money in exchange for sexual services. In addition, a quarter reported that they sometimes accepted payment in the form of cannabis or other illicit drugs. Thirteen per cent of the males and 20 per cent of the females sometimes accepted alcohol in exchange for sex. Twenty of the males and ten females reported that they were not currently engaged in prostitution.

Table 6.4 Locations of work

Locations worked	Males	Females
	N	N
Edinburgh only	68	56
Glasgow	16	30
Rest of Scotland	7	17
London/SE England	17	26
Midlands	1	–
Merseyside	1	3
NE England	4	2
NW England	1	–
Wales	4	–
Outside UK	2	6

Note Some respondents reported working in several locations.

The sex distribution of the respondents' clients is shown in Table 6.5.

Table 6.5 The sex of respondents' clients

Clients	Respondents	
	Males N	Females N
Males	79	90
Females	4	2
Males and females	11	10
Total	94	102

As this table shows, the majority of both male and female sex workers catered exclusively for male clients. A minority, eleven males and ten females, were prepared to have clients of either sex and a smaller group, four males and two females, catered for female clients.

Condom use

Some details of self-reported condom use and AIDS-related risk among this study group have already been reported elsewhere (Morgan Thomas *et al.* 1989). Respondents were asked whether or not they asked their clients to use condoms for penetrative sex. Their pattern of responses is shown in Table 6.6.

Table 6.6 Frequency of requesting clients to use condoms for penetrative sex

Frequency	Males N	Females N
Always	63	62
Usually	11	14
Sometimes	7	15
Rarely/never	5	8
Total	86	99

It is emphasized that the information in Table 6.6 does not indicate the level of client condom use. Even so, it is notable that a small minority of both males and females reported that they rarely or never requested their clients to use condoms. Only a third of the male sex workers and a quarter of the females reported that clients never refused to use condoms. The majority of the study group reported that at least some of their clients did not use condoms. Approximately half of the study group reported encountering clients who specifically asked for *unprotected* penetrative sex. Twenty-six males and thirty-one females reported that they at least occasionally charged more money to engage in unprotected sex. A total of thirty-nine males and forty females, 38.5 per cent of the study group, reported that they sometimes had unprotected intercourse with clients.

Respondents were asked to estimate the proportions of clients with whom they used condoms for penetrative sex. Females reported that on average they did so on 56 per cent of occasions for vaginal intercourse. The corresponding proportion of condom use among males having vaginal intercourse with female clients was 79 per cent.

More specific information was elicited on client contacts in the week preceding interview. This revealed that male sex workers had used condoms for only 25 per cent of vaginal and 89 per cent of anal intercourse. Female workers reported having used condoms for 87 per cent of vaginal and 100 per cent of anal intercourse.

A third of the males and a fifth of the females reported having experienced at least one condom failure during the months preceding interview. At least some of these failures were probably due to the use of inappropriate condoms. For example, those suitable for anal sex were not readily available in Edinburgh during the study period. In addition, 79 per cent of the males and 45 per cent of the females reported that they used lubricants with condoms. Some of these individuals stated that they used oil-based preparations which have been reported to perish condom latex.

These results indicate that the majority of men and women interviewed in this study had adopted risk-reduction measures related to the spread of HIV infection and other sexually transmitted diseases. Nevertheless, a considerable proportion had not adopted such precautions all of the time. The reports given indicated that in most cases where unprotected sex occurred it was in response to client request. Only 7 per cent of the males and 4 per cent of the females reported that they themselves at least sometimes refused to use condoms. Other factors which restricted condom use included the availability of condoms at the time of client contact and difficulties in obtaining condoms suitable for specific purposes (such as anal and oral sex). In addition, some of the men and women interviewed reported allergic reactions to condoms or to other prophylactic devices. The major constraint appeared to be the reluctance of some clients to use condoms. The above findings clearly indicate that there is considerable scope for improvement. Even so, 53 per cent of the males and 66 per cent of the females reported using condoms more since they had become aware of AIDS than they had done previously. In addition, 23 per cent of the males and 21 per cent of the females reported that they had always used condoms.

Another AIDS 'risk reduction' measure which sex workers could employ would be to offer alternatives to penetrative intercourse. However, only 15 per cent of the males and 28 per cent of the females reported a change in the sexual services they provided. This is not, in fact, that surprising as it would also have meant a considerable reduction in income levels. Among the males who reported a change in the services they provided, 59 per cent stated that this reflected a change in the clients' requests, 12 per cent ascribed it to their own insistence, and 29 per cent reported that it was a joint decision. Among the females who reported a change, 32 per cent stated that it was at the clients' request, 6 per cent at their insistence, while 62 per cent felt it was a joint decision.

The study group was asked whether or not they had continued to see the same number of clients since the publicizing of the AIDS epidemic. Approximately half reported that this publicity had not affected the number of clients with whom they had contact. A quarter reported seeing fewer clients. In contrast, 7 per cent of the males and 18 per cent of the females stated that they had more client contacts since the AIDS publicity than they had before. These responses doubtless reflect a variety of factors and are rather difficult to interpret.

Non-paying partners

Sixty-eight males and seventy-nine females reported that they had engaged in sexual activities with at least one lover or non-paying partner in the month preceding interview. Thirty-five males and fifty-six females stated that they currently had a regular partner. Of the latter, five males and ten females reported that their regular partners had engaged in sexual activity with someone else during their association. Twenty-six of the males and thirty-one of the females with regular partners reported that they never or only rarely used condoms with their partners. Ninety-one respondents reported that they had a regular non-paying partner. Of these nineteen males and five females were in gay relationships. The remaining sixteen males and fifty-two females had heterosexual partners.

Psychoactive drug use

Respondents were asked a battery of questions on their use of alcohol, tobacco, and illicit drugs such as cannabis (marihuana), LSD, cocaine, and heroin.

Tobacco

Seventy-three per cent of the males and 87 per cent of females reported that they smoked tobacco. Even taking into account the general youthfulness and low socio-economic status of the study group, this is an atypically high level of tobacco use. Among those aged 20–24 in the overall Scottish population only 37 per cent smoked during 1986 (Scottish Committee, Action on Smoking and Health 1989).

Alcohol

The self-reported alcohol consumption of the study group has already been described elsewhere (Plant *et al.* 1989). Only six males and eight females claimed to be total abstainers. In fact, a high proportion of the study group were regular and heavy drinkers. Details of alcohol consumption were recorded in 'units' of alcohol. Each unit is roughly equivalent to half a pint of normal strength beer, stout, cider, or lager or to a single 'public bar' measure of spirits or to a glass of wine. Each unit contains approximately one centilitre or 7.9 grammes of absolute alcohol.

Approximately two-thirds of those interviewed reported having drunk during the previous week. Among the males who had done so the mean week's alcohol consumption was 63.8 units, equivalent to thirty-two pints of beer or to two bottles of spirits. The corresponding mean for females was 48.1 units, equivalent to twenty-four pints of beer or to a bottle and a half of spirits.

Respondents also provided details of the amount of alcohol they had consumed on their last drinking occasion. Since most had drunk in the past week this was not an independent measure, but was, for most, included in their week's total. Male drinkers reported consuming a mean of 17.7 units and female drinkers reported consuming a mean of 13.9 units. Even taking into account the general youth of the study group, their alcohol consumption levels, like their tobacco smoking, were highly atypical. Both the drinking and smoking certainly reflect the fact that most of those interviewed spent much of their working time in and around licensed premises. Some of the interviewers reported that many of the study group were conspicuously heavy drinkers.

A quarter of the study group, twenty-four males and twenty-eight females, had, in the week preceding interview, consumed quantities of alcohol which have been identified as exposing those who regularly imbibe such quantities to high levels of risk from adverse consequences. These levels are 50 units for males and 35 units for females (Royal College of Psychiatrists 1986; Royal College of General Practitioners 1986; Royal College of Physicians 1987). It must be noted that a considerable proportion of the study group was interviewed during December 1988. This fact certainly served to increase alcohol consumption levels. Approximately 40 per cent of the study group reported that they 'always' or 'usually' drank while working and fewer than a quarter stated that they never did so.

Illicit drugs

Consistent with their very high levels of tobacco and alcohol use, the study group also reported a high degree of illicit drug use. For the purpose of this study 'illicit' drugs were defined as substances such as cannabis or heroin which are controlled by the Misuse of Drugs Act

(1971) as well as glues and solvents or other substances used recreationally.

The overall levels of self-reported use of a list of seventeen types of drugs are shown in Tables 6.7a and 6.7b.

Table 6.7a   Levels of self-reported illicit drug use (males)

Type of drug	Ever used	Used at least once each month
	%	%
Cannabis	90	58
LSD	31	2
Barbiturates	14	–
Ativan	5	–
Librium	4	1
Valium	26	4
Mogadon	15	–
Glues/solvents	28	–
Amphetamines	59	24
Amyl/butyl nitrate	55	22
Heroin	11	4
Methadone	7	6
Cocaine	28	4
PCP (Angel dust)	3	–
Temazepam	7	1
Pain-killers	17	1
Other sleeping tablets/ tranquillizers	18	3

Note Percentages are calculated in relation to the number of males who answered each question. These varied from 80 to 96.

As these tables indicate, the study group had engaged in high levels of drug use, including regular use. Differences between the drug experiences of the sexes were not great. Even so, females were markedly more likely to report having used benzodiazepines (e.g. Ativan and Valium) as well as heroin, cocaine, and substances such as pain-killers and sleeping tablets than were males. The latter, however, were more likely to have used amphetamines.

Intravenous drug use

Forty-one respondents, a fifth of the study group, reported having at some time used drugs intravenously. Females were significantly more likely than males to report such drug use, twenty-eight out of 101 compared with only thirteen out of 100 (Morgan Thomas *et al.* 1989). Eighteen women and six men were still injecting drugs at the time of interview. Thirty-nine of the forty-one people who had used drugs intravenously had shared their injecting equipment with other people since 1980. This is important, since, as emphasized throughout this book, such sharing practices are one of the two major ways whereby HIV infection may be transmitted.

Table 6.7b Levels of self-reported illicit drug use (females)

Type of drug	Ever used	Used at least once each month
	%	%
Cannabis	83	53
LSD	28	1
Barbiturates	29	–
Ativan	25	8
Librium	19	1
Valium	55	32
Mogadon	24	2
Glues/solvents	18	–
Amphetamines	62	20
Amyl/butyl nitrate	47	4
Heroin	33	9
Methadone	23	10
Cocaine	48	9
PCP (Angel dust)	8	–
Temazepam	28	12
Pain-killers	49	20
Other sleeping tablets/ tranquillizers	41	13

Note Percentages are calculated in relation to the number of females who answered each question. These varied from 90 to 99.

Fewer than a third of those who were still using drugs intravenously reported that they never shared injecting equipment. All of them reported having shared equipment in the past. The most recent sharing episodes ranged from 1983 to 1988.

The remaining seventeen respondents who currently used intravenous drugs and who still shared their injecting equipment were asked about the frequency with which they did so. The five males reported sharing equipment on average five times per month with an average of

2.3 people. The twelve females reported sharing on average 7.5 times per month with an average of 6.3 different people. Their sharing was not confined to Edinburgh. Three males and nine females reported sharing in other parts of the UK.

As already noted, a total of ninety-one respondents reported that they currently had a lover or non-paying sexual partner. Fifteen of these, six males and nine females, reported that their partners had used drugs intravenously. A further five males and four females either did not know or declined to answer this question.

Alcohol and drug problems

Approximately half the study group reported having experienced some form of adverse consequence associated with their alcohol or illicit drug use. These are shown in Table 6.8.

Table 6.8 Experience of alcohol or drug problems

Problem	Males N	Females N
Financial	30	35
Domestic	32	34
Legal	26	34
Health	22	26
Social	16	23
Work	11	20
Total	58	48

Note Some individuals reported more than one problem. The totals relate to those who reported one or more such problems.

HIV status

Approximately 60 per cent of the study group, half the males and nearly three-quarters of the females, reported having had an HIV antibody test (Morgan Thomas *et al.* 1989). Five males and twelve females reported that they had received a positive test result. Three males and five females reported that they did not know the result of the tests. In addition, two males and seven females declined to disclose the result of their tests. The others who had been tested reported receiving negative results. The males who reported having a positive test result had all used drugs intravenously and stated that they had shared injecting equipment with someone who was HIV seropositive. However, only nine out of the twelve HIV seropositive females reported a personal history of intravenous drug use and sharing injecting equipment with someone who was HIV seropositive. The remaining three females attributed their HIV infection to sexual transmission. One reported that her regular partner was a seropositive intravenous drug user. The other two reported that their former sexual partners included people whom they knew were HIV seropositive. Both women also reported having had hepatitis B at least once. It is therefore probable that their sero-conversions were also related to intravenous drug use by their partners. Three of the twelve HIV seropositive females reported that they were not currently working as prostitutes.

Health care

The study group was asked whether or not they contacted medical practitioners for routine health checks. Only 109 out of 205 replied that they did so. Fifty-three individuals further reported that they did not always seek medical advice even if they had genital or anal symptoms which could have been attributable to sexually transmitted disease. Half the males and a third of the females reported that they had never attended the local genito-urinary medicine clinic. In addition fourteen males and sixteen females reported that they had failed to keep appointments at this agency. Most respondents reported that if they had persisting symptoms they eventually sought medical help. Even so, some stated that if symptoms disappeared then they did not visit a doctor.

HIV and AIDS-related knowledge and beliefs

Respondents were asked to rate the risks of HIV transmission through twenty-four methods. These included several, such as shaking hands and sharing cutlery, which, on the basis of current evidence, appear to involve no risk or only a very tiny risk of infection. The overall responses to these items are presented in Table 6.9.

As this rather complex table shows there were some areas of confusion and uncertainty. Even so, the study group as a whole was reasonably well informed on the theoretical risks of specific possible (or unlikely) modes of HIV transmission.

Table 6.9 Assessment of levels of risk of possible modes of HIV transmission

Possible modes of transmission	Sex of respondent	Safe %	Low risk %	Medium risk %	High risk %	Don't know %
Toilet seats	M	87	9	1	–	3
	F	76	16	3	1	4
Sharing crockery and cutlery	M	82	12	2	1	3
with an infected person	F	68	15	6	2	9
Shaking hands with an	M	87	10	1	–	2
infected person	F	80	14	1	1	4
Germs in the air	M	83	10	4	–	3
	F	75	15	–	1	9
Deep kissing an infected	M	56	30	10	1	3
person	F	48	24	18	4	6
Unprotected vaginal inter-	M	–	2	9	88	1
course from infected man to woman	F	1	1	9	89	–
Unprotected vaginal inter-	M	1	4	8	86	1
course from infected woman to man	F	2	5	14	79	–
Vaginal intercourse with	M	48	17	31	3	1
infected person using a condom	F	34	32	27	6	1
Unprotected anal	M	1	2	14	81	2
intercourse with infected person – passive	F	1	3	15	77	4
Unprotected anal	M	4	3	11	81	1
intercourse with infected person – insertive	F	–	3	6	88	3
Anal intercourse with infected	M	49	13	31	5	2
person using a condom	F	25	27	26	19	3
Fisting infected person	M	23	12	34	26	5
	F	16	15	20	23	26
Being fisted by infected	M	26	14	29	26	5
person	F	14	16	21	24	25
Rimming infected person	M	32	7	31	23	7
	F	21	9	24	29	17
Being rimmed by infected	M	39	10	31	14	6
person	F	24	15	23	20	18
Sharing sex toys with	M	30	13	17	36	4
infected person	F	11	12	17	47	13
Injecting drugs, sharing	M	–	1	5	94	–
equipment with infected person	F	–	–	1	99	–
Injecting drugs, without	M	63	9	11	15	2
sharing injecting equipment	F	55	19	9	15	2

Table 6.9 (continued) Assessment of levels of risk of possible modes of HIV transmission

Possible modes of transmission	Sex of respondent	Assessment				
		Safe %	Low risk %	Medium risk %	High risk %	Don't know %
Giving blood	M	76	14	2	–	8
	F	69	14	5	4	8
Receiving blood transfusion	M	40	22	17	9	12
	F	28	34	16	12	10
Swallowing infected person's tears	M	63	23	6	2	6
	F	62	19	4	4	11
Swallowing infected person's saliva	M	56	16	19	4	5
	F	47	31	14	5	3
Swallowing infected person's semen	M	5	8	13	67	7
	F	5	6	9	77	3
Swallowing infected person's vaginal fluid	M	7	7	13	66	7
	F	5	6	15	67	7

Note Percentages relate only to the number of respondents who replied to each question. These varied from 172 to 204.

Respondents were asked it they thought one could tell that a person was HIV seropositive from their appearance. Eight males and six females stated (incorrectly) that they believed that they could do this. In addition, three-quarters of the males and nearly half of the females reported that they had not had penetrative sex with anyone who was HIV seropositive. In fact, such statements appear to be very dubious since any of the study group might have had contact with infected but asymptomatic clients.

Conclusions and discussion

As expected, these results confirm the fact that the men and women in this study group were atypically heavy users of alcohol, tobacco, and illicit drugs. As already indicated, the subjects of this study were not selected as a representative random sample of those in the sex industry. They were disproportionately bar/street workers. Those who worked through escort agencies were under-represented as were those who worked mainly from saunas and massage parlours. The latter are distinctive in many ways from the bar/street workers largely featured in this chapter.

Alcohol and illicit drug use were commonplace accompaniments of client contact. In view of the disinhibiting effects of alcohol and other psychoactive substances (see Chapter 1), this fact presents problems for AIDS prevention. Approximately a fifth of the study group had used drugs intravenously and 8 per cent of those interviewed were, by their own reports, HIV seropositive. None of these results is unexpected in the light of earlier evidence about the drug scene in Edinburgh and the overlap between drug use and prostitution.

Overall, the men and women interviewed were fairly well informed about the risks of HIV infection. In spite of this, a considerable number were at risk, as were their clients, due to their acquiescence to pressure to engage in unprotected penetrative sex. A second major area of risk related to the very low rate of condom use with lovers and non-paying partners. This has already been highlighted in Chapter 4 and elsewhere in this book.

The information reported above was all derived from self-reports. Such data are inevitably flawed by bias, poor memory, denial, and other limitations. It has been shown that epidemiological studies of self-reported alcohol use are sometimes seriously biased by over-reporting, under-reporting, or by logical inconsistencies (Pernanen 1974; Midanik 1982a, 1982b; Plant *et al.* 1986). Even so, Singh (1979) has concluded that, in general, the subjects of studies of 'deviant' groups, such as drug users, are reasonably honest when responding to survey inquiries. A similar view has been expressed by Clark and Tifft (1966) and Ball (1957). Spanier (1976) has concluded that self-report data, if handled with caution, are a useful source of information about sexual behaviour. Reading and Wiest (1984) have reported, from a study of men, that such data are highly consistent.

The 'snowballing' method employed in this study had the considerable merit of identifying a group of men and women who were known to be sex workers. The interviewers included researchers, workers in statutory and non-statutory health and social services, and people who had worked in the sex industry. All respondents were either previously known to interviewers or were introduced to them by other respondents who vouched for both the suitability of the new interviewees and the credibility and trustworthiness of the researchers. 'Snowballing' has the possible defect of producing a rather homogeneous study group, since initial contacts may lead researchers to similar people. In the present exercise twelve very different interviewers were used but the study group, as already emphasized, was disproportionately of street and bar workers. Respondents, as already noted, were not paid for their participation in a long and fairly complex interview. Such payment is not normal in British social research, though it is more commonplace elsewhere, such as in the USA. Most people clearly co-operated with the study because they were interested in and often concerned about AIDS risks. Co-operation was certainly fostered by the friendly demeanour of the interviewers, many of whom were previously known to and trusted by their respondents.

The results presented above give a useful indication of some of the characteristics, behaviours, and beliefs of the 205 men and women who have been described. Even so, it is important to emphasize that these results are certainly not wholly accurate and, like all comparable survey data, must be interpreted with a degree of caution.

Prostitution is as old as civilization. Commercial sex has survived even the most draconian and repressive attempts to eradicate it. In addition, AIDS is not the first incurable, fatal sexually transmitted disease. Syphilis once had a very similar position to the one that is occupied by AIDS today. Past experience suggests that neither the threat of disease nor the risks of stigma, abuse, imprisonment, or violence have deterred people from working as prostitutes. The sex industry is extensive. Moreover, those who sell sexual services are vastly outnumbered by those who buy such services. This study and the others described elsewhere in this book were mounted because of fears that prostitution might be a medium through which HIV infection is transmitted into the general population. The results outlined above suggest that there is potentially a risk of such infection, largely associated with intravenous drug use by both sex workers and their sexual contacts. It is important to acknowledge the differences between sex workers who have used drugs intravenously and those who have not. These two subgroups run very different risks. Interview data and more general information indicate that intravenous drug use was far less common among sauna, massage parlour, and escort agency workers than among those who worked through bars and streets.

The most alarming conclusion is probably the fact that large numbers of clients (mainly males) actively request unprotected sex. Many are frequently prepared to pay more for such 'high-risk' activities. Approximately a quarter of the study group were prepared to participate in unprotected sex for additional payment, even though many clearly recognized the risks. Some engaged in unprotected sex with clients without charging more.

Several urgent policy options are indicated by these findings. These are prefaced by emphasizing that public health will not be enhanced by attempts to curb or to proscribe prostitution. As indicated by Darrow (1984), past repression in this field has often been entirely counter-productive, driving activities further underground and discouraging men and women from seeking medical advice.

It is important that those who engage in commercial sex should attempt to minimize the risk to themselves and their partners. Risk education is not helped if people fear that possession of condoms will be used as evidence of prostitution or brothel keeping.

The men and women who work in the sex industry and the vast numbers of people who use their services must be acknowledged to be priority groups for AIDS education and prevention. Strategies are needed to ensure the promotion of less dangerous drug use and sexual behaviours. Health information should be devised and delivered to sex workers and their clients as a matter of urgency. There is clearly a need to foster far more extensive condom use. Availability must be greatly increased. This should particularly extend the accessibility of condoms suitable for anal and oral sex. Condom use should be fostered not only on the basis of safety, but also by eroticizing condoms and enhancing their overall image as an essential accompaniment of sexual behaviour. Condom manufacturers have a major public health responsibility in these respects and sadly some are failing to meet the new demands imposed by the advent of AIDS.

Some of the men and women interviewed in this study indicated that they were inhibited from seeking regular medical checks. This poses an important challenge to the health and social services. The latter could usefully emulate their counterparts in the Netherlands who actively encourage sex workers to visit their 'user-friendly' services.

At the time of writing there is little evidence that HIV infection has been spread through prostitution in the study area. Even so, the extent of such infection in the local population has by no means yet been charted. AIDS threatens the whole community and not only small 'deviant' subgroups. These results emphasize the urgency of implementing preventive strategies before AIDS becomes as widespread as syphilis has been in the past.

Acknowledgements

This study is funded by the Medical Research Council. Additional support has been provided by the Alcohol Research Group, the Bill Kenyon Education Trust, the Scottish Health Education Group, the Scotch Whisky Association, and by an anonymous charitable trust. Dr Ron Stall and Dr Barbara Leigh are thanked for permission to use or adapt a number of survey questions for inclusion in this study.

Dr Moira Plant and Mrs Angelica Warner are thanked for assistance and support. Thanks also go to the interviewers, the respondents, and the many people who gave this study their enthusiastic support.

Some of the information in this chapter has been published in the *British Medical Journal*. The editor and his colleagues are thanked for giving permission to reproduce this.

References

Ball, J.C. (1957) 'The reliability and validity of interview data obtained from 59 narcotic addicts', *American Journal of Sociology* 72: 650–4.

Clark, J.P. and Tifft, L. (1966) 'Polygraph and interview validations of self-reported deviant behavior', *American Sociological Review* 31: 516–23.

Darrow, W.W. (1984) 'Prostitution and sexually transmitted diseases', in K.K. Holmes, P.-A. Mardh, P.F. Sparling, and P.J. Weisner (eds) *Sexually Transmitted Diseases*, New York: McGraw-Hill, pp. 109–15.

Goldberg, D. (1989) Personal communication.

Midanik, L. (1982a) 'The validity of self-reported alcohol consumption and alcohol problems: a literature review', *British Journal of Addiction* 77: 357–82.

Midanik, L. (1982b) 'Over-reports of recent alcohol consumption in a clinical population: a validity study', *Drug and Alcohol Dependence* 9: 101–10.

Morgan Thomas, R., Plant, M.A., Plant, M.L., and Sales, D. (1989) 'AIDS risks amongst sex industry workers: some initial results from a Scottish study', *British Medical Journal* 299: 148–9.

Morrison, V. (1988a) Personal communication.

Morrison, V. (1988b) 'Observation and snowballing: useful tools for research into illicit drug use?', *Social Pharmacology* 2: 245–71.

Pernanen, K. (1974) 'Validity of survey data on alcohol use', in R.J. Gibbins, Y. Israel, H. Kalant, R.E. Popham, W. Schmidt, and R.G. Smart (eds) *Research Advances in Alcohol and Drug Problems*, Vol. 1, New York: Wiley.

Plant, M.A. (1975) *Drugtakers in an English Town*, London: Tavistock.

Plant, M.A., Peck, D.F., and Samuel, E. (1986) *Alcohol, Drugs and School-Leavers*, London: Tavistock.

Plant, M.L., Plant, M.A., and Morgan Thomas, R. (1989) 'Alcohol, AIDS risks and commercial sex: results from a Scottish study', *Drug and Alcohol Dependence* (in press).

Polsky, N. (1969) *Hustlers, Beats and Others*, Harmondsworth, Middx: Pelican.

Reading, A. and Wiest, W. (1984) 'An analysis of self-reported sexual behaviour in a sample of normal males', *Archives of Sexual Behaviour* 131: 69–82.

Robertson, J.R. (1986) *Heroin, AIDS and Society*, London: Hodder & Stoughton.

Robertson, J.R. (1988) Personal communication.

Robertson, J.R., Bucknall, A.B.V., Welsby, P.D., Roberts, J.J.K., Inglis, J.M., Peutherer, J.F., and Brettle, R.P. (1986) 'Epidemic of AIDS related virus (HTLV III/LAV) infection amongst intravenous drug abusers', *British Medical Journal* 292: 527–9.

Royal College of General Practitioners (1986) *Alcohol: A Balanced View*, London: Royal College of General Practitioners.

Royal College of Physicians (1987) *A Great and Growing Evil*, London: Tavistock.

Royal College of Psychiatrists (1986) *Alcohol: Our Favourite Drug*, London: Tavistock.

Scottish Committee, Action on Smoking and Health (1989) Personal communication.

Scottish Office (1984) *Scottish Abstract of Statistics*, Edinburgh: HMSO, Table 7.1.

Singh, A. (1979) 'Reliability and validity of self-reported delinquency studies: a review', *Psychological Reports* 44: 987–93.

Spanier, E.B. (1976) 'Use of recall data in survey research on human sexual behaviour', *Social Biology* 23: 244–53.

Chapter seven

Intravenous drug use and syringe-sharing practices of call men and hustlers

Dan Waldorf and Sheigla Murphy

Introduction

As a result of the AIDS epidemic, male homosexuals, intravenous drug users, and female prostitutes have received considerable attention in the scientific literature as possible carriers and transmitters of HIV. Homosexual and bisexual males along with intravenous drug users constitute the two highest-risk groups to contract AIDS and ARC in the United States. Female prostitutes are known to be active transmitters of the virus in Africa (Kreiss *et al.* 1986; Mann *et al* 1987; Piot *et al.* 1984; Van de Perre *et al.* 1985) but, at present, there is only limited information about their role in transmission of the virus in Europe (Papaevangelou *et al.* 1985, 1988; Barton *et al.* 1985; Tirelli *et al.* 1987, 1988) and the United States (Smith and Smith 1986; Wallace *et al.* 1987; Fischl *et al.* 1987; Padian *et al.* 1987; Centers for Disease Control 1987; Rosenberg and Weiner 1988). This has been elaborated in Chapter 1. In fact, the majority of studies about female prostitutes in both Europe and the United States indicate that the drug-injecting female prostitute is more likely than her non-drug-using professional sisters to be HIV sero-positive (Papaevangelou *et al.* 1985, 1988; Wallace *et al.* 1987; Tirelli *et al.* 1987, 1988; Cohen *et al.* 1988; Seidlin *et al.* 1988; Rosenberg and Weiner 1988).

Male prostitutes have *not* received the same attention as have females despite the fact that there are large numbers of male prostitutes in most cities and that their clients are a mix of homosexual and bisexual men who are considered to be at very high risk of acquiring AIDS and ARC (Tirelli *et al.* 1987; Chiasson *et al.* 1988; Waldorf *et al.* 1988; Lauderback *et al.* 1988). Furthermore, a high proportion of the clients of male prostitutes are family men from middle-class communities so that male prostitutes may serve as an epidemiological bridge to females and children just as well as intravenous drug users.

This chapter presents new quantitative information about the intravenous drug use and injecting equipment-sharing practices of male prostitutes in the San Francisco Bay area. Interviews were conducted with 360 prostitutes – 180 hustlers and 180 call men – and descriptive information is presented on the following topics:

The incidence of intravenous drug use;
Syringe-sharing practices;
Availability of needles and syringes for prostitutes who are intravenous drug users; and
Self-reports about HIV testing.

The findings should be useful to both planners and practitioners in the field and most particularly to AIDS prevention programmes.

Prostitutes and intravenous drug use

In general, most of the current research related to female prostitutes has been concerned with the incidence of HIV, AIDS, and ARC among various ill-defined subgroups. The proportion of HIV seropositive female prostitutes ranges from zero to 65 per cent and varies from locale to locale and from sample to sample (Barton et al. 1985; Brenky-Faudeux and Fribourg-Blanc 1985; Centers for Disease Control 1987; Papaevangelou et al. 1985, 1988; Padian et al. 1987; Seidlin et al. 1988; Rosenberg and Weiner 1988). The rates of AIDS vary from 9.6 to 526.2 per one million (Centers for Disease Control 1987). Most of the studies of female prostitutes have been made with convenience samples that give little consideration of the various types of prostitutes. Those who solicit clients in public places have generally received more attention than call girls, agency affiliated workers, and erotic masseuses. Convenience samples recruited in jails and drug treatment programmes reveal a higher incidence of HIV seropositive prostitutes than do 'community samples' (Centers for Disease Control 1987; Cohen et al. 1988).

Male prostitutes have been nearly ignored by AIDS researchers for unknown reasons. At present, there have been only two studies that tested male prostitutes: one in New York City (Chiasson et al. 1988) and one in north-eastern Italy (Tirelli et al. 1988; Tirelli et al. 1987). The New York study was conducted at a venereal disease clinic and included eighty-four male prostitutes. Of the thirty-two who reported having sex with males, seventeen people, or 53 per cent, were HIV seropositive; of those fifty-two who reported serving female clients only, five individuals, or 10 per cent, were positive. The Italian study was conducted in Udine, Pordenone, and Treviso, and twenty-seven male prostitutes were tested and compared with seventy-five homosexual men and 106 male intravenous drug addicts. Three of the twenty-seven prostitutes (11.1 per cent) were positive compared with 17 per cent of the homosexual controls and 49 per cent of the addict controls. Both studies concluded that male prostitutes were a high-risk group. Another study of homeless youth in New York City attending a health clinic, many of whom were males who resorted to prostitution to support themselves, found that 6.7 per cent of 1111 tested were HIV seropositive (Daley 1988). The only other information on male prostitutes to date is that generated by the study described in this chapter and by the Edinburgh study described in the previous chapter. Earlier information on the Californian study related to intravenous drug use, injecting equipment sharing, and voluntary testing of 'hustlers' (Waldorf *et al.* 1988; Lauderback *et al.* 1988). There are plans for another HIV testing study of male prostitutes to be conducted in San Francisco and other ongoing research with male prostitutes in Holland and the United Kingdom (Davies 1989; Morgan Thomas 1989; Visser 1989).

Method

Prior to the selection of the study group, there was considerable information about the world of male prostitutes provided by the previous ethnographic research of one of the principal staff (Marotta 1982, 1984, 1985, 1986). This indicated that 'hustlers' or male prostitutes who solicit customers in baldly sexual encounters could be found at cruising areas, in gay bars, and erotic bookstores. Initial information about 'call men', or men who solicit customers over the telephone, via call books and advertisements, was more rudimentary. It was known that many of them advertised in speciality newspapers in the area, but the authors did not know the range of the different types of male prostitutes.

During the processes of locating respondents for the study a typology of male prostitutes was devised which served as a theoretical basis for selecting individuals to be included. Very briefly, male prostitutes in San Francisco can be organized into two different general types with various subtypes within each group (Marotta *et al.* 1988). The first type is the most visible and the most obvious to the casual observer. This type utilizes face-to-face encounters with potential clients in public places such as cruising areas, arcades, theatres, bookstores featuring erotica, and gay bars. For the purposes of this chapter these are called 'hustlers' and the principal subtypes are delineated according to erotic styles. Very briefly, they are:

Trade Hustlers – usually heterosexual ('straight') or bisexual males who express a rather ostentatious and aggressive masculinity, who trade sex for money, do not admit homosexual inclinations, and often profess no enjoyment of sex with men.
Drag Queen Hustlers – transvestites and transsexuals who assume an exaggerated female identity, usually specialize in oral sex, and are localized in particular streets and bars in the Tenderloin, a sex trade zone.
Youths – young, often gay-identified males who present themselves as being innocent and naïve in the ways of the world, but who participate in a wide spectrum of sexual activities.

The second subgroup who are identified are 'call men'. The organization of 'call men' is not based upon erotic styles, but on the ways that they locate clients and the types of services they provide. Call men subtypes are as follows:

Call Book Men who are predominantly gay-identified and bisexual. They generally work from a call book or regular customers. There are also 'drag queen call girls' who are transvestites who work from a call book.
Erotic Masseurs who advertise for new clients while serving 'regulars' and who provide some elements of the legitimate massage business with an erotic twist. They are often certified by licensed massage schools and are guided by well-developed philosophical rationales for their work. They also charge relatively low prices compared to other 'call men'.
Models and Escorts are men who generally obtain customers through advertisements placed in mainstream and special interest publications. They often entertain clients socially as well as sexually. They tend to develop networks of regular customers and may also operate simultaneously from a call book.
Stars of the Erotic Industry – of stage, screen, and magazines –

are the élite group among male sex workers and are very small numerically. The most common of this type of prostitute in the San Francisco Bay area are erotic dancers who strip in local nightclubs and theatres for both male and female audiences. Customers, both female and male, are often solicited at such events, and services are provided at other locations. They also command the highest prices in the industry.

It is noted that, concurrent with the AIDS epidemic, there has been a substantial increase in the number of call men advertisements appearing in San Francisco newspapers. This suggests that there are more call men than there were before the AIDS epidemic. Explicit erotic massage advertisements are also a fairly recent phenomenon in San Francisco newspapers and have increased dramatically since the AIDS epidemic began. Unlike in the female prostitution scene in San Francisco, there are very few agency-operated male prostitution businesses in the city and few pimps. Only ten of the people interviewed during this study reported agency affiliations and those had been in the past rather than the present. Some youths had pimp-like 'sugar-daddies' who provided them with clients, but such relationships were usually short-lived. There were no accounts of males who corresponded to the traditional pimps of female prostitutes. The latter may supervise several prostitutes in more or less formal arrangements.

All respondents were located by the chain referral method, which is a technique used by sociologists, psychologists, and ethnographers to locate hard to find groups (Biernacki and Waldorf 1981). This method is also known as 'snowballing' and has also been discussed in Chapter 6. The project hired several knowledgeable interviewers to locate different types of prostitutes and employed indigenous locaters from the various types of prostitutes to assist in the location efforts. The typology of male prostitutes in San Francisco served as a theoretical overview and guide to locate male sex workers for the project.

In general, the project has generated considerable ethnographic information about both the 'hustler' and the 'call men' scenes in San Francisco, and the study group obtained provided a reasonable representation of male sex workers in that city. Substantial numbers of six of the seven types of sex workers were interviewed. There was difficulty locating and interviewing 'stars of the erotic industry' and only one person was located who consented to be interviewed who fitted that type. The study group was *not* a random or representative sample since there are no known lists or populations of male prostitutes. Furthermore, it is doubtful whether any random or representative samples can ever be drawn of male prostitutes since the very nature of the work requires that it be clandestine.

Quantitative data were gathered by means of a screening and a life history interview schedule. Additional qualitative information was gathered (about various aspects of their occupation, their clients, and sexual practices) from a focused interview guide which was tape-recorded. The interview took approximately two and a half to four hours to complete.

Results

The mean age of the study group was 27.9 years, with call men being on average five years older than hustlers. The range in age, however, was 18–56 years. It should be noted that there are younger hustlers, but the project did not attempt to locate them as the focus was on adults – those 18 years and over. In terms of ethnicity and race, the majority (70.3 per cent) were white. Roughly three out of ten were from minority groups with Blacks comprising nearly one in seven (14.2 per cent) and Latinos nearly one in eleven (8.9 per cent). In general, the educational level of the study group was low. Most of the 'hustlers' left school before graduation from high school, before the twelfth year. Call men had tended to stay in school longer; the median year that they left school was thirteen (the equivalent of a year in college). By no means all of the study group were gay-identified; only slightly more than half (56.1 per cent) described themselves as gay. A sixth (16.9 per cent) were bisexual. Another sixth were transvestites (15.8 per cent), and 8.6 per cent were heterosexual. This is elaborated in Table 7.1. Please note that there were some data missing for some variables. The numbers presented below vary very slightly.

Drug use

In general, male sex workers were quite experienced with illicit drugs. Among the 360 people interviewed for the project, none could report that they had never used any illicit drug. Most persons began to experiment with illicit drugs, usually marijuana, at an early age (mean age for the total study group was 15.3 years) and most were using illicit drugs regularly (again usually marijuana) by the time they were 17 years old. The extent of this drug use was generally indicated by responses to two questions about their drug experiences. More than half (53.3 per cent) reported that they had felt addicted to an illicit drug at some time in their lives and nearly a quarter (24.2 per cent) reported that they had been to a drug treatment agency for problems associated with illicit drug use.

Table 7.1 Characteristics of the study group by type of sex worker

	Hustlers		Type of sex worker Call men		Total	
Number	180		180		360	
Age						
Mean	25.3 years		30.6 years		27.9 years	
Median	24.0		30.0		26.0	
Range	17–49		18–56		17–56	
Ethnicity	N	%	N	%	N	%
Black	27	15.0	24	13.4	51	14.2
Latino	19	10.6	13	7.3	32	8.9
White	121	67.2	132	73.7	253	70.5
American Indian	4	2.2	3	1.7	7	1.9
Other	9	5.0	7	3.9	16	4.5
Education						
Mean	11.1 grades		12.9 grades		11.9 grades	
Median	11.0		13.0		12.0	
Range	2–17		1–20		1–20	
Sexual Identity	N	%	N	%	N	%
Gay-identified	80	45.2	122	68.9	202	57.1
Bisexual	32	18.1	29	16.3	61	17.2
Transvestite	44	24.8	13	7.3	57	16.1
Heterosexual	19	10.7	12	6.8	31	8.6
Other	–	–	1	0.6	1	0.3

Intravenous drug use was reported by more than half (53.3 per cent) of the study group. Hustlers reported intravenous drug use more than call men; more than two out of every three of the hustlers (67.8 per cent) reported having injected drugs, while only a third of the call men (38.9 per cent) did. The most frequently reported injected drugs were methamphetamine, followed by cocaine and heroin. This is shown in Table 7.2.

Table 7.2 Self-reported intravenous drug use by type of sex worker

| | Type of sex worker | | | | | |
	Hustlers		Call men		Total	
Number	180		180		360	
Ever Injected an						
illicit drug	N	%	N	%	N	%
Yes	122	68.9	70	39.5	192	54.1
No	56	31.5	107	60.5	163	45.9
Methamphetamine						
injection (ever)	N	%	N	%	N	%
Never	9	7.4	8	11.4	17	8.9
Once	4	3.3	5	7.1	9	4.7
2–10 times	16	13.1	7	10.0	23	12.0
11–250 times	26	21.3	21	30.0	47	24.5
More than 250 times	67	54.9	29	41.4	96	50.0
Total	122		70		192	
Cocaine injection						
(ever)	N	%	N	%	N	%
Never	50	40.7	25	36.2	75	39.1
Once	7	5.7	8	11.6	15	7.8
2–10 times	22	17.9	12	17.4	34	17.7
11–250 times	26	21.1	16	23.2	42	21.9
More than 250 times	18	14.0	8	11.6	26	13.5
Total	123		69		192	
Heroin injection (ever)	N	%	N	%	N	%
Never	70	57.9	44	63.8	114	60.0
Once	6	5.0	6	8.7	12	6.3
2–10 times	19	15.7	9	13.0	28	14.7
11–250 times	3	2.5	9	13.0	12	6.3
More than 250 times	23	19.0	1	1.4	24	12.6
Total	122		69		190	

Age was not associated with intravenous drug use but education was. People who had left school early were significantly more likely to have used drugs intravenously than were those who had remained at school longer. Most (70.7 per cent) of all respondents who had left school before the twelfth grade reported injecting illicit drugs, while only half (54.9 per cent) of the high school graduates and a fifth (21.9 per cent) of those who had attended college did so. This finding held for both hustlers and call men. This is elaborated in Table 7.3.

Table 7.3 Self-reports of illicit drug injection by education (N = 360)

	Less than high school graduate		High school graduate		Some college	
	N	%	N	%	N	%
Ever injected an illicit drug						
Yes	94	70.7	56	54.9	42	34.7
No	39	29.3	46	45.1	79	65.3
Total	133		102		121	

Syringe sharing[1]

Questions about needle and syringe sharing posed some problems for the project.[2] After the first hundred interviews it was noted that there was considerable discrepancy between the proportion of persons who said that they had ever injected illicit drugs and the proportion who reported that they had shared injecting equipment. The staff of the project knew from long experience with drug users that it is most unusual for intravenous drug users not to share syringes, particularly when they are beginning to inject drugs. New injectors do not, as a rule, possess either syringes or the requisite knowledge of how to inject drugs. Most often such sharing of syringes occurs for some months and in some cases for years.

The initial question about needle sharing followed the questions about intravenous drug use. It was a standard filter question that asked, 'Have you ever shared needles or syringes, by sharing we mean with anyone?' For what may be a variety of reasons respondents were reluctant to report needle sharing – different definitions of needle sharing, some reluctance to admit risky behaviour, and a certain hesitation on the part of some of the interviewers to challenge respondents when they reported intravenous drug use but no sharing. The initial review supported the conclusion that respondents were generally under-reporting their needle-sharing activities. At that point the question was rephrased in order, it was hoped, to produce better data. This had little effect. None the less in the authors' view needle sharing probably was generally under-reported.

Despite the problems with the initial needle-sharing question, more than seven out of every ten persons (71.3 per cent) who reported that they injected illicit drugs reported that they had shared needles and syringes. Unlike the responses to the questions about intravenous drug use, where there were considerable differences between hustlers and call men, syringe sharing was reported just as often by call men who had injected illicit drugs as by hustlers. While call men may report injecting illicit drugs less than hustlers, when they injected illicit drugs, they reported syringe sharing just as often.

Syringe sharing occurs in a variety of social situations – with friends, room-mates, intimates, and in communal settings such as shooting galleries[3] and bath houses. The last two, shooting galleries and bath houses, were of particular interest to the project because it is expected that the syringe sharing that takes place at such locations can place the injector at risk of becoming infected with HIV (Des Jarlais *et al.* 1986). Three out of every ten persons who reported needle sharing reported that they had shared syringes at shooting galleries. Another sixth (16.9 per cent) reported that they had injected at bath houses and sex clubs. The differences between call men and hustlers were not statistically significant. The needle-sharing patterns that were reported are illustrated further in Table 7.4.

Availability of syringes and how they were used

In the United States possession of a hypodermic syringe without a physician's prescription is against the law in some states; California is one of those states. (It should be noted that the State of Minnesota does *not* have laws prohibiting the possession of syringes and does *not* have large numbers of intravenous drug use-attributed AIDS cases, unlike other states that restrict possession of syringes, most particularly New York, New Jersey, and Massachusetts.) In addition, many states have paraphernalia laws that have been used by the police against addicts and other intravenous drug users for years; California also has a paraphernalia law. As a consequence of these laws many drug injectors find it difficult to find or buy syringes and often resort to using syringes in shooting galleries or use syringes discarded by other users. Many intravenous drug users do not normally carry their outfits or syringes on their person for fear of being stopped by the police and being arrested for possession of an illegal syringe.

Table 7.4 Self-reports of needle and syringe sharing by type of sex worker

| | Type of sex worker | | | | | |
	Hustlers		Call men		Total	
Ever shared	N	%	N	%	N	%
Had shared	88	71.0	51	71.8	139	71.3
Did not share	5	4.0	7	9.9	12	6.2
Suspect shared	31	25.0	13	18.3	44	22.6
Total	124		71		195	
Ever shared at						
shooting gallery	N	%	N	%	N	%
Never	56	65.1	38	76.0	94	69.1
Once	5	5.8			5	3.7
2–25 times	11	12.8	6	12.0	17	12.5
26–100 times	5	5.8	1	2.0	6	4.4
More than 100 times	9	10.5	5	10.0	14	10.3
Total	86		50		136	
Ever shared at bath						
house or sex club	N	%	N	%	N	%
Never	75	87.2	38	76.0	113	83.1
Once	2	2.3	4	8.0	6	4.4
2–25 times	7	8.2	5	10.0	12	8.8
26–100 times			1	2.0	1	0.7
More than 100 times	2	2.3	2	4.0	4	2.9
Total	86		50		136	

Note Percentages may not equal 100 per cent due to rounding.

In order to explore the availability of syringes and how they were used each person in this study group was asked a series of questions:

* about ownership of a syringe,
* how they obtained it,
* who else used it,
* and what percentage of the time they used it exclusively or shared it with others.

These questions revealed that half (47.9 per cent) of all those who reported that they had shared syringes owned their own equipment. Most (57.7 per cent) bought or obtained these syringes from other users who were designated as a 'street source'. Another quarter (23.1 per cent) reported that they had bought them from a pharmacy, but the meaning of this is that they have presented themselves to a pharmacist as a diabetic or a relative of a diabetic and bought the syringe through misrepresentation. Diabetics and the relatives of diabetics can routinely buy syringes at pharmacies without a prescription despite the laws which prohibit such practices. It should also be noted that diabetics are often sources for much of the underground supply of syringes available on the street.

Of the respondents who said that they owned syringes three out of ten (29.6 per cent) reported that other persons used this syringe. When asked with whom they shared, the most frequent responses were friends, room-mates, and intimates.

Pursuing the issue of sharing syringes, respondents were asked to estimate the proportion of the time that they: used their own syringe; used their own syringe, but shared it with others; and, last, used someone else's syringe. The mean percentages of these estimates indicate that ownership of one's own syringe does not mean exclusive use of one's own syringe. The mean proportion of the time that respondents used their own syringes was 71.6 per cent. Roughly a quarter of the time (24.5 per cent) they used someone else's syringe and a fifth (22.3 per cent) of the time they used their own syringe but shared it with others. This is elaborated in Table 7.5.

Reasons for sharing syringes

Availability, convenience, and fears of being arrested for paraphernalia laws were the most frequently mentioned reasons given for sharing syringes. These reasons were explored with six questions. The first was an open-ended question that simply asked: 'Tell me the reason or reasons why you share needles?' The most frequently mentioned answer was that there was only one syringe available, and this comprised more than half (58.9 per cent) of all responses.

This was followed by a series of five closed-ended questions that sought to generate greater details about the reasons for sharing. The answers to these questions indicate that the cost of syringes was not a major concern. Only 5.1 per cent reported that 'needles were too expensive'. Syringes were relatively inexpensive, selling for $2–$3 on the street, which was considerably more than the price at a pharmacy. The most frequently mentioned reason for sharing was availability. More than eight out of ten (87.6 per cent) answered 'yes' to the reason 'Needles are not available'. Convenience was suggested by two items: 'It is more convenient to use other people's needles' and 'Sometimes can't wait to use your own outfit'; half of the needle sharers answered 'yes' to the first and two out of five answered 'yes' to the second question. This is shown by Table 7.6.

Table 7.5 Self-reports of ownership of injecting equipment, where this was procured, and how this was used by type of sex worker

| | Type of sex worker | | | | | |
	Hustlers		Call men		Total	
Do you currently have your own outfit?	N	%	N	%	N	%
Yes	49	49.5	26	51.0	75	50.0
No	50	50.5	25	49.0	75	50.0
Total	99		51		150	
How did you get your outfit?	N	%	N	%	N	%
From street	32	62.7	13	48.1	45	57.7
Bought at pharmacy	8	15.7	10	37.0	18	23.1
Other	8	15.7	2	7.4	10	12.8
No answer	3	5.9	2	7.4	5	6.4
Total	51		27		78	
Does anyone else use your outfit?	N	%	N	%	N	%
Yes	19	37.2	5	17.9	24	30.3
No	32	62.8	23	82.1	55	69.6
Proportion of Time (Mean)		%		%		%
Used own outfit		69.1		77.3		71.6
Used someone else's outfit		27.4		17.6		24.5
Used own, but shared with other		22.8		21.1		22.3

Racial variations

Recent research in the United States has noted that blacks and hispanics have higher rates of intravenous drug use-attributed AIDS than do whites, most particularly in north-eastern cities such as Boston, Buffalo, New York City, and Newark (Peterson and Bakeman 1988). The authors of that study speculated that the reasons for such high rates among minorities are '1) the higher prevalence of needle sharing among non-white IV drug users, 2) the greater inability of minority needle users to obtain sterile drug equipment, and 3) the lower health status of non-white populations in the United States'. Other researchers have reiterated minority differences (Weinberg and Murray 1987; Koplan *et al.* 1985; Bakeman *et al.* 1986a, 1986b, 1987; Centers for Disease Control 1986a; Rogers and Williams 1987).

Table 7.6 Self-reports of reasons for sharing injecting equipment

| | Type of sex worker | | | | | |
	Hustlers		Call men		Total	
Tell me the reason or reasons why you share needles. (open-ended question)	N	%	N	%	N	%
Only one needle available	56	65.1	40	78.4	96	70.1
Needles are hard to get	8	9.3	4	7.8	12	8.8
Don't own a needle	8	9.3	4	7.8	12	8.8
Needles are too expensive	3	3.5	1	2.0	4	2.9
Other	19	22.1	16	31.4	35	25.5
Some persons say that they share needles for the following reasons. Tell me which ones apply to you.	N	%	N	%	N	%
Needles are not available	79	90.8	41	82.0	120	87.6
Needles are too expensive	4	4.6	3	6.0	7	5.1
Sometimes can't wait to use own outfit	41	47.1	14	28.0	55	40.1
It is more convenient to use other people's needles	48	55.2	20	40.0	68	50.0
You don't want to be arrested by the police for paraphernalia laws	32	36.3	9	18.0	41	29.9

Note Many respondents gave more than one answer to the questions so the numbers will not necessarily equal the total number of respondents.

To test this theory, several variables used in this analysis were examined in relation to race and ethnicity. To facilitate the analysis and overcome the relatively small size of the study group, respondents were simply dichotomized into 'whites' and 'minorities'. This analysis revealed that there was little difference between whites and minorities. Minorities did not report injecting illicit drugs more than whites, they owned their own syringes just as often as whites, and they did not share their syringes more than whites. There were some differences between whites and minorities in the utilization of shooting galleries but these were not significant. This is elaborated in Table 7.7.

Table 7.7 Self-reports of sharing injecting equipment in shooting galleries and drug houses by ethnicity

Shared injecting equipment at a shooting gallery or drug house	Whites		Ethnic minorities		Total	
	N	%	N	%	N	%
Never	70	75.3	24	55.8	94	69.1
1–10 times	8	8.6	7	16.3	15	11.0
11–100 times	9	9.7	4	9.3	13	9.6
More than 100 times	6	6.5	8	18.6	14	10.3

HIV testing and AIDS diagnoses

San Francisco has a very active, voluntary, anonymous HIV testing programme. In some ways it has served as a model for other testing efforts in the United States. And from the inception of this project the authors offered free, anonymous testing to all of the respondents who were interviewed (it was not required by the project). Very few accepted this offer. One of the principal reasons why so few did so was that the majority had already been tested; nearly two-thirds (65.8 per cent) reported that they had been tested for HIV infection prior to the interview. There was little difference between hustlers and call men in this respect.

Of those who had been tested, 94.5 per cent had received the results of the test. Of those who had received the results, only thirty-seven people or 16.5 per cent were HIV seropositive. Call men reported positive tests more often than hustlers; one in five of the call men (22.9 per cent) and one in ten of the hustlers (10.6 per cent) were HIV seropositive. Call men may have had a higher seroprevalence rate for several reasons. They had been working as prostitutes longer, were gay-identified, and had participated in anal sex more than had the hustlers.

In addition to questions about HIV testing, respondents were also asked whether or not they had ever been diagnosed for AIDS or ARC by a physician. Twenty people reported that they had been diagnosed for AIDS or ARC. Table 7.8 provides further details of the HIV testing results, AIDS and ARC diagnoses reported by the study group.

Table 7.9 examines the association between intravenous drug use and the combinations of HIV seropositivity and diagnoses. In terms of sheer percentages it appears as if there is a strong association (two-thirds of all those who were either HIV seropositive and/or diagnosed reported intravenous drug use), but statistical tests were not significant. The most that can be inferred from this table would be that there is a tendency for persons who were seropositive or diagnosed also to report intravenous drug use. This tendency might have become significant with a larger study group.

Table 7.8 HIV testing and AIDS diagnoses by type of sex worker

	Hustlers		Call men		Total	
	N	%	N	%	N	%
Have you ever taken a blood test for AIDS (HIV)?						
Yes	124	68.9	113	62.8	223	65.8
Did you find out the results of the test?						
Yes	114	92.7	109	96.5	223	94.5
HIV test results						
Positive	12	10.6	25	22.9	37	16.7
Negative	101	89.4	84	77.1	185	83.3
Total	113		109		222	
Diagnosed by physician						
AIDS	1	0.6	2	1.1	3	0.8
ARC	12	6.7	5	2.8	17	4.7
Neither	167	92.7	172	95.1	339	94.4
Total	180		179		359	

Table 7.9 Self-reports of HIV seropositivity or AIDS or ARC diagnoses by intravenous drug use

HIV status or AIDS/ARC diagnosis	Intravenous drug users		Respondents who had not used drugs intravenously	
	N	%	N	%
Yes	31	16.1	15	9.1
No, neither	161	83.9	149	90.9
Totals	192	100.0	164	100.0

Summary and policy implications

Male prostitutes, unlike their female counterparts, have been virtually ignored by AIDS researchers. This chapter delineates a typology of male prostitutes which served as the theoretical basis for the study's selection procedures. The two main categories are hustlers and call men. Within the main categories are seven subtypes. Substantial numbers of six of the seven subtypes of sex workers were interviewed. The study group were neither a random nor a representative sample but a reasonable representation of the various types of male sex workers in San Francisco.

All of the sex workers interviewed had at some time used an illicit drug. Most respondents began smoking marihuana by the time they were 15 years old and by 17 were using it regularly. More than half of the respondents had felt addicted to an illicit drug at some point in their lives with a quarter of the study group having had treatment for their drug use. Two out of every three hustlers reported some intravenous drug use, while only a third of the call men did. The most frequently injected drugs were methamphetamines, followed by cocaine and heroin.

Although there were considerable difficulties with the set of syringe-sharing questions more than seven out of ten sex workers who reported intravenous drug use reported that they had shared needles and syringes. There was no difference between call men and hustlers in reports of syringe sharing. In the context of the AIDS epidemic the locations in which sex workers share syringes has a bearing on the transmission of the virus. More than three out of ten persons who reported sharing syringes reported sharing in shooting galleries. Another sixth had injected at bath houses or sex clubs.

In California, as well as twelve other states, possession of a hypo-dermic syringe is illegal; therefore intravenous drug users are under-standably reluctant to carry drug paraphernalia on their persons. Many intravenous drug users have difficulty procuring syringes and resort to sharing and/or renting syringes in shooting galleries or using syringes discarded by others. Owning one's own syringe did not preclude sharing since nearly half of the respondents who reported that they had shared owned their own syringes. The lack of available syringes was the most frequently given reason for sharing injecting equipment. The expense of such equipment was not an abiding concern for most of the persons who reported syringe sharing.

Recent research has noted higher rates of intravenous drug use-related AIDS cases among minority populations. Minorities among male sex workers did *not* report injecting illicit drugs more than whites, they owned their own syringes just as often as whites, and they did not share their syringes more than whites.

These findings are of considerable importance to planners and practitioners of AIDS prevention and service provision. The findings on drug injectors and syringe sharing suggest that male sex workers in the San Francisco area may be doubly at risk of HIV infection. These patterns of intravenous drug use need not apply to other groups of sex workers. This is because high levels of drug injecting probably reflect factors within each local community. Many of the present study group lived and worked in the Tenderloin, a long-standing community of sex workers and drug users.

The results about reasons for sharing injecting equipment – availability, convenience, and fears of arrest – suggest that development of needle exchange programmes might be a viable way to reduce syringe sharing among male sex workers. Existing needle exchange programmes should consider targeting male sex workers to reduce the risk of HIV infection. Recently, a group of volunteers, called Prevention Point, have begun to exchange needles in San Francisco for intravenous drug users in the south of Market Street area in San Francisco. While their activities are against the law, it would appear that neither the city nor the police will act to curtail their actions. Injecting equipment exchanges have already been established in Britain, the Netherlands, Switzerland, and Australia.

Lastly, the two major categories of sex workers, hustlers and call men, require different kinds of outreach and prevention measures due to a number of important differences between the two groups. Call men are on the average older, better educated, generally gay-identified, and more likely to move in special circles where conventional life-styles are the norm.

Hustlers, on the other hand, are younger, more likely to have less than a high school education, more diverse in their sexual identifications (gay, bisexual, transsexual, and heterosexual), and are more likely to be injecting illicit drugs than call men. Hustlers tend to live a much more street-orientated life-style; often living in the street or in transient hotels. They frequently live from day to day with poor nutrition, inadequate housing, and various problems associated with their drug use.

Call men are probably being contacted through traditional public health outreach efforts and public information campaigns. Hustlers, and particularly young hustlers, are a much more difficult population to target. Hustlers, because of their youth, are less confident of their gay identities if they are gay-identified and are more likely to be somewhat ambiguous in their sexual identifications. Sensitivity to issues of hustlers' gay identities and heterosexual identities is essential to successful prevention efforts. For example, public information campaigns aimed at homosexual males will not be effective with drag queens or trade hustlers who are not gay-identified. Drag queens often view themselves as women and trade hustlers as heterosexuals. General sensitivity to the differing sexual identities of drag queens *vis-à-vis* trade hustlers *vis-à-vis* youths is a mandatory component of any public health intervention with male sex workers.

Hustlers, particularly young hustlers, are alienated from traditional public health communication media. Many are runaways who are, for various reasons, reluctant to contact 'official agencies'. Although the present study was confined to people over the age of 18 many had been runaways in their early teens.

Criminal activities such as drug use and petty theft foster an outlaw orientation on the part of these street hustlers that distances them from mainstream medical and other kinds of service providers.

Service providers and prevention policy planners need to be willing to use unconventional methods of locating their targeted populations and communicating their important information. Ex-sex workers could be recruited and trained as outreach workers. Because of their knowledge and entrée into sex worker scenes, they would be invaluable in alerting active sex workers of their risk of AIDS, in providing them with information, and in directing them to available services.

Notes

1 For a detailed review of the literature on syringe and needle sharing see an earlier article generated by the project (Waldorf *et al.* 1988).
2 California intravenous drug users do *not* use the traditional needle, eye dropper, and baby pacifier that are often used by addicts and other drug injectors in New York City, but rather a disposable syringe that is intended for one-time use.
3 Shooting galleries are locations where intravenous drug users gather to rent or use needles and syringes for injection of illicit drugs. Very often they are located near cruising areas and are both formal and informal in their organization. Most shooting galleries are located in private apartments/houses or abandoned buildings (Murphy and Waldorf 1989).

References

Bakeman, R., Lumb, J.R., and Smith, D.W. (1986a) 'AIDS statistics and the risk for minorities', *AIDS Research* 2: 249–52.

Bakeman, R., Lumb, J.R., and Smith, D.W. (1986b) 'AIDS risk group profiles in whites and members of minority groups', *New England Journal of Medicine* 315: 191–2.

Bakeman, R., McCray, E., Lumb, J.R., Jackson, R.E., and Whitley, P.M. (1987) 'The incidence of AIDS among blacks and hispanics', *Journal of the National Medical Association* 79: 931–8.

Barton, S.E., Underhill, G.S., Gilchrist, C., Jeffries, D.J., and Harris, J.R.W. (1985) 'HTLV-III antibody in prostitutes' (letter), *Lancet* 2: 1424.

Biernacki, P. and Waldorf, D. (1981) 'Snowball sampling: problems and techniques of chain referral sampling', *Sociological Methods and Research* 10: 141–61.

Brenky-Faudeux, D. and Fribourg-Blanc, A. (1985) 'HTLV-III antibody in prostitutes' (letter), *Lancet* 2: 1424.

Centers for Disease Control (1986a) 'Acquired immunodeficiency syndrome (AIDS) among black and hispanics – United States', *Morbidity and Mortality Weekly Report* 35: 655–66.

Centers for Disease Control (1986b) 'Positive HTLV-III antibody results for sexually active female members of social/sexual clubs – Minnesota', *Morbidity and Mortality Weekly Report* 35: 45.

Centers for Disease Control (1987) 'Antibody to human immunodeficiency virus in female prostitutes', *Morbidity and Mortality Weekly Report* 36: 157–60.

Chiasson, M.A., Lifson, A.R., Stoneburner, R.L., Ewing, W., Hildebrandt, D., and Jaffe, H.W. (1988) 'HIV-1 seroprevalence in male and female prostitutes in New York City', *Abstracts from the Sixth International Conference on AIDS*, Stockholm, Sweden, June.

Cohen, J., Hauer, L., and Poole, W. (1987) 'Risk factors for HIV infection in 500 sexually active women in San Francisco', paper presented at the annual meeting of the American Public Health Association, New Orleans, 18–22 October 1987.

Cohen, J., Alexander, P., and Wofsy, C. (1988) 'Prostitutes and AIDS: public policy issues', *AIDS and Public Policy Journal* 3: 16–22.

Daley, S. (1988) 'New York City youth: living in the shadow of AIDS', *New York Times* 14 November.

Davies, P. (1989) Personal communication.

Des Jarlais, D., Friedman, S., and Strug, D. (1986) 'AIDS and intravenous drug users: a socio-cultural perspective', in T. Feldman and T. Johnson (eds) *The Social Dimensions of AIDS: Methods and Theory*, New York: Praeger.

Fischl, M.A., Dickinson, G.M., Flanagan, S., and Fletcher, M.A. (1987)

'Human immunodeficiency virus (HIV) among female prostitutes in South Florida', *Abstracts from the Third International Conference on AIDS*, 1–5 June 1987, Washington, DC: US Department of Health and Human Services and the World Health Organization.

Koplan, J., Hardy, A., and Allen, J. (1985) 'Epidemiology of acquired immunodeficiency syndrome in intravenous drug abusers', *Journal of Psychoactive Drugs* 5: 13–23.

Kreiss, J.K., Koech, D., Plummer, F.A., Holmes, K.K., Lightfoote, M., Piot, P., Ronald, A.R., Ndinya-Achola, J.O., D'Costa, L.J., Roberts, P., Ngugi, E.N., and Quinn, T.C. (1986) 'AIDS virus infection in Nairobi prostitutes: spread of the epidemic to East Africa', *New England Journal of Medicine* 314: 414–17.

Lauderback, D., Waldorf, E., Marotta, T., and Murphy, S. (1988) 'HIV testing, attitudes and AIDS awareness among male prostitutes in the San Francisco Bay Area: preliminary findings of the Prospero Project', submitted for publication. San Francisco, CA: Institute for Scientific Analysis.

Mann, J., Quinn, T.D., Piot, P., Bosenge, N., Nzilambi, N., Kalala, M., Francis, H., Coleburders, R.L., Byers, R., Kasa Azila, P., Kabeya, N., and Curran, J.W. (1987) 'Condom use and HIV infection among prostitutes in Zaire', *New England Journal of Medicine* 316: 345.

Marotta, T. (1982) 'Adolescent male prostitution, pornography and other forms of sexual exploitation', San Francisco: Urban and Rural Systems Associates.

Marotta, T. (1984) *Tracking and Sexual Revolution*, unpublished book manuscript.

Marotta, T. (1985) *The Last Bath House*, unpublished book manuscript.

Marotta, T. (1986) *Promised Land*, unpublished book manuscript.

Marotta, T., Waldorf, D., and Murphy, S. (1988) 'Males doing sex work in the San Francisco Bay Area – a typology and description', submitted for publication, San Francisco, CA: Institute for Scientific Analysis, Prospero Project.

Morgan Thomas, R. (1989) Personal communication.

Murphy, S. (1987) 'Intravenous drug use and AIDS: notes on the social economy of needle sharing', *Contemporary Drug Problems* 3.

Murphy, S. and Waldorf, D. (1989) 'Kickin' down to the street doc: shooting galleries in the San Francisco Bay Area', submitted for publication. San Franscisco, CA: Institute for Scientific Analysis.

Padian, N., Carlson, J., Browning, R., Nelson, L., Grimes, J., and Marquis, L. (1987) 'Human immunodeficiency virus (HIV) infection among prostitutes in Nevada', *Abstracts from the Third International Conference on AIDS*, 1–5 June 1987, Washington, DC: US Department of Health and Human Services and the World Health Organization.

Papaevangelou, G., Roumelioitou-Karayannis, A., Kallinikos, G., and

Papouptsakis, G. (1985) 'LAV/HIV-III infection in female prostitutes', *Lancet* 2: 1018.

Papaevangelou, G., Roumelioutou, G., Kallinikos, G., Papouptsakis, G., and Stefanou, T. (1988) 'Education in preventing HIV infection in Greek registered prostitutes', *Journal of Acquired Immune Deficiency Syndromes* 1: 386–9.

Peterson, J.L. and Bakeman, R. (1988) 'AIDS and IV drug use among ethnic minorities', San Francisco, CA: Center for AIDS Prevention Studies.

Piot, P., Quinn, T.D., and Taelman, H. (1984) 'Acquired immunodeficiency virus (HIV), infection and related disease in a cohort of Nairobi prostitutes', *Abstracts from the Third International Conference on AIDS*, 1–5 June 1987, Washington, DC: US Department of Health and Human Services and the World Health Organization.

Rogers, M.F. and Williams, W.W. (1987) 'AIDS in blacks and hispanics: implications for prevention', *Issues in Science and Technology* 10: 12–16.

Rosenberg, M.J. and Weiner, J.D. (1988) 'Prostitutes and AIDS: a health department priority?', *American Journal of Public Health* 78: 418–23.

Seidlin, M., Krasinski, K., Bebenroth, D., Itro, V., Paolinao, A.M., and Valentin, F. (1988) 'Prevalence of HIV infection in New York call girls', *Journal of Acquired Immune Deficiency Syndromes* 1: 150–4.

Smith, G.L. and Smith, K.F. (1986) 'Lack of HIV infection and condom use in licensed prostitutes' (letter), *Lancet* 2: 1392.

Tirelli, U., Vaccher, E., Diodatao, S., Biosio, R., De Paoli, P., and Crotti, D. (1987) 'HIV infection among female and male prostitutes', *Abstracts from the Third International Conference on AIDS*, 1–5 June 1987, Washington, DC: US Department of Health and Human Services and the World Health Organization.

Tirelli, U., Errante, D., and Serraino, D. (1988) 'HIV-1 seroprevalance in male prostitutes in Northeastern Italy' (letter), *Journal of Acquired Immune Deficiency Syndromes* 1: 414–15.

Van de Perre, P., Clumeck, N., Careal, M., Nzabihimana, E., Robert-Guroff, M., De Mol, P., Freyeus, P., Butzler, J.-P., Gallo, R.C., and Kanyamupira, J-B. (1985) 'Female prostitutes: a risk group for infection with human T-cell lymphotropic virus type III', *Lancet* 2: 524–7.

Visser, J. (1989) Personal communication.

Waldorf, D., Murphy, S., Lauderback, D., Reinarman, C., and Marrota, T. (1988) 'Needle sharing among male prostitutes: preliminary findings of the Prospero Project', submitted for publication to Social Problems, Alameda, CA: Institute for Scientific Analysis.

Wallace, J.E., Christonnikos, N., and Mann, J. (1987) 'HIV exposure in New York City streetwalkers (prostitutes)', *Abstracts from the Third International Conference on AIDS*, 1–5 June 1987, Washington, DC: US Department of Health and Human Services and the World Health Organization.

Weinberg, D.S. and Murray, H.W. (1987) 'Coping with AIDS: the special problems of New York City', *New England Journal of Medicine* 317 (23): 1469–73.

Chapter eight

Female prostitutes, AIDS, drugs, and alcohol in New South Wales

Christine Harcourt and Ross Philpot

Introduction

AIDS in Australia

The advent of HIV infection and its major end point, the acquired immune deficiency syndrome (AIDS), has added yet another alarming dimension to questions which have vexed the public, police, and legislators in New South Wales for a great many years. Prostitution, drugs, alcohol, and sexually transmitted diseases have been continuing themes (though rarely openly acknowledged) in the history of white Australia. They feature particularly in the history of Sydney, which as the first established European settlement also has the unhappy distinction of being the drug capital of Australia and the city with the most extensive prostitution trade. Sydney is now the Australian city with the most people suffering and dying from AIDS, and presumably (although the full numbers are unknown) the highest population in Australia of people infected with HIV.

The first recognized case of AIDS in Australia was diagnosed late in 1982. Three years later, by the end of 1985, 112 cases and sixty-two deaths had been reported (Whyte *et al.* 1987: 66). A number of people, including four babies, had developed AIDS from contaminated blood supplies, and the public had been subjected to a good deal of panic by newspaper headlines and statements from politicians indicating that the disease would spread rapidly to the heterosexual community via the prostitution trade. It was in this climate that a reliable and practical test for the presence of HIV antibody (an enzyme-linked immunosorbent assay – ELISA) was brought into use in Australia. When the test was introduced, staff at Sydney Sexually Transmissible Disease (STD)[1]

Centre began to keep a coded register of the numbers of female prostitutes tested. They also enrolled 132 female prostitutes in a questionnaire survey to find out their risk factors for HIV infection and history of other sexually transmitted diseases, including hepatitis B, which, it was thought, might be associated as co-factors.

Sydney STD Centre: 1985 survey of female prostitutes

Sydney STD Centre is situated on Macquarie Street in the heart of Sydney's central business district. It is close to Sydney Hospital, State Parliament, the State Library, and numerous senior medical and legal practices. It is the oldest and busiest clinic dealing exclusively with sexually transmitted diseases in Australia, having been opened in 1933, one year before a similar facility in Newcastle (Lewis 1988: 7). Both were designed primarily as 'blue light' port facilities to treat sailors and other itinerant workers coming into the docks, which were at that time the communication centres of New South Wales.

It was not until 1971 that a female clinic was opened adjacent to the male clinic, but within a few years it was attracting a large number of prostitutes for regular health checks and counselling. Most of these women worked in the numerous parlours and clubs in the city centre and inner suburbs. Some others worked in small terrace-house brothels or solicited from the streets of Darlinghurst and neighbouring Kings Cross, a popular tourist area and *de facto* red light district adjacent to the central business district. However, in general, street workers were less inclined than parlour workers to seek regular medical advice.

By the time the first survey of female prostitutes was conducted at the Centre in 1985 it was estimated that about 40 per cent of the Centre's annual registration of 2100 new female patients were prostitutes, and over 300 of them had been tested for HIV infection. In spite of many early alarms through false positive results, by the end of the year none was found to have been infected with the virus. However, concern about the spread of AIDS via prostitution continued to be high and in 1986 the New South Wales Department of Health made a grant of money to one of the authors (RP), the Centre's Director, to conduct further research into the prevalence of HIV infection among female prostitutes. Research staff were appointed and began work on a prospective study which was based on an updated version of the questionnaire used in 1985. It has thus been possible to record and compare data on an almost continuous basis since the first months of HIV antibody testing.

Early results showed that prostitutes were seriously at risk of infection through a number of factors relating to their work and to their behavioural and social contexts. Principally they were at risk through having unprotected penetrative sex with clients and with non-paying partners. From their estimates it appeared that as many as one-third of their sexual partners may have been bisexual. Furthermore, around 10 per cent of women were at direct risk through using intravenous drugs, and an even greater number, nearly 30 per cent, through having sexual partners who injected drugs. A third area of risk was apparent in the high number of sexually transmitted diseases which affected these women (Philpot *et al.* 1988). Conditions such as herpes, genital warts, gonorrhoea, syphilis, and also trauma, which resulted in skin lesions and fragile and damaged mucosal surfaces, were obviously a cause for concern. There was also evidence from overseas that some of the diseases may be in themselves ço-factors for the development of HIV infection (Weber *et al.* 1986).

The behavioural problems associated with prostitution included a very high level of illicit and legal use of non-injectable substances, including prescription drugs as well as those taken without prescription. In addition, tobacco use was very widespread and some women had serious alcohol problems (Philpot *et al.* 1989).

Prostitution, drugs, and alcohol in the history of New South Wales

There is, unfortunately, nothing unusual about the conjunction of high levels of prostitution, drug abuse, and sexually transmitted diseases in Australia's recent history. The white invasion and colonization of Port Jackson and the foundation of Sydney were inextricably linked with the excessive use of alcohol and the sexual and economic exploitation of women. Even the impressive new Sydney Hospital, opened in 1816, was known as the 'Rum Hospital' because it was funded by a franchise on the importation of that liquor. In its early years, the colony's internal economy ran on alcohol, and wealth and political power wavered between the military and the civil administration as the rum monopoly changed hands.

Between 1788 and 1852 the labour force of the colony was provided by convicts taken from the prison hulks of Britain and sent, in most cases, to a lifetime of separation from family and home. Only one in seven of these transportees was female and, for obvious reasons, few 'respectable' non-convict women found their way ashore in the first decades (Hughes 1988). Although their sexual services were greatly in demand, the primitive, convict-based, frontier economy had little room for women in legitimate employment, even as domestics or farm labourers. Prostitution, sexual bartering, cohabitation, or concubinage were the most accessible forms of income and support for poor women and their children for a large part of the nineteenth century. Conditions established in the earliest penal settlements of New South Wales and Tasmania had repercussions throughout Australia well into the twentieth century. The relationship between prostitution and the white invasion of Australia is succinctly described in the report of the Select Committee upon Prostitution.

In the 1820s it is alleged that there were over twenty brothels in Sydney, although the adult male population of the colony was only 14,344. Prostitution was widely regarded and generally tolerated as an inevitable aspect of the convict system. The imbalance between the sexes was held to justify the male demand for prostitutes, while female recruitment reflected the fragility of marital and de facto relationships as well as the extremely limited opportunities for women in the contemporary economy. If prostitution was an integral part of the convict system, it easily outlived that system, taking new forms, but always being sustained by the demographic and economic conditions of a migrant, mobile society.

(Select Committee 1986: 242)

By the end of the nineteenth century prostitution was still a highly visible part of Sydney life. No adequate estimate can be made of the size of the trade, which was unorganized, casual, and probably to some extent seasonal. However, in 1908, agitators for public order law reform estimated that there might have been as many as 3000 street prostitutes in Sydney (Allen 1984: 204). 'Common prostitutes' were subject to police control under the Vagrancy Act, and historians have argued that these powers were used selectively against the older and poorer women on the streets, and also in such a way as to contain prostitution largely within a *de facto* red light district in the inner city. These are themes which reappear throughout the history of prostitution in this state.

The Police Offences (Amendment) Act of 1908 greatly increased police powers over prostitution, by creating new crimes of soliciting, living on the earnings of prostitutes, and brothel keeping. Prostitution became less visible on the streets but women with no other adequate legitimate source of income sought the protection of pimps and other organized racketeers who found the trade to be lucrative in spite of fines and bribes to police and officials.

Changes also occurred in the patterns of drug use in the eastern states. Alcohol continued to be widely consumed in great quantities. Beer was widely promoted as a health food for men, and women were tempted with 'tonics' which often contained a good deal more alcohol than did beer. Other drugs were also very popular. In the 1890s laws had been passed to control Chinese opium dens in the cities and on the goldfields. Opiates in patent medicines and elixirs came under legislative scrutiny early in the twentieth century but the legal consumption of narcotics remained very high: 'in 1936 [Australia] had the highest legitimate consumption of addictive drugs in the western world – twice the per capita cocaine consumption of Britain and three times its heroin usage' (McCoy 1980: 42).

Cocaine was particularly in demand after World War I since many returning soldiers had been exposed to the drug while on active service. Organized gangs traded in sly grog (bootleg alcohol) and drugs, and, as legislation restricted the legal supply of opiates and cocaine in New South Wales and Victoria, prostitutes became the major consumers, thus providing a docile as well as a profitable work-force for their pimps. Nevertheless, one of the best known dealers of the time was a woman, Kate Leigh, known as the 'Snow Queen'.

Eventually, in the 1930s, the law-makers and the police were able to control the illegal distribution of narcotics. But, just as prostitution had simply changed its guise and persisted in new forms under harsher legislation, so with the decline in opiates and cocaine use, there was a dramatic rise in the use of minor analgesics, barbiturates, and amphetamines. Chemists and drug companies continued to promote potent dependence-producing drugs in fancy packages and again women and 'women's conditions' were their major targets. In the 1960s and 1970s Australia was breaking new records with the highest consumption of aspirin in the world and an analgesic-related renal failure rate fifty times higher than in other countries (McCoy 1980).

For most of this period, prostitution remained largely confined to its traditional inner-city locale. Public awareness of the trade increased greatly in the late 1960s when the use of Sydney as a Rest and Recreation centre for American servicemen from Vietnam contributed to a rapid growth in visible prostitution, and again in the late 1970s when legislative changes repealed the offence of soliciting. Unfortunately, this attempt at partial decriminalization coincided with a massive increase in illicit drug use (mainly related to heroin) by young people, and, for a variety of social and economic reasons, a rise in the number of teenagers and young adults drifting homeless and unemployed into Kings Cross.

The spectacle of numerous drug-affected young prostitutes soliciting in the residential streets of Darlinghurst was intolerable and an Amendment to the 1979 Prostitution Act was introduced in 1983. This prohibited soliciting near residences and public buildings. An incoming Conservative government strengthened this provision in 1988 by also proscribing soliciting in non-residential areas which were in the view of 'a dwelling, school, church or hospital'. The Prostitution Act (1979) was largely repealed and replaced by the Summary Offences Act (1988). In keeping with its historical associations, there is a concerted attempt by councils, the police, and the public to restrict conspicuous street prostitution to the main streets of Kings Cross. The great majority of the 'invisible' trade has recently been conducted well away from the city centre.

During the 1970s, brothels (generally referred to as 'parlours') began to spread far into the suburbs. Most of these premises were discreet and discouraged drunkenness and disorderly behaviour. Some were selective about the type of clients they accepted and operated under a variety of inoffensive business names which facilitated credit card payments. In spite of some well-publicized, but not very successful, attempts by local councils to close parlours which were brought to their attention, there has been very little public reaction to this shift to the suburbs. It has been estimated that before 1975 over two-thirds of prostitution took place in central Sydney. By 1985 more than 60 per cent occurred in the suburbs – mainly in brothels (parlours, studios, clubs) and to a much lesser extent in private homes and units and through the services of escort agencies (Select Committee 1986: 268).

Prostitution in New South Wales in the 1980s

The current situation in New South Wales is that prostitution itself is legal, as it always has been, for women over the age of 18 years. However, the practice of prostitution is severely curtailed by a number of laws which interact to regulate the trade. These include, primarily, the Summary Offences Act (1988), the Crimes Act (1900), and the Disorderly Houses Act (1943). In addition, other legislation regulating the liquor trade, advertising, tenancy, child and community welfare, and local government includes sections which limit the ways in which prostitutes can work within the law. The most comprehensive barrier to the establishment of legal brothels is the section of the law dealing with living on the earnings of prostitution. This makes it illegal to own, manage, or work as a receptionist or sitter in a brothel, or in any other way to derive income from prostitution without actually being a prostitute.

The inherent contradictions in current social attitudes to prostitution and the attempts to control the trade through legal intervention were recognized by the Select Committee of the Legislative Assembly upon Prostitution. This was appointed in 1983 'to investigate and report upon the public health, criminal, social and community welfare aspects of prostitution in New South Wales' (Select Committee 1986: xi). It reported in April 1986, putting forward suggestions for the decriminalization of prostitution and its regulation through local government and planning laws. The Report has never been fully debated in Parliament, although a number of successful health, welfare, and anti-corruption initiatives have stemmed directly from its recommendations.

Also early in 1986, in a radical departure from traditional government attitudes towards prostitution, the State Government and the Federal Government jointly funded the New South Wales branch of the Australian Prostitutes' Collective (APC). The APC had been founded by a group of prostitutes, ex-prostitutes, and women supportive of prostitutes' rights, following the successful growth of similar groups in Holland, the USA, Britain, and France. Their primary aim was to fight for the decriminalization of prostitution and the enhancement of workers' control over the trade. They also provided support, advice, and information to working prostitutes and attempted to build up a sense of collective identity and unified aims among the very disparate and sometimes antagonistic individuals who are employed in many different forms of commercial sex.

Government funding enabled the APC to lease premises centrally located in Kings Cross and to employ several members of staff on a long-term basis. Its role included collating and disseminating information through posters and publications, a telephone service, workshops, and outreach visits to parlours and clubs. The Government was particularly anxious from the outset that the APC should take a leading role in educating prostitutes about the risks of AIDS and in the methods of prevention of AIDS and other sexually transmitted diseases. Over two years of funded operation the APC has had some major organizational difficulties, but it was successful in its primary aim of contacting a very large number of prostitutes throughout the Sydney metropolitan area and beyond, and in raising their awareness and understanding of AIDS. Outreach workers have distributed many thousands of condoms in city and suburban parlours, given advice and help in finding safer working environments, and encouraged many women to seek regular medical advice. Much of their educational work was done in conjunction with staff from Sydney STD Centre and from other sexual health clinics in the state. Sadly, the APC lost its funding and ceased its operations in 1989.

Female prostitutes and the incidence of AIDS in Australia

Since 1985, when the first serious alarm was raised about the danger of AIDS spreading into the female prostitute population, the total number of AIDS cases in Australia has continued to rise dramatically. Figures for January 1989 showed 1168 people affected, of whom 564 have died. Seven hundred and fifty-four (64.5 per cent) of the reported cases occurred in New South Wales. However, 88.3 per cent of all the victims in Australia were homosexual/bisexual men. Only approximately 4 per cent (42 out of 1168) were women. Of these, fewer than 20 per cent (eight women) were infected through heterosexual activity and fewer than 12 per cent (five women) were infected through intravenous drug use. Only partial figures were available for HIV infections in which AIDS had not developed. Even so, it was apparent that the proportion of those infected with HIV through heterosexual transmission or intravenous drug use was four to eight times higher than the number presenting with AIDS, indicating that by early 1990 there may be 'approximately 50 heterosexual and 35 intravenous drug user cases' (National Health and Medical Research Council 1989).

There have been no cases of AIDS diagnosed in female prostitutes in Australia, although several young women who have worked as prostitutes are known to be HIV seropositive. In each case the woman had been using drugs intravenously for some time before the diagnosis and the circumstances indicate that this was the source of infection. There is no conclusive evidence so far that any female prostitutes have been infected with HIV through their sexual activity. However, the potential for spread by this means is clearly apparent from the current epidemiological data. Moreover, the authors' own investigations indicate that the risk factors for infection of female prostitutes, identified in 1985, are still relevant. These include intravenous drug use; having unprotected penetrative sex with men who may themselves be at risk through bisexuality or intravenous drug use; and having a high incidence of sexually transmitted diseases.

Study conducted at three STD clinics in Sydney (1987 and 1988)

The questionnaire

In the course of a prospective study, begun in 1987, interview data have been elicited from 334 English-speaking prostitutes. In addition, ninety-six Thai-speaking prostitutes answered a questionnaire in their own language. One hundred and eighty-one interviews in English were conducted at Sydney STD Centre in 1987, and in 1988 the study was broadened to include two other metropolitan clinics (see Table 8.1). A further forty-nine respondents were enrolled at the Sydney STD Centre, forty-eight at the Kirketon Road Centre, Kings Cross, and fifty-six at the Parramatta Hospital Sexual Health Clinic, Parramatta. Of the ninety-six Thai-speaking prostitutes, forty-nine were interviewed at the STD Centre, forty-two at Parramatta, and five at the Kirketon Road Centre, but because of the language and cultural difficulties involved in surveying these women, their data have been analysed separately and, unless otherwise specified, are not included in the results presented below.

Questions were asked about demographic background – age, marital status, education, previous employment, and place of work; behavioural aspects such as drug taking, tobacco and alcohol use, private and 'business' sexual activity and condom use; and about medical conditions and history of sexually transmitted diseases. An attempt was also made to discover how much the women knew about AIDS and other sexually transmitted diseases, about their prevention and treatment, and from where they obtained their information. Seventy women at the STD Centre answered a follow-up questionnaire between four and twelve months after the first to indicate what changes, if any, had taken place in that time. Medical records held at the Centre were used, wherever possible, to validate details provided by self-reports.

As anticipated, some differences emerged between the clientele of each clinic, confirming that they provide services to somewhat different populations of prostitutes. Table 8.1 provides some comparative demographic details of prostitutes interviewed in each clinic during 1988.

Table 8.1 Demographic background of female prostitutes

	Sydney STD Centre n = 49		Kirketon Road Centre n = 46		Parramatta Clinic n = 56	
	N	%	N	%	N	%
Median age in years	28		23		26.5	
Mean no. of years in prostitution	1.3		2.1		2.5	
Place of work: street	1	2.0	10	21.7	0	0
parlour	36	73.5	33	71.7	54	96.4
escort	6	12.2	1	2.2	0	0
private	6	12.2	2	4.4	2	3.6
Supporting children 0–18 years old	11	22.4	7	14.6	28	50.0

Sydney STD Centre

The historical background and central location of Sydney STD Centre have been described above, and some of the basic data relating to the age, working conditions, and health of prostitutes seen at the Centre have been recorded in earlier publications (Philpot et al. 1988, 1989). The data analysed from the smaller cohort in 1988 are consistent with information derived from 150 interviews in 1987. These showed that the women had a mean age of 29.1 years, had been working in prostitution for a median of just over two years, and that the great majority worked in brothels (parlours) in the inner suburbs of Sydney. Four women were working from the street at the time of interview in 1987.

Kirketon Road Centre, Kings Cross

The Kirketon Road Centre was opened in 1986, specifically to offer a health care service which would be appropriate for an area which has a very high number of itinerant young people, including many tourists, students, and casual workers employed by local businesses, and above all a very high population of 'street kids' – drug users, prostitutes, homeless juveniles, and runaways, as well as those simply looking for entertainment. The clinic is small and operates on an informal and friendly basis, offering counselling, testing, treatment, and information on AIDS and sexually transmitted diseases, as well as a range of general practitioner services. It is also an access point for referral for drug treatment, accommodation, and a variety of other welfare services. The clientele includes many very young teenagers, and a number of somewhat older female prostitutes, as well as local residents and business people who find the evening opening hours convenient. As indicated by Table 8.1, the female prostitutes interviewed at Kirketon Road tended to be younger than those interviewed at Sydney STD Centre. More of the former worked on the streets and fewer were supporting young children.

Parramatta Hospital Sexual Health Clinic

By contrast the Parramatta Hospital Sexual Health Clinic is situated in the demographic centre of the greater Sydney metropolitan area, approximately 20 kilometres west of the central business district. Parramatta is a commercial and administrative centre for the extensive and rapidly growing western residential suburbs of Sydney. The town is pleasant and prosperous but many of the areas it serves have socially disadvantaged populations with a high level of poverty, unemployment, health and social problems, and often a paucity of accessible services to meet their needs. High school retention rates are often lower than elsewhere and youth unemployment and juvenile crime are long-term problems in some suburbs. Housing is much cheaper in the western suburbs than in more central areas (though still very expensive by non-Sydney standards) and they have a large population of young families and of people earning less than average wages. The major difference between prostitutes interviewed in Parramatta and those in the city is that 50 per cent of those in Parramatta were supporting (or helping their partners to support) young children. This is more than twice the proportion of mothers seen at the Centre, and more than three times as many as at Kirketon Road. A very high proportion worked in brothels and none worked on the street. This is not surprising as there has been a very determined attempt by local councils and police to keep street prostitution away from the western suburbs.

Results

Condom use by clients of prostitutes: AIDS-induced behavioural change

In spite of demographic differences however, the information gained in 1988 confirms that at least one significant behavioural change had occurred throughout the prostitution trade. This could reasonably be attributed to AIDS publicity and the educational work of health professionals and the Australian Prostitutes' Collective (APC). Prostitutes working in parlours were much more likely to use condoms with their clients than they were two or more years earlier.

The Select Committee upon Prostitution found that condom use varied considerably between prostitutes working in different areas of the trade. Almost all street workers and most independent prostitutes (working from home or rented rooms) insisted on their clients using condoms. Independent workers, however, often included a large number of 'regulars' among their clients. Such clients were less likely to be encouraged to use condoms than were other clients. Prostitutes from all levels of prostitution agreed that street workers in particular used condoms nearly all the time. The rationale for this was that street workers were more often desperate for money and well aware that they could not afford time off through sickness. At the same time they may be reluctant, for a variety of economic, social, and legal reasons, to seek medical advice through recognized channels. A similar point has already been noted in Chapter 6. The workers themselves said that as freelance prostitutes they had more choice of whom they accepted as clients and more freedom to arrange their own terms (Select Committee 1986: 166–7).

Parlour workers were less well placed in this respect. The Select Committee reported that,

> Doctors, workers (prostitutes), managers, and clients of brothels said that generally condoms were not used, and that often their use was actively discouraged. One reason given for this is that the discovery by police of condoms on premises or on a person may be used as evidence that prostitution has taken place. More commonly it was argued that clients do not like using condoms, and if asked to do so would take their custom elsewhere. In the Committee's survey of client attitudes, 42 out of 58 said they would prefer not to wear a condom when having sex with a

prostitute, and 19 of these 42 said they would go elsewhere if asked to use a condom.

(Select Committee 1986: 165)

These conclusions contrast with the Scottish experience noted in Chapter 6. The Edinburgh study indicated that massage parlour workers were generally less inclined to forgo condom use than were street workers. The London study described in Chapter 4 concluded that most escort agency workers were using condoms.

The 1985 survey at Sydney STD Centre tended to confirm the observation that condoms were used infrequently by parlour workers. Of the 132 women questioned in 1985 only 11 per cent (fourteen women) said they used condoms with all their partners (clients and non-paying partners), and 49 per cent (sixty-five women) used condoms on one occasion in five or less often (Philpot et al. 1988). Staff who were working at the STD Centre at the time reported that even this was an overestimate and that a more accurate figure for the trade overall was that fewer than 5 per cent of female prostitutes insisted on their clients using condoms.

A similar situation persisted throughout 1986. Most women, on questioning, would say that they preferred their clients to use condoms, but that brothel managers invariably allowed clients to choose and would not employ workers who caused problems. The APC tried to assist prostitutes by publishing lists of parlours which encouraged the use of condoms but these places were always very much in the minority.

A dramatic change occurred a few months after the initiation of this study. In April 1987 a well-publicized, multi-media AIDS awareness campaign was mounted throughout Australia. The campaign was badly received in many quarters because, like a comparable British campaign, it apparently had more effect in frightening members of the general public who were at low risk of infection than in alerting people at high risk (Dwyer et al. 1988; Morlet et al. 1988). Condom use by the clients of the prostitutes in this study did increase markedly during this time and many workers reported that the change was a direct response by the brothel managers to the AIDS publicity campaign (Harcourt et al. 1988a). The majority of managers in Sydney City and suburbs began to encourage the use of condoms on their premises, arguing that it was now good business practice and beneficial for the sex industry to do so. Reportedly, most clients, having few alternative venues, have acquiesced to this change.

In 1987, 46 per cent (sixty-nine out of 150) of prostitutes interviewed said they used condoms with all their paying clients though not with their non-paying partners. In addition, 18.7 per cent (twenty-eight out of 150) said they used condoms for all sexual contacts, including those with non-paying partners (Philpot *et al.* 1987). These rates continued to climb and by 1988 a total of 87.8 per cent of the STD Centre respondents reported using condoms with all clients and 32.7 per cent used condoms for every heterosexual contact. This is illustrated by Table 8.2. APC outreach workers have been able to confirm that clients are asked to use condoms in the great majority of brothels in the Sydney metropolitan area.

Table 8.2 Condom use by partners of prostitutes

	Sydney STD Centre n = 49		Kirketon Road Centre n = 48		Parrramatta Clinic n = 56	
	N	%	N	%	N	%
With all paying partners	43	87.8	46	95.8	47	83.9
With paying and non-paying partners	16	32.7	10	20.8	26	46.4
For contraception	16	32.7	14	29.2	20	35.7

Sexually transmitted diseases

The increased use of condoms in brothels may be having a beneficial effect on the prevalence of some sexually transmitted diseases, particularly acute infections such as chlamydia, gonorrhoea, and pelvic inflammatory disease (PID). It is not possible to assess accurately the proportion of sexually transmitted diseases in Australia which are associated with prostitution, although 10–15 per cent is generally accepted as a reasonable estimate. A comparison at Sydney STD Centre between female prostitutes and other women attending the clinics showed that the former had eight times as much gonorrhoea and twice as much chlamydia and PID as did the other women (Harcourt *et al.* 1988b). High levels of sexually transmitted diseases were also reported in a year-long survey of women working in a single house of prostitution in Sydney during 1981–82, where the commonest conditions seen were vulvo-vaginitis, gonorrhoea, genital herpes, pelvic inflammatory disease, non-gonococcal genital infection, and genital warts. Unwanted pregnancies and a range of general medical problems were also noted in that study (Donovan 1984a, 1984b).

Many of these conditions have the potential to lead to long-term ill health. Some may cause infertility, and others are associated with life-threatening conditions such as cancer and AIDS. Gonorrhoea, chlamydia, syphilis, and hepatitis B (which is sometimes sexually transmitted) have all been identified as possible co-factors for HIV infection and the subsequent development of AIDS. In vivo studies have shown that latex condoms are impervious to the organisms causing these conditions and should be effective in reducing the infection rate if used correctly. The authors have recently compared the incidence of sexually transmitted diseases in a group of fifty female prostitutes before and after they began using condoms with all their clients and found that acute infections fell by more than 66 per cent in a one-year period when condoms were used. Chronic and recurrent infections, such as genital warts, herpes, and cervical cytology, were less obviously affected (Harcourt *et al.* 1988c).

Thai prostitutes in Australia

Some establishments which employ large numbers of Thai-speaking prostitutes and have a mainly Asian clientele still do not encourage the use of condoms. There is evidence that many of their workers have a much higher incidence of gonorrhoea, chlamydia, and other sexually transmitted diseases, than do English-speaking prostitutes (Harcourt *et al.* 1988b). STD Centre staff and members of the APC have estimated that up to 400 Thai women in Australia have been working as prostitutes at any one time. Nearly all are working illegally, having entered the country on visitors' permits, which do not allow the holder to undertake paid employment. There is evidence that many are victimized and exploited by the men who recruit them into prostitution. Their interview responses made it clear that very few were experienced prostitutes, they had very little understanding of sexually transmitted diseases or the ways to avoid them, and were confused about, or unaware of, the risks of HIV infection.

Health professionals have found that the problems of treatment and infection control are exacerbated by the pressure on the women to keep working to pay off debts to their employers and often to support siblings and parents in Thailand. Mobility also affects treatment programmes since women are moved from one brothel to another or even from one city to another to avoid police and immigration officials. Most Thai women stay in Australia for between three and six months, although some return for a similar period over several years by applying annually for a new temporary visa. A current priority in the battle against AIDS in Australia is to persuade these women, their managers, and clients of Asian background that HIV infection does threaten the general population and is not confined to one or two well-defined groups.

Non-paying partners of prostitutes

Another subject of concern is the possibility of the sexual spread of HIV infection to prostitutes from their non-paying partners. For women in the USA, one of the significant risk factors for becoming infected is known to be having a partner who is at risk (D'Aquila and Williams 1987). Clearly, improvements in the level of condom use with clients only will not provide sufficient protection for prostitutes in the long term, although it will undoubtedly help to stem the spread of infection via their clients to the wider community.

As already noted in Chapters 4 and 6, most of the women questioned would not consider asking their lovers to use condoms because of the effects of such a request on the relationship; their own desire to distinguish clearly between sex for money and sex for pleasure; and sometimes because non-paying partners were not aware of the prostitute's occupation. Nevertheless, well over one-third of the women had knowingly had partners who were at risk of infection either because they were bisexual or, more frequently, because they used drugs intravenously. Approximately a quarter of the women interviewed said they knew at least one of their non-paying partners in the previous five years had used drugs intravenously. This is elaborated in Table 8.3. The problem appeared to be greater with the younger prostitutes. Only 20 per cent of those interviewed at the Kirketon Road Centre said they used condoms with non-paying partners, and yet they were even less likely to be in stable, long-term relationships than older women. Perhaps as a result of increased condom use over all, it was noticeable that, as shown in Table 8.2, approximately one-third relied primarily on condoms for contraception.

The increased acceptance of condoms and safer sex practices at work, combined with the current low level of heterosexually transmitted HIV infections, suggests that New South Wales may have won a temporary breathing space as far as the sexual spread of AIDS into the prostitution population is concerned. But spread through drug injection is dangerously poised, with educational and publicity campaigns

147

apparently having little behavioural impact on most intravenous drug users. A paper published early in 1988 showed that 12 per cent of the users surveyed at one centre in Sydney were HIV seropositive (McLaws *et al.* 1988). Overall, the proportion of Australian AIDS cases attributable to intravenous drug use doubled between January 1988 and January 1989 (National Health and Medical Research Council 1989).

Table 8.3 Female prostitutes having sexual partners at risk of HIV infection

Risk factor of partners	Sydney STD Centre n = 49		Kirketon Road Centre n = 48		Parramatta Clinic n = 56	
	N	%	N	%	N	%
Intravenous drug user	12	24.5	12	25.0	15	26.8
Bisexuality	8	16.3	7	14.6	7	12.5

Prostitutes and intravenous drug use

The evidence from Europe and Asia indicates that intravenous drug use is rapidly becoming the single most significant source for the spread of HIV infection, and that female prostitutes are among those most at risk.

In Australia, a relatively high proportion of female prostitutes are, or have been, intravenous drug users. A few are introduced to illicit drugs through prostitution, where their quasi-legal status throws them into contact with the criminal underworld. However, many more enter the trade in order to finance previously established dependence. Prostitution is one of the most lucrative sources of income open to all women, and is an obvious source of the very high daily income needed by some drug dependants. The Select Committee found that 'the great majority of drug dependent prostitutes in Sydney acquired their habit before entering the trade' (Select Committee 1986: 202) and, as noted in Chapter 1, a similar conclusion has been reached by Goldstein (1979).

Of seventeen drug-injecting prostitutes interviewed at Sydney STD Centre in 1987, four had worked as prostitutes for some time before their first 'taste'. Four had started using at approximately the same time that they became prostitutes, while nine had begun injecting drugs at least one year before they entered prostitution. The presence of a number of heavily dependent young women in the sex industry greatly intensifies the risk of the spread of HIV infection, both through drug use and through unsafe sex. Young people who engage in prostitution to finance a drug habit may be more likely to acquiesce to demands for services such as anal sex, which are known to carry a high risk of HIV infection. Apart from their need to earn, the disinhibiting effects of the drugs they use may well override their knowledge of safer sex practices. Whatever she may say to the contrary, it is difficult to believe that a young woman dropping asleep over the interview table will always remember to insist that her clients use condoms. Addict-prostitutes are often very young. They work in the least salubrious locations, have little prior experience of managing clients, and are isolated from older, more sophisticated prostitutes who could instruct them in ways to avoid infection.

Nearly a quarter of the women surveyed at the STD Centre had injected drugs in the previous five years and approximately 11 per cent were still injecting. The Select Committee upon Prostitution estimated that up to 10 per cent of all prostitutes (fewer than 300 individuals) in New South Wales were seriously involved with illicit drugs at the time of its investigation (Select Committee 1986: 197–8). It did not offer an assessment of the number of prostitutes who were occasional or recreational drug users, although it is estimated that over 10,000 people in the state might fall into that category.

The highest levels of intravenous drug use were found among street prostitutes. Many parlour managers adopt a very strict attitude towards drug use on their premises, because drug-using prostitutes often cause problems with clients, and may draw unwanted police attention to the brothel. From the prostitute's point of view a heavy drug habit may interfere with her ability to work regular hours, and will probably require more money than can be earned even in a busy parlour where at least half her income will have to be given to management. Freelance street prostitutes charge less for services but keep all they earn. Recent estimates of the proportion of street prostitutes in Sydney with a heavy drug habit range from 60–90 per cent. The Select Committee accepted a figure of 80 per cent as being approximately correct (Select Committee 1986: 198).

Two of the women interviewed at Sydney STD Centre in 1987 were obviously drug affected at the time. The remainder showed no physical signs of heavy drug use and mainly maintained their drug habits by working four or five shifts per week in parlours and clubs without having to resort to more stressful street work. One parlour worker had been using heroin with varying intensity for seventeen years since the age of 11. The majority of drug-injecting female prostitutes attending the STD Centre were not dependent or intensive users (Philpot *et al.* 1989).

A similar proportion of current drug users was identified at the Centre in 1988. This is shown in Table 8.4.

Table 8.4 Intravenous drug use by female prostitutes

	Sydney STD Centre n = 49		Kirketon Road Centre n = 48		Parramatta Clinic n = 56	
	N	%	N	%	N	%
Current intravenous drug user	5	10.5	12	25.0	5	8.9
Former intravenous drug user	13	26.5	4	8.3	7	12.5
Number (%) of current users sharing injecting equipment	4/5	80.0	11/12	91.6	5/5	100.0

However, as this table shows, there was an unusually high proportion (43.4 per cent) of former drug users, when compared with 1985 (8.3 per cent) and 1987 (10.6 per cent). There is no obvious explanation for this, unless it reflects the fact that recent publicity given to the danger of sharing injecting equipment had induced more former users to attend for HIV antibody tests. The numbers of users and former users at Parramatta were very close to those previously noted in Sydney. In contrast, 25 per cent of those interviewed at Kirketon Road were currently using drugs, and several were showing signs of recent drug intake during the interview. Six (half) of the women who used drugs intravenously worked on the street. Four other street workers had no apparent drug problem.

Attitudes to sharing 'fits'

Whether they were heavily dependent or were occasional users, all the intravenous drug users questioned were greatly at risk of HIV infection because of their attitudes to sharing 'fits' (needles and syringes). Fifteen out of seventeen (88.2 per cent) intravenous drug users had shared injecting equipment within the previous six months in 1987. A similar high proportion of current drug injectors were sharing in 1988. Four out of five drug injectors interviewed at Sydney STD Centre, all five at Parramatta, and eleven out of sixteen at the Kirketon Road Centre had recently shared injecting equipment. One woman denied sharing but had requested an HIV antibody test because she had used a syringe which she found in a public park.

Irrational and emotive attitudes towards sharing were common, and paralleled in many ways previously described attitudes towards condom use with partners with whom the women had emotional ties. Most women stressed that they shared injecting equipment only with close friends, husbands, or siblings and expressed their confidence that they were 'safe'. However, on questioning they sometimes expressed doubts about the behaviour of their partners. One woman said she was fully aware of the dangers of AIDS, had no sexual partners apart from clients with whom she always used condoms, and only ever shared 'fits' with her twin sister. She then went on to add confidentially that she was worried for her sister who seemed not to have the same concern about AIDS and shared with anyone available. Inconsistency in applying 'safer sex' and 'safer drug use' practices to partners in a close personal relationship were almost universal and contrasted strongly with the self-assurance and AIDS-awareness consciously projected by most of the women interviewed. Needle and syringe sharing with close friends had continued in spite of the existence of several well-patronized injecting equipment exchange outlets which had been operating in the Kings Cross and city areas for nearly two years. Clearly much work is needed to bring about significant behavioural change.

Intravenous and non-intravenous drug use by prostitutes

The numbers of drug injectors in prostitution are boosted by those who enter the trade after acquiring a habit. In addition, the occupation itself is very stressful and is conducive to over-reliance on drugs for rest and relaxation and to cope with the tensions associated with the life-style it demands. Many of the drugs used are legally obtained (with or without prescription). Some others, such as amphetamines and barbiturates, may be injected and are generally cheaper and more harmful than heroin and cocaine. It is noticeable that women interviewed at Parramatta in 1988 (who were more likely to be supporting children, and to be in difficult economic circumstances) were much less likely to use heroin or cocaine than women at the other two centres. However, the former did have a high level of amphetamine use and appeared more likely to resort to tranquillizers. This is shown in Table 8.5.

Table 8.5 Number of prostitutes using prescription and recreational drugs in the six months prior to interview

	Sydney STD Centre n = 49		Kirketon Road Centre n = 48		Parramatta Clinic n = 56	
	N	%	N	%	N	%
Barbiturates	2	4.1	3	6.3	0	0
Sleeping pills	8	16.3	11	22.9	8	14.3
Tranquillizers	5	10.2	4	8.3	10	17.8
Antidepressants	1	2.0	2	4.2	0	0
Amphetamines	6	12.2	14	29.2	13	23.2
Amyl nitrite	0	0	1	2.1	0	0
Marijuana	24	49.0	19	39.6	23	41.1
Cocaine	10	20.4	9	18.8	3	5.4
Crack	0	0	1	2.1	0	0
Heroin	5	10.2	10	10.8	3	5.4
Methadone	2	4.1	0	0	1	1.8
None of the above	15	30.6	20	41.6	23	41.1

Taking all the 1988 interviews together, up to 23 per cent of female prostitutes had resorted to using sleeping tablets in the six months before interview, and 18 per cent had used antidepressants and tranquillizers. Barbiturate use, which was a serious problem ten or fifteen years ago, was currently much less common.

As noted in Chapter 1, drugs such as amphetamines, caffeine, alcohol, and tobacco are used extensively by prostitutes to relieve the tedium, stress, and, in some cases, their intense dislike of the work they do. Stimulants and tobacco are most likely to be used on the job. Seventy-six per cent (116 out of 153) of the prostitutes studied smoked cigarettes and 50 per cent (seventy-seven out of 153) smoked more than twenty per day. This is shown by Table 8.6. In interviews the women clearly related this high level of smoking to work. Many said it relieved the boredom between clients, helped them and their clients to relax, and calmed their nerves. Most agreed that their work-places contained a majority of smokers, making it difficult to give up or cut down while working, and tempting non-smokers to take up the habit. Again, women from the western suburbs scored very heavily in cigarette consumption.

In spite of big reductions in smoking levels by the Australian population at large, young women have continued to take up smoking at a relatively faster rate than ever before.

Table 8.6 Tobacco smoking among the study group

Number of cigarettes smoked daily	Sydney STD Centre n = 49		Kirketon Road Centre n = 48		Parramatta Clinic n = 56	
	N	%	N	%	N	%
0	18	36.7	13	27.1	6	10.7
1– 9	7	14.3	4	8.3	2	3.6
10–19	9	18.4	7	14.6	10	17.8
20–29	12	24.5	12	25.0	19	33.9
30 and over	3	6.1	12	25.0	19	33.9

By far the most popular illegal drug for relaxation, used by nearly 43 per cent (sixty-six out of 153) of those questioned, was cannabis (marijuana). Women sometimes share marijuana cigarettes with regular clients, but for the most part marijuana is used away from work at weekends and in socially relaxed situations with friends and lovers.

About 15 per cent of women were using cocaine, 12 per cent used heroin, and approximately 5 per cent were using methadone, either legally as part of a treatment programme and/or illegally, pethidine, morphine, or designer drugs such as Ecstasy (XTC) and crack (smokable cocaine). The women who used opiates or injectable drugs often used more than one such substance, particularly if there were local shortages of their preferred drug. The earlier survey in 1987 found that twenty-six out of 150 women (17.3 per cent) used three or more substances, not counting tobacco and alcohol, and that some drug users had been using as many as ten different substances in the previous six months. Poly-drug use among young prostitutes was noted by the Select Committee upon Prostitution as a growing problem and one which is particularly difficult to treat because of the unpredictable effects of a mixture of substances.

Alcohol consumption

In contrast to smoking, excessive alcohol consumption by prostitutes is discouraged in most brothels, as it can obviously interfere with a woman's ability to work and to maintain the discretion necessary in her occupation. However, in some parlours and clubs, drinking with clients is regarded as part of the prostitute's duty, and a climate of drinking to relax and to enhance social interaction is fostered by these premises. Many prostitutes have a few drinks before work to ease tension, and those who drink heavily often do so at home after completing a shift, in order to wind down. Binge drinking was mentioned by some who otherwise did not drink heavily on a daily basis, and a history of past alcohol abuse was noted in a number of women who no longer had a drinking problem.

In several case studies of AIDS in homosexual men, alcohol abuse has been linked to failure to use condoms and to avoid known high-risk behaviour (Carr 1988). Women who drink heavily may well be similarly affected, particularly as they often expressly use alcohol to release inhibitions and tensions. In view of their previously described attitudes towards condom use, the fact that alcohol is mostly consumed in leisure time may further enhance their risk of infection by non-client contacts.

Binge drinking and wide fluctuations in the amount of alcohol consumed made it very difficult for some women to estimate their daily intake. Drinkers have therefore been classified according to their estimated daily intake, averaged over the six months prior to interview. Intake was measured in 'standard' drinks containing ten grams of alcohol, and an average consumption of from two to four drinks per day (14 to 28 per week) was described as 'medium', and more than four drinks per day was deemed to be 'high risk'. This is elaborated in Table 8.7. Altogether 28.8 per cent (forty-four out of 153) of those surveyed in 1988 drank two or more standard drinks per day. Twelve out of 153 (7.8 per cent) were binge drinkers who otherwise had a negligible daily intake. White wine and beer were the alcoholic drinks most often consumed by the respondents, but those who drank heavily frequently preferred whisky or whisky-based liqueurs.

It was again noticeable that the women interviewed at Parramatta Sexual Health Clinic were much more likely than those from the inner suburbs to be heavy drinkers. Half of all those drinking at high-risk levels and half of the binge drinkers were in the Parramatta group. However, this probably reflects, as much as anything, the socio-economic background of the women surveyed in the western suburbs. Several recent investigations of urban life-styles and official reports on health needs have highlighted the fact that people in socially disadvantaged areas have more life-style-related health problems than those in more prosperous suburbs. Often this reflects the lack of social amenities in the poorer areas and the overriding importance of bars and clubs as centres of leisure activities.

Table 8.7 Risk levels of prostitutes who drank alcohol

	Low risk		Medium risk		High risk	
	N	%	N	%	N	%
STD Centre (n = 49)	37	75.5	8	16.3	4	8.2
Kirketon Road Centre (n = 48)	30	62.5	10	20.8	5	10.4
Parramatta Clinic (n = 56)	33	58.9	8	14.3	9	16.1

As with tobacco, beer and wine are relatively cheap in Australia. The country's long tradition of excessive alcohol consumption and its current position as the consumer of more alcohol per head of population than any other English-speaking nation indicates that this is a broad-based cultural phenomenon and not a problem specifically related to prostitutes and their work (Wodak 1986). There can be no doubt that prostitution is a highly stressful, dangerous, and health-threatening occupation which, for many individuals, is associated with an excessive use of drugs and alcohol. However, there is plenty of historical and contemporary evidence to show that drug use by prostitutes is simply an amplified reflection of drug use in the population as a whole. The Select Committee upon Prostitution was told that 'many years ago street workers were as badly affected by alcohol as they now appear to be by heroin' (Select Committee 1986: 192). Barbiturates have gone out of favour in recent years while cocaine is becoming more popular with all drug users in the state. Inevitably other changes will occur over time.

Conclusions

Intravenous drug use by prostitutes has been targeted by the media and local councils in Australia as being of particular concern since the advent of AIDS, because prostitutes are a link between high- and low-risk groups. However, as health professionals tirelessly reiterate, it is individuals' behaviours, rather than membership of a group, which pose the highest risk of infection with HIV. Prostitutes who share needles and syringes or who engage in risky sexual behaviour while under the influence of alcohol or other drugs represent only a small minority of all the women in the sex industry. They do, however, have a lot in common with thousands of other non-prostitutes who engage in the same risky behaviours. All these people and all their sexual contacts are at risk unless further behaviour modification is achieved.

This study of female prostitutes attending STD clinics in the Sydney metropolitan area and other evidence from Australia show that the known level of HIV infection among these women is very much lower here than in many other parts of the world. Over 1100 prostitutes visiting the Centre between January 1985 and January 1989 have been tested for HIV antibody and at the time of writing none has been found to be HIV seropositive.

This study has also shown that the potential for rapid spread of disease through prostitution into the wider community is very great. The data described above, and those collected in medical centres in other states, cannot present the full picture. Many of those people most at risk of HIV infection, in particular the very young 'street kids' and heavily dependent male and female prostitutes, rarely show up in statistics because they avoid, or are ignorant of, established STD and drug referral centres. There is currently no equivalent study of male prostitutes in Australia, although it is known that a number of drug-dependent youths who are HIV infected work casually as prostitutes in Sydney and elsewhere. Other men who have at one time or another worked as prostitutes are included in the risk categories of 'homosexual/bisexual' for statistical purposes.

There is no cause for complacency. Even so, there is some hope that the safer practices adopted by most prostitutes might allow a little extra time to learn more about the hidden areas, and perhaps to induce some behavioural change where it is most needed.

Notes

1 The National Venereology Council of Australia has approved the terminology 'sexually *transmissible* diseases'. This emphasizes the fact that such infections can also be transmitted by non-sexual means. This is the accepted usage in Australia.

References

Allen, J. (1984) 'The making of a prostitute proletariat in early twentieth century New South Wales', in K. Daniels (ed.) *So Much Hard Work: Women and Prostitution in Australian History*, Sydney: Fontana.

Carr, A. (1988) 'Drugs and alcohol: reasons or excuses for unsafe sex', *National AIDS Bulletin* (Australian Federation of AIDS Organisations Inc.) February: 14–20.

D'Aquila, R.T. and Williams, A.B. (1987) 'Epidemic human immunodeficiency virus (HIV) infection among intravenous drug users (IVDU)', *Yale Journal of Biology and Medicine* 60: 545–67.

Donovan, B. (1984a) 'Gonorrhoea in a Sydney house of prostitution', *Medical Journal of Australia* 140: 268–71.

Donovan, B. (1984b) 'Medico-social aspects of a house of prostitution', *Medical Journal of Australia* 140: 272–5.

Dwyer, D.E., Howard, R., Downie, J., and Cunningham, A.I. (1988) 'The "Grim Reaper" campaign' (letter), *Medical Journal of Australia* 149: 49.

Goldstein, P.J. (1979) *Prostitution and Drugs*, Lexington: Lexington Books.

Harcourt, C., Edwards, J., and Philpot, R. (1988a) 'On the "Grim Reaper" campaign' (letter), *Medical Journal of Australia* 149: 162–4.

Harcourt, C., Philpot, R., and Edwards, J. (1988b) 'Effects of lifestyle and sexual practices on the health of prostitutes', paper given at the Bicentenary Health Care Congress, Sydney Hospital, Sydney, October.

Harcourt, C., Philpot, R., and Edwards, J.C. (1988c) 'The effects of condom use by clients on the incidence of STDs in female prostitutes', *Venereology* 2: 4–7.

Hughes, R. (1988) *The Fatal Shore*, London: Pan.

Lewis, M. (1988) 'From Blue Light Clinic to Nightingale Centre: a brief history of the Sydney STD Centre and its forerunners', Part 1, *Venereology* 1: 3–9.

McCoy, A.W. (1980) *Drug Traffic, Narcotics and Organised Crime in Australia*, Sydney: Harper & Row.

McLaws, M.-L., McGirr, J., Croker, W., and Cooper, D.I. (1988) 'Risks of human immunodeficiency and hepatitis B viral infections in intravenous drug abusers' (letter), *Medical Journal of Australia* 148: 263–5.

Morlet, A., Guinan, J.J., Diefenthaler, I., and Gold, J. (1988) 'The impact of the "Grim Reaper" national AIDS educational campaign on the Albion Street (AIDS) Centre and the AIDS Hotline', *Medical Journal of Australia* 148: 282–6.

National Health and Medical Research Council (Special Unit in AIDS Epidemiology and Clinical Research) (1989) *Monthly Cumulative Analysis of Cases in Australia*, January.

Philpot, C.R., Harcourt, C., and Edwards, J. (1987) 'Sexually transmissible diseases (STDs) and human immunodeficiency virus (HIV) infection in

Australian prostitutes', paper given at the 5th Regional Conference (South East Asian and Western Pacific Branch) of the International Union Against the Venereal Diseases and the Treponematoses, Bali, Indonesia, October.

Philpot, C.R., Harcourt, C., and Edwards, J. (1988) 'Human immunodeficiency virus and female prostitutes, Sydney 1985', *Genitourinary Medicine* 64: 193–7.

Philpot, C.R., Harcourt, C.L., and Edwards, J.L. (1989) 'Drug use by prostitutes in Sydney', *British Journal of Addiction* 84: 499–506.

Report of the Select Committee of the Legislative Assembly upon Prostitution (1986) Parliament of New South Wales.

Weber, J.N., McCreaner, A., Berrie, E., Wadsworth, J., Jeffries, D.J., Pinching, A.J., and Harris, J.R.W. (1986) 'Factors affecting seropositivity to human T cell lymphotropic virus type III (HTLV-III) or lymphadenopathy associated virus (LAV) and progression of disease in sexual partners of patients with AIDS', *Genitourinary Medicine* 62: 177–80.

Whyte, B.M., Gold, J., Dobson, A.J., and Cooper, D. (1987) 'Epidemiology of acquired immunodeficiency syndrome in Australia', *Medical Journal of Australia* 146: 65–9.

Wodak, A. (1986) 'Australian alcohol consumption', *Medical Journal of Australia* 144: 1–2.

Chapter nine

Prostitution and AIDS risks among female drug users in Frankfurt

Dagmar Hedrich

Introduction

The first known cases of AIDS in the Federal Republic of Germany (FRG) in 1980–81 included homosexual men and intravenous drug users. Haemophiliacs and other people who had received transfusions of infected blood or blood products were also affected. The first 'full-blown' cases of AIDS were registered with the German health authorities in 1982. Since October 1987 test laboratories have notified the authorities of the anonymous results of positive HIV antibody tests (Deutscher Bundestag 1988).

Eighteen thousand HIV seropositive test results had been reported by March 1988. By the end of that month there were 2779 registered AIDS cases. At the time of writing, 72 per cent of AIDS cases were homosexual men and 10 per cent were intravenous drug users. Only approximately 7 per cent of those with AIDS were females. Recently there has been a dramatic increase in the number of female AIDS cases. These rose from sixty-six in mid-1987 to 190 by the end of 1988. More than half of these females were known to have been intravenous drug users.

Since the exact number of intravenous drug users in the community is unknown it is not possible to assess accurately the rate of infection among drug users in general. The police have estimated that there are between 50,000 and 60,000 people dependent upon illicit drugs in the FRG, of whom 90 per cent are opiate users (Wille 1987a; Deutscher Bundestag 1988: 184). Unofficial estimates of the extent of illicit drug use have been far higher (e.g. Schmerl 1984; Boellinger 1987). A study of drug dependants in long-term therapeutic agencies in 1987 revealed HIV infection rates of 15–20 per cent (Kindermann 1989).

AIDS prevention programmes

There are several programmes in the FRG designed to curb the spread of HIV infection among drug users. These include extensions of advice and counselling facilities at established drug agencies, increasing outreach work with groups such as intravenous drug users and prostitutes, and the improvement of in-patient care for people with AIDS. In addition, a new programme, 'Women and AIDS', was initiated in December 1988, which, among other things, specifically targeted female drug users.

The main thrust of Ministry of Health AIDS prevention campaigns has been through education. This has focused upon informing the public about the ways in which HIV infection may be transmitted. Such campaigns have been designed with the intention of changing behaviours. They have been conducted on the premise that education can be effective only in a climate of co-operation, agreement, and tolerance. If such a climate did not exist, 'high-risk groups' particularly would be deterred from seeking advice and from contacting health and social agencies (Deutscher Bundestag 1988: 45).

Drug policies

The primary emphasis of treatment for drug dependence in the FRG is upon abstinence-orientated therapy designed to facilitate the cessation of drug use. The therapeutic response consists of an integrated network of supervision and care facilities. These offer services for problem drug users which facilitate withdrawal, after-care, and rehabilitation (Wille 1987a).

Alternative therapeutic approaches which employ drug substitution have been tried (Lotze 1978). Even so, drug substitution is not normally part of the response to drug dependence and has lacked general support from Government, medical authorities, and drug agencies.

Until recently problem drug users were offered help and support only if they accepted the goal of total abstinence. This long-established policy has undergone several changes. There has been increasing emphasis upon the provision of support which does not necessarily involve total cessation of drug use. Such support is intended to minimize the adverse effects of drug use which is viewed as only a temporary phase in the individual's life. Drug users in the process of reducing their drug involvement are encouraged to make social contacts beyond the drug scene.

The impact of HIV infection on drug services

The main mode of HIV infection among drug users has been through sharing injecting equipment. Sexual transmission appears to have played a lesser role (Wille 1987b; Plaut and Ramloch-Sohl 1987). In response to this situation central Government and regional health ministers unanimously consented to the free provision of sterile needles and syringes for intravenous drug users. This agreement was reached at a special conference in March 1987 (Wille 1987b). Since then, sterile injecting equipment has been available, without prescription, from chemists' shops. Drug workers have distributed free supplies of needles and syringes and drug injectors have also been able to obtain injecting equipment from vending machines strategically placed in various locales. Such provision has become good in urban areas, but drug users in rural areas may still encounter difficulty in obtaining sterile needles and syringes.

The rapid spread of HIV infection among intravenous drug users has rekindled interest in drug substitution programmes as a method of rehabilitation. A pilot scheme has been set up in North Rhine-Westphalia. Seventy-five drug users have been given a substitute drug, 1-Polamidon (Levo-Methadon). This is legally available only on prescription. Strict admission criteria have been applied to those included in this venture. Other German states have also been modifying their drug treatment programmes to incorporate substitution approaches.

The AMSEL Project

A long-term study of drug dependence and related conditions was set up in Frankfurt in 1985. This is the largest city in Hesse and has a population of 600,000. Most of the 6000 identified drug dependants in Hesse obtain their drugs in Frankfurt. The Verein Jugendberatung und Jugendhilfe (Young People's Advice and Support Centre) is conducting this study, which is funded by the social services in Hesse, Frankfurt City Council, and the Diocese of Limburg.

This study is designed to ascertain how some drug-dependent people cease drug use. In addition, it is hoped to identify the demographic, social, and therapeutic correlates of such cessation. The AMSEL Project aims to combine research with practical action. Social workers from youth and drug advice centres have been involved with the project from its inception and conduct data collection together with members of the AMSEL Project team.

Method

The development of 324 drug dependants is being monitored over a five-year period. Details of these individuals are elicited either from an intensive yearly interview or, if the individual agrees, from one to one supervision such as out-patient therapy. The project's social workers may also arrange for in-patient care. In such cases follow-up data are collected in the in-patient facilities. Participation in this study is completely voluntary (Projektgruppe Rauschmittelfragen 1986).

Each year the project workers develop a list of questions to be included in interviews. Data are collected by tape-recording interviews. The variables included in the interview included biographical data, drug histories, use of drug agencies, contact with the legal system, HIV status, and experience (if any) of prostitution. These recordings are used to conduct qualitative as well as quantitative analyses. If, for any reason, a respondent is not available for re-interview, some data may be collected from a third person such as a relative, friend, or drug counsellor. Such people are used only if the respondent in question has provided consent. Clients are not paid to participate in this study.

The Frankfurt area: the setting for the study

Frankfurt has had an important drug scene since the early 1970s. The drug problems of Frankfurt are comparable to those of larger cities such as Berlin and Hamburg. Frankfurt has become one of the main centres for drug dealing in the FRG. This reflects several factors, including the presence of an international airport. Frankfurt has a good network of drug advice and therapeutic agencies.

Between 1985 and mid-1988 2000 cases of HIV infection were recorded in Frankfurt. At the time of writing between thirty and fifty new cases of infection were being identified each month (Doerr et al. 1988). Frankfurt has an above average number of women among those who have been identified as HIV seropositive. Three hundred and twenty-five (20.6 per cent) of the 1580 HIV seropositive people recorded at the Hygiene-Institut in Frankfurt were female. According to official statistics, approximately half of these seropositives were intravenous drug users. Clinical experience suggests that the latter figure was an underestimate and that 75 per cent would be more accurate. This situation is similar to that in Edinburgh, described in Chapter 6.

Doerr *et al.* (1988) have suggested that 'almost all HIV infected prostitutes have been or still are drug addicts'. They further concluded that half of the HIV-infected women in Frankfurt were at least occasionally involved in prostitution.

This situation prompted Frankfurt Health Authority to introduce a drug substitution programme for drug users in January 1989. This is exclusively for HIV-infected prostitutes with a long drug use history. The programme is intended to curb the spread of HIV infection through commercial sex. Prostitutes with AIDS receive prescribed methadone. Asymptomatic HIV-infected women receive a temporary drug substitute to ease or to facilitate drug withdrawal. The women are to be given social and therapeutic support and help to find accommodation and employment. This venture reflects self-help programmes initiated and co-ordinated by prostitutes in several German cities (e.g. HYDRA in Berlin and the HWG in Frankfurt).

The general association between drug use and prostitution has been reviewed in Chapter 1. Wille (1987b) cites an unpublished study by Jaeger *et al.* This indicated that 64 per cent of female drug dependants had worked as prostitutes. The same authors asserted that a much lower proportion of male drug dependants were engaged in prostitution.

Stein-Hilbers (1988) has further emphasized the importance of prostitution as a method of paying for the drug requirements of female drug dependants. The AMSEL Project was established because of the drug use–prostitution connection.

Prostitution in the Federal Republic of Germany

Prostitution is not illegal in the FRG. Regular health examinations are compulsory if people are to work legally in prostitution. This system is based on a law designed to prevent the spread of sexually transmitted diseases. This does not acknowledge that prostitutes are an occupational group but refers to them as 'persons who are suspected of spreading venereal diseases'. Prostitutes' organizations have discovered that the application of this law is vaguely delineated. It is administered in a variety of ways in different local settings. Communities with fewer than 50,000 inhabitants do not have to accept legal prostitution and a city may be declared a prohibited area for commercial sex.

Prostitutes have to pay income tax even though their occupation lacks official recognition. As prostitutes they cannot pay for health insurance or a pension plan directly. Many problems may arise in relation to illness or to old age. For several years a number of self-help groups of prostitutes have been trying to solve such problems. Their major goal has been to obtain for prostitutes similar rights to those enjoyed by other workers in service industries.

Anybody (male or female) who wishes to work as a prostitute in Frankfurt has to be examined every two weeks by the Public Health Department. Every twelve weeks these examinations include an HIV antibody test. Health checks give clearance to work in parts of the city, the so-called 'tolerance districts', in which prostitution is allowed.

Since good looks and health are their working assets, most prostitutes are not eager to expose themselves to health risks, for example, by engaging in unprotected penetrative sex. Income and health are important considerations which influence the types of activities engaged in with clients.

Bilitewski (1987) has suggested that female prostitutes may be divided into the following three subgroups:

1. Professional prostitutes. These are mostly registered, are health conscious, and know the dangers of HIV infection.
2. Women who work temporarily as prostitutes but who do not regard themselves as prostitutes. These mainly engage in such work only when short of money. They often work at home and are not officially registered.
3. Women who are intravenous drug users and who engage in prostitution to pay for regular drug supplies. They distinguish between themselves and other prostitutes on the grounds that they cannot understand anyone working as a prostitute without being drug dependent. They do not view prostitution as a professional activity and most are not registered with health authorities. They take little care of their health.

It appeared that heterosexual 'professional prostitutes' in Frankfurt were generally not HIV seropositive. Prostitutes who were infected were mainly intravenous drug users. The latter were also more at risk from clients who requested high-risk sexual practices such as intercourse without using a condom. Drug-dependent women (or men) may be more likely than other prostitutes to acquiesce to such requests, especially if paid more to comply (Plaut and Ramloch-Sohl 1987). In addition, drug-using prostitutes' judgement and bargaining capacity are likely to be further impaired when under the effects of heroin or other substances.

Very little is known about the clients of prostitutes. Even so, it has been suggested that there are differences between those who contact drug-dependent sex workers and those who contact non-drug-dependent sex workers (Gersch *et al*. 1988).

Since the outbreak of the AIDS epidemic prostitutes have repeatedly been accused of being potential carriers of HIV infection. In the context of the FRG this has yet to be proven (Froeschl and Braun-Falco 1987). Mass media coverage of alleged AIDS risks among prostitutes led to a fall in the demand for their services. This resulted in vicious competition for clients. Initially the clients who were discouraged were those who had previously required sex with a condom. This situation probably increased the claims that clients who wanted unprotected sex would be successful in finding women who were prepared to agree to this.

The AMSEL study group

Eighty-five women and 239 men took part in the first series of AMSEL interviews. This ratio is broadly consistent with more general evidence of the involvement of males and females with drug use. The mean age of both males and females was 26.

When first interviewed, 95 per cent of females and 89 per cent of males were heavily drug dependent. The remainder had extensive and heavy involvement with legal and illicit drugs. Even so, they were not (or no longer) dependent. The largest subgroup (274) was of intravenous heroin users with long drug careers. On average, these individuals had made two attempts to cease drug use in association with in-patient therapy.

The average age at which both males and females had become involved with illicit drugs was 18. The transition from initiation to regular drug use had taken six months for over 80 per cent of the study group.

Over 70 per cent of the respondents had been in drug therapy at least once. The average age of such therapeutic contact was 22 for females and 23 for males. Half of those receiving such care had broken off treatment before it had been completed. These experiences were a reflection of how respondents were contacted. They were sought out several years after initial therapeutic attempts or when they were renewing contact with drug agencies. Others were contacted while imprisoned for drug-related offences. Seventy-two per cent of males and 64 per cent of females were either in treatment agencies or penal institutions when interviewed initially. Respondents who were outside institutions were contacted by the 'snowballing' method which has been described in Chapters 6 and 7.

Drug-using prostitutes

The AMSEL Project has been particularly concerned with prostitution and HIV infection among female drug users. Data are currently available on only the first three years of this five-year study. This information relates to eighty-five women in the investigation. Of these thirty-nine (46 per cent) were classified as having worked as 'prostitutes'. The latter term is not used pejoratively. It would be more appropriate to use it to refer to women who had derived income from selling sexual services during particularly critical phases of their drug careers.

Biographical characteristics

The thirty-nine prostitutes ranged in age between 18 and 37. Their mean age was 25.2 while that of the forty-six non-prostitutes was 27.2 years. The marital status of these two subgroups is shown in Table 9.1.

Table 9.1 Marital status

Marital status	Prostitutes		Non-prostitutes	
	N	%	N	%
Single	27	69.2	24	52.2
Married	5	12.8	7	15.2
Separated	2	5.1	2	4.3
Divorced	5	12.8	13	28.3
Total	39	99.9	46	100.0

As this table shows, two-thirds of the prostitutes were unmarried, compared with only half of the non-prostitutes. The prostitutes were also less likely than the other women to have children. This is shown in Table 9.2.

Table 9.2 Proportion of respondents who had children

Number of children	Prostitutes		Non-prostitutes	
	N	%	N	%
No children	27	69.2	24	52.2
1 or more children	10	25.6	19	41.3
Not known	2	5.1	3	6.5
Total	39	99.9	46	100.0

The prostitutes were markedly more likely than other women to have experienced parental separation when they were young. By the ages of 11 to 15 only a third of the former compared with two-thirds of the latter subgroup were living with both parents.

Twenty-five (64.1 per cent) of the prostitutes and twenty-five (54.3 per cent) of the non-prostitutes reported having had at least one close family member with drug problems.

The overall educational level of the study group was low. This is elaborated in Table 9.3.

Table 9.3 Educational level

Education	Prostitutes		Non-prostitutes	
	N	%	N	%
Did not finish school	7	17.9	4	8.7
Finished Hauptschule[1]	19	48.7	19	41.3
Finished Realschule[2]	11	28.2	19	41.3
Abitur[3]	2	5.2	3	6.5
No data	–	–	1	2.2
Total	39	100.0	46	100.0

[1] Nine-year elementary school.
[2] Middle school/high school.
[3] Final examination qualifying for university entrance.

Consistent with the information depicted in Table 9.3, very few respondents had completed professional training of any kind. Only six of the prostitutes and fifteen of the non-prostitutes had completed such training.

Twenty (51.3 per cent) of the prostitutes were unemployed one year before the first interview and a further thirteen were not working for other reasons, such as imprisonment or long-term therapy. This is illustrated by Table 9.4.

Table 9.4 Employment status

Employment	Prostitutes		Non-prostitutes	
	N	%	N	%
Unemployed	20	51.3	17	37.0
Unemployed due to imprisonment, long-term therapy, etc.	13	33.3	16	34.8
Working	1	2.6	3	6.5
School/training	5	12.8	10	21.7
Total	39	100.0	46	100.0

At that time 64 per cent of the prostitutes and 26 per cent of the non-prostitutes lived either alone or in a therapeutic community. Half of the non-prostitutes lived with family or partners, while only ten (25.6 per cent) of the prostitutes did so.

Alcohol and drug use

By the age of 14, twenty-two (56.4 per cent) of the prostitutes and seventeen (37 per cent) of the non-prostitutes had been regular drinkers and/or at least irregular users of illicit drugs. By the age of 18, thirty (77 per cent) of the prostitutes and thirty-one (67.4 per cent) of the other women reported such involvement with psychoactive drug use. By the age of 18 approximately half the overall study group had been regular opiate users. This is amplified by Table 9.5.

As this table shows, a substantial minority of respondents reported having been regular opiate users while still very young. The prostitutes were particularly likely to have been regular opiate users below the age of 16. The prostitutes were more likely than the other women to have had use of amphetamines and barbiturates as well as heroin and other opiates while young. Overall, thirty-six (92.3 per cent) of the thirty-nine prostitutes and thirty-nine (84.8 per cent) of the forty-six non-prostitutes were intravenous drug users or had been taking heroin several times a day for longer than six months at initial interview. Most women were also using tranquillizers and sleeping pills rather than cocaine or other stimulants.

Table 9.5 Regular[1] consumption of opiates between the ages of 13 and 18 (heroin dependants only)

Age	Prostitutes (N = 36)		Non-prostitutes (N = 39)	
	N	%	N	%
13	1	2.8	–	–
14	4	11.1	1	2.6
15	7	19.4	2	5.1
16	7	19.4	7	17.9
17	12	33.3	15	38.5
18	19	52.8	18	46.1

[1] Regular use was defined in relation to scores 8 to 10 on a drug use intensity scale, ranging from 1 (drug-free) to 10 (severe opiate dependence).

Prostitution and drug use

The average age at which the study group of thirty-nine prostitutes had begun to provide sex for payment was 20. Twenty-two of these women had already been drug dependent for at least one year. Only three women reported having engaged in prostitution before developing drug dependence. A further seven respondents did not provide clear information.

Two-thirds of the prostitutes stated that an important reason for selling sexual services was the need to raise money to buy drugs. Six women further stated that their income also purchased drug supplies for their partners. Ten per cent of the women also noted that prostitution was important simply to earn a living. Forty per cent of the women reported that by 'selling sex' they were avoiding crime and at the same time managing to buy drugs. The author and her colleagues formed the impression that for most of these women prostitution was a source of income only at times of heavy drug use. On average, these respondents had begun using drugs seven years before admission to the study. This, also on average, was one to two years before the women reportedly began to work as prostitutes.

Prostitution served as a means of obtaining money at times when alternative sources of drug supply were exhausted. Sometimes a woman organized her drug supplies in co-operation with a partner. If the latter was imprisoned, prostitution served as an emergency method of securing funds. It was, however, uncommon for women to engage in long-term prostitution to secure drug supplies.

The milieu of drug-dependent prostitutes is quite different from that of 'professional' prostitutes. The latter may be defined as female sex workers who are not heroin dependent and who derive their incomes solely from prostitution. In most areas drug-dependent women prostitutes work on the street. Some had worked in bars or brothels. Few had worked from an apartment, meeting clients at home or by telephone arrangement. Some of the drug-using prostitutes lived with men who were drug dealers.

Less than a third of the women interviewed had regular customers and only three out of thirty-nine were officially registered. In Frankfurt pimps are uncommon for drug-using prostitutes; only three reported having worked with pimps. The male partners of some women, who were also drug users, could arguably be regarded as pimps (Hoigard and Finstad 1987: 187).

In general, the thirty-nine women engaged in prostitution when they were using drugs. Only a few appeared to do so during drug-free periods. Twenty women provided an assessment of their perceptions of prostitution. None regarded it as positive. Thirteen viewed it as negative and seven were ambivalent.

Twenty-one women have provided details of what they regarded as negative aspects of prostitution. Eleven of these reported experiencing adverse effects while they were working as prostitutes. A further ten experienced such effects only after they had ceased to work as prostitutes. The most common of the adverse effects that were reported were feelings of guilt and shame and also disgust with clients. Over a third of the women reported experiencing problems with their partners as well as disturbed sexual relationships. Most of those in this study group had clearly experienced adverse and sometimes serious consequences because of their involvement in prostitution. Most clearly regarded commercial sex, not as intrinsically appealing, but simply as a means to an end.

In spite of this, it cannot be inferred that the cessation of opiate use will invariably motivate women to leave prostitution. Some engage in prostitution for reasons not related to drugs. These include a general need for money, to pay debts, rent, or to care for children. Such needs are particularly pressing when women live drug free but fail to find alternative employment.

If services which provide support for drug-using prostitutes insist upon cessation of prostitution it is probable that they will exclude many people who occasionally provide sex for payment. It is more realistic to accept that some drug users do sometimes sell sex and to foster and maintain contact with such people. One of the goals of the future drug policy should be to enable those women who do sell sexual services to 'professionalize' their negotiation with clients. As noted elsewhere in this book, such negotiations have major implications for the practice of 'safer sex'.

HIV infection

The males and females included in the AMSEL study were asked whether or not they had had HIV antibody tests and if so what the results of these had been. None of those who were not heroin users (N = 50) were reportedly HIV seropositive. A total of eighteen out of the seventy-five heroin-using women (24 per cent) and fifty out of 199 males (25 per cent) reported that they had received positive antibody tests. Sixty-three of the heroin-using women had been tested. One hundred and eighty-five of the 199 males had been tested. Thirty-three of the thirty-six female prostitutes in this heroin-using group had been tested. Fourteen of these women, 42.4 per cent, had received positive results and a further four were currently awaiting tests. Thirty of the thirty-nine female heroin users who were not prostitutes had been tested. Only four (13.3 per cent) were HIV seropositive.

The female drug-using prostitutes had the highest HIV infection rate of all those drug users in the AMSEL study group. This may simply have reflected greater exposure to the virus. These data do not indicate whether or not infection was linked with specific living conditions, with prostitution, drug use, or other characteristics of these women. It is also uncertain whether or not additional factors such as physical health or stress predisposed some people to becoming HIV seropositive.

Another German study of drug users has noted higher HIV seroprevalence rates among females than among males (Grosse-Aldenhoevel and Kunze 1986, cited in Wille 1987b: 87). This difference was attributed to greater female involvement in prostitution.

The present study indicated that, within the drug scene, women had a subordinate position. One result of this is that females were often the last to get the 'works' (needle and syringe) when those were being shared by a group of injectors. The 'junkie whore' is on the lowest level of the drug scene's hierarchy and such women are often despised by male drug users. Many women do not have their own accommodation and have nowhere to keep their injecting equipment. Many work on the streets and do not retain their own needles and syringes because of possible police action. Accordingly, female drug-using prostitutes are often forced to borrow injecting equipment when they obtain drugs.

Conclusions

At the time of writing contact had been retained with twenty-nine of the thirty-nine drug-using prostitutes. Two women had died, three had withdrawn from the project. Only six women had not been contacted. Roughly half of those with whom contact was maintained had stayed in touch with some form of drug therapy. Many did sometimes use drugs but only eight continued in prostitution and twenty-one reported having ceased to do so. It was apparent that the cessation of drug use was strongly related to an individual's social relationships and the emotional support available from other people. Social support is especially important for HIV-infected drug users. Froeschl and Braun-Falco (1987) have noted the problems posed for such people by social isolation and lack of income. These authors cited US data indicating that HIV seropositive females are at a considerable disadvantage compared with males. Such disadvantages are often compounded by the need to care for children (Froeschl and Braun-Falco 1987: 189).

For many of the women in this study their first positive experiences had been their relationships with males who were often drug dependants. Only a few of these couples had succeeded in giving up their drug use. There is a clear need for therapeutic initiatives that are flexible enough to cater for couples who may require help and support at the same time.

The rehabilitation of drug dependants frequently requires a resumption of work or education. It is often very difficult for former drug users to obtain training or employment. The female prostitutes in this study were especially disadvantaged in relation to education and professional qualifications (Hedrich 1989). Relapse prevention should emphasize training and education. A number of self-help organizations have already been active in this regard.

During the present study, considerable improvements have been noted in the use of sterile injecting equipment by both males and females. This has been due both to information and to increasing the availability of sterile equipment. Eleven of the fourteen HIV seropositive female prostitutes have been monitored for an average of two years. Four have not experienced drug problems during this time. Six of the remaining seronegative drug-using prostitutes ceased using illicit drugs during the investigation period.

This study, like the others cited in this book, shows that many drug-dependent women were financing their drug use through prostitution. As noted by other contributors, there was also a high level of identified HIV infection among the study group. The latter were characterized by a lack of social and economic support and by poor working conditions. Among these women in the study, prostitution was perceived in a very negative way and many reported having experienced adverse consequences either while working as a prostitute or thereafter.

The top priority for AIDS prevention in relation to the sex industry is to foster and to maintain contacts with drug-using prostitutes. Such action should aim to reduce the pressures which encourage unsafe sex and unsafe drug use. Services should not cater only for drug users who are prepared to abstain from drug use. Provision should be flexible and 'user-friendly'. This is the only way that this important high-risk group of people will be drawn into counselling and care.

Acknowledgements

Ms Jocelyn Mack and Ms Antje Fulqhum are thanked for translating this chapter from the original German.

References

Bilitewski, H. (1987) 'Aids, Otto und die Nutte', *Hydra Nachtexpress, Zeitung fuer Bar, Bordell und Bordstein*, HYDRA: Kantstrasse 54, D-1000 Berlin 12.

Boellinger, L. (1987) *Drogenrecht, Drogentherapie: Ein Leitfaden fuer Drogenberater, Drogenbenutzer, Aerzte und Juristen*, Frankfurt am Main: Schriftenreihe Fachhochschule.

Deutscher Bundestag (ed.) (1988) *AIDS: Fakten und Konsequenzen: Zwischenbericht der Enquete-Kommission 'Gefahren von AIDS und wirksame Wege zu ihrer Eindaemmung' des Deutschen Bundestages*, Bonn: Referat Oeffentlichkeitsarbeit.

Doerr, H.W., Forssbohm, M., Peters, M., Braun, W., and Valenteijn, A. (1988) 'Zur Epidemiologie der HIV-Infektion im Frankfurter Raum', *AIDS Forschung* 11: 618–21.

Froeschl, M. and Braun-Falco, O. (1987) 'Frauen und AIDS', in H. Jaeger (ed.) *AIDS: Psychosoziale Betreuung von AIDS und AIDS-Vorfeldpatienten*, Stuttgart/New York: Thieme, pp. 182–94.

Gersch, C., Heckmann, W., Leopold, B., and Seyrer, Y. (1988) *Drogenabhaengige Prostituierte und ihre Freier*, Sozial-paedogigisches Institut Berlin, Hallesches Ufer 32–38, D-1000 Berlin 61.

Hedrich, D. (1989) *Drogenabhaengige Frauen und Maenner: Eine Vergleichsstudie*, Frankfurt (in press).

Hoigard, C. and Finstad, L. (1987) *Seitenstrassen*, Reinbek b. Hamburg: Rowohlt.

Kindermann, W. (1989) 'Zur HIV-1-Antikoerperpraevalenz bei Drogenabhaengigen in der Bundesrepublik Deutschland', *Suchtgefahren* 35: 50–3.

Lotze, J. (1978) 'Ambulatnes Therapieprogramm mit Methadon', *Niedersaechisches Aerzteblatt* 9.

Plaut, G. and Ramloch-Sohl, M. (1987) 'Zur Infektionsprophylaxe der AIDS-Erkrankung bei intravenoes applizierenden Drogenabhaengigen durch die Vergabe von sterilem Injektionsbesteck', *Suchtgefahren* 33: 281–5.

Projektgruppe Rauschmittelfragen (1986) *Materialien zum Projekt AMSEL*, Jugendberatung und Jugendhilfe, Corneliusstrasse 15, D-6000 Frankfurt am Main 1.

Schmerl, C. (1984) *Drogenabhaengigkeit: Kritische Analyse psychologischer und soziologischer Erklaerungsansaetze*, Opladen: Westdeutscher Verlag.

Stein-Hilbers, M. (1988) 'Der Teufelskreis aus Drogen, Prostitution und Aids', *Frankfurter Rundschau* 26 February: 14.

Wille, R. (1987a) 'Drug addiction in the Federal Republic of Germany: problems and responses', *British Journal of Addiction* 82: 849–56.

Wille, R. (1987b) 'AIDS und Drogenabhaengigkeit', in H. Jaeger (ed.) *AIDS: Psychosoziale Betreuung von AIDS und AIDS-Vorfeldpatienten*, Stuttgart/New York: Thieme, pp. 81–110.

Chapter ten

Prostitution in Accra

Alfred Neequaye

Introduction

In Africa, AIDS was first reported to be mainly transmitted by heterosexual intercourse. Those with many sexual partners were at an increased risk of infection, and in East Africa 'bar girls' and female prostitutes were found to serve as a reservoir of infection, with a high percentage being HIV-1 positive (Kreiss *et al*. 1986). In 1985 very little was known about AIDS in Ghana and West Africa in general. From the East African experience it was thought that some information about the situation could be obtained by studying prostitutes.

Prostitution is illegal in Ghana but it is openly practised in certain places. For example, in Accra, an area called Korle Wokon is noted for its prostitutes. Although prostitutes practise quite openly, Ghanaian society in general disapproves of their activities. Prostitutes are therefore open to harassment, for example by the police and city council officials and by some members of the public. Prostitutes are therefore very suspicious of any official contact and of 'do-gooders'. The initial research approaches to prostitute groups were unsuccessful, but within the Ministry of Health's Communicable Diseases Unit there were field-workers who had contacts with some prostitutes because of their work in the clinics for sexually transmitted diseases. These field-workers therefore set up informal meetings with the leaders of a group of home-based prostitutes in Labadi, Accra. After lengthy meetings, they agreed to participate in a study which was designed to examine the social circumstances of the prostitutes and also to take blood samples for analysis for HIV infection. Other prostitute groups were difficult to approach because they were not as well organized as were the home-based women. The other women were prostitutes who operated from bars and night-clubs. After numerous unsuccessful attempts to enrol such people in the study, it was suggested that the researchers should discuss the project with the proprietors or managers of the night-clubs. Two popular night-clubs were identified in Accra and Tema. The author and his colleagues met the managers of these establishments and provided them with information about AIDS. After a full explanation of the purpose of the study, they agreed to co-operate. They arranged dates for the researchers to meet and interview the women working in their respective clubs. Interviews were conducted in the evenings in the managers' offices as discreetly and quickly as possible in order not to waste the women's time. It is probable that women may have been encouraged to co-operate because they could operate in the night-clubs only with the consent of the managers.

Results

The initial results of this study have already been reported (Neequaye *et al.* 1987a). Two distinct groups of prostitutes were observed. The first group operated from their own rooms or from brothels in one area and were organized into an association. These were classified as 'home-based' or 'low class prostitutes'. The other group operated from night-clubs, discos, bars, and hotels, and these were classified as 'high-class prostitutes'. Of the eighteen home-based prostitutes who were interviewed, sixteen were the bread-winners for their families and were the heads of their households. Fifteen were divorced or separated and one was widowed. Two were married and were working as prostitutes with the consent of their husbands. The home-based women tended to be older than the night-club prostitutes, with an average age of 39.3 years (range 27–50 years). They had more children to support, with an average of 5.5 per person. They had very little education. Half had not had any schooling; 28 per cent had attended only primary school and 22 per cent had completed middle school. All eighteen cited financial reasons for working as prostitutes. They had neither the skills nor the capital to engage in many other occupations. They charged the equivalent of $0.50 per client per sexual act and each had several clients each day or evening. On average, they reported having two or three clients each day. On their 'lucky days' they sometimes doubled this number. They engaged in only vaginal intercourse with clients. None admitted to oral or anal sex. Half of them had never used condoms before and the others had used them only very rarely.

The high-class prostitutes were a heterogeneous group, quite different from the home-based women. The high-class prostitutes probably represented the majority of prostitutes in Accra since such women can be found in almost every bar in the city. Tema is the major port in Ghana and the visiting seamen, both Ghanaian and foreign, attract many prostitutes. Such women are very mobile both within the country and abroad. Most high-class prostitutes solicit from hotels, night-clubs, or bars. Ninety-eight were interviewed. They were much younger than the home-based women. Some had travelled outside Ghana. In contrast to the home-based women, many of whom originated from other areas of Ghana, a good proportion of the high-class prostitutes came from Accra but worked in suburbs far from their homes. They had received more extensive education than had the home-based women. Eighty-one per cent of the high-class prostitutes had received some schooling, of whom 27 per cent had finished primary school, 42 per cent had attended middle school, and 10 per cent had attended secondary school. The reasons they gave for being prostitutes were varied. Half reported doing so in order to support their families. Seven out of forty-two worked as prostitutes to acquire money to establish themselves in other trades. Five reported working as prostitutes to pay for their education in vocational institutes. Five attributed their prostitution to marital sexual dissatisfaction. Three stated that they worked as prostitutes for fun and entertainment. When asked about their sexual practices with clients the majority reported only vaginal sex, but a few practised oral sex. One reported that she would engage in anal intercourse with clients if the price was right. Condom use in 1986 was very low. Approximately 60 per cent of the women had never used condoms and the other respondents reported doing so only sometimes.

The high-class prostitutes can be further subdivided into three subgroups. The most sophisticated operated only from international class hotels and night-clubs in Accra and Tema. These were better educated and all spoke good English to facilitate communication with their clients. Quite a few such women ultimately marry clients. Marriage to a client, usually an expatriate, serves as one of the main attractions of prostitution for women. The majority of these women drank some alcohol, both beer and spirits. The researchers did not, however, encounter any respondents with overt signs of severe alcohol problems. Some women in this group smoked cigarettes and there have been recent reports of cocaine sniffing by high-class prostitutes. Such reports were largely anecdotal but a chef in one of the fashionable night-clubs frequented by prostitutes has been arraigned before a public tribunal for allegedly supplying cocaine. This was a new trend in Ghana and it is disturbing because some prostitutes may earn enough to be able to afford regular cocaine use. They usually spend the night with one client and may charge the equivalent of $5–$15.

Members of the next subgroup of high-class women were similar in outlook to those described above but were less sophisticated and geared their trade to local clients. They also operate from discos, night-clubs, and hotels. The majority of this subgroup preferred to spend the whole evening or night with a client and charge the equivalent of $5–$10. A few of these women ascribed their involvement in prostitution to the need to accumulate enough money to start trading businesses. Indeed, the author and his colleagues know of a few prostitutes who have used their earnings to establish themselves selling food and other items in the local market. Many prostitutes never have enough money to enable them to do this. Some of these women also marry clients. One 28-year-old woman married a client who originated from a neighbouring country. She has since settled down with this man and has given birth to a baby. She was a very articulate woman who favoured the legalization of prostitution and the taxation of prostitutes as a solution to the harassment of prostitutes by the police.

The third subgroup of high-class prostitutes was far the largest. They were found in bars, cheap night-clubs, and hotels. These women may have several clients in a day and earned on average fees of approximately $5 per day. The majority of these women had other daytime jobs. Some were petty traders in the market or worked as housemaids. This subgroup was more difficult to reach because they were scattered over the city.

Of the two main groups, the home-based women turned out to be more interesting. During planning for a second programme the researchers discovered that all of these women belonged to a registered association called the Ghana Widows' Association. This had been in existence for over thirty years. There were over six subsidiary branches operating in different parts of Accra. Each area had its local branch with elected leaders and officers, usually those who could read and write. The local associations met once a week. Attendance at such meetings was usually high. Business included the reading of statements of accounts. News from other associations and the national offices was shared and problems of members were discussed. The local leaders represented branches at the district level at monthly meetings. The local associations were mainly intended to look after the welfare of their members. Each member paid weekly contributions to the treasurer. From these contributions a proportion was paid to the national association's coffers. The remainder was retained and used for the local members. From these contributions each member was entitled to a fitting funeral should she die in service. In addition, a lump sum was given for the support of her family. Also, each member was entitled to a loan to meet the funeral expenses of close relatives. Some of the money was also used for welfare purposes, such as payment for protection from harassment from local thugs and drunks. The national association has links in almost every major city in Ghana. The researchers were informed of links between associations in Accra, Tema, Kumasi, Tamale, Sunyani, Koforidua, Takoradi, and Ho.

The national association has a national president or 'Queen Mother' who is very influential. The national association has tried to get successive governments to recognize prostitution but has failed, and at the time of writing it was experiencing difficulties mainly because of quarrels over funds. The money that was paid to the national association was used at the discretion of the Queen Mother and her council, for administrative expenses and disbursement to local associations in need. Discord arose over the distribution of funds. The author was informed that the association has split along tribal lines, since some tribes believed that they had not received fair allocations. The Queen Mother and various officials in the association, having grasped the importance of AIDS prevention, were very co-operative, and the foundation has been laid for future intervention projects which would need the collaboration of these women.

HIV infection and AIDS

The initial study of prostitutes was carried out in early 1986. At that time less than 1 per cent of the women were seropositive for HIV-1 and all were healthy. However, at around this time it became evident that the first cases of AIDS were appearing in Ghana. Almost all were young women who had come back to Ghana for medical treatment. From their case histories it emerged that they had all been working in the Ivory Coast (Côte d'Ivoire) as prostitutes (Neequaye et al. 1987b). It was reported that many young Ghanaian women were practising prostitution in almost every major capital or seaport in West Africa. In Lagos there were tales of hotels in Agege full of Ghanaian prostitutes. In Abidjan the low-class prostitutes were mostly Ghanaian, as also were the high-class women in the smart hotels (Denis *et al.* 1987). There were also reports of Ghanaian women working as prostitutes in Dakar, Ouagadougou, Monrovia, Lome, and in Europe. These women were part of the mass exodus from Ghana in the late 1970s and early 1980s during the period of severe economic depression and political uncertainty. Ghanaian men and women left to look for work in neighbouring countries, but most of them were unskilled and therefore not readily employable. Some of the women found their way into prostitution as a means of survival. The unskilled men also took all kinds of work in order to survive. There were even reports of some Ghanaian men working as prostitutes in Europe because it paid very well. Most of these migrants earned foreign exchange which, because of the black market operating at that time, could be changed into large sums of local money when remitted home.

These migrant workers visited home on holiday during major festivities such as Christmas, Easter, or the major local festivals. They came home flushed with foreign exchange. They also returned with a lot of personal items such as clothes, radio cassettes, and videos which were the envy of the friends and relatives whom they had left behind. They attracted a lot of attention from the opposite sex. It was therefore only a question of time before these returning workers, both male and female, introduced HIV infection and other sexually transmitted diseases into their communities. They posed two main dangers. First, they could spread any acquired disease and, second, by their life-styles they helped recruit other Ghanaians to work abroad, by either passive recruitment or active enticement. There have been reports in Ghanaian newspapers of Ghanaian businessmen and women recruiting young girls ostensibly to work in restaurants in neighbouring countries but then forcing them to work in brothels. Here are three examples of this.

Case 1: Ms O.Q. This 15-year-old girl had lived in a neighbouring country for about twenty months working as a prostitute. She was working in Ghana as a housemaid when her mistress took her to the Ivory Coast and left her with the owner of a brothel. Her belongings and clothes were taken from her and she was left in a room to entertain clients. She did not speak the language and she was told that because she did not have any travel documents she would be arrested on sight by the local police. She was also refused food until she agreed to have sex with the clients. She later agreed to this and worked until she was able to save enough money to escape back home. She is now HIV seropositive.

Case 2: Mrs R.T. This 33-year-old mother of three was having serious financial problems four years earlier. An acquaintance extolled the benefits of working in the Ivory Coast. She expressed interest and was actively recruited by an agent who paid her fare and handed her over to her employer for a fee. The employer gave her a room and after a few days told her what she was expected to do. She refused but she was threatened with police action and she was asked to refund her fare, rent, and living expenses. She worked as a prostitute for about a year and saved enough to return to Ghana. She is now HIV seropositive.

Case 3: Ms A.S. This 23-year-old woman died of AIDS. She ran away from home in 1983 because of the things she could get for herself in a neighbouring country. She had seen and heard many friends returning home with beautiful clothes and plenty of money. She knew before going that she would be working as a prostitute.

There are certain communities in Ghana where prostitution is tolerated. Indeed, going to neighbouring French-speaking countries is part of the folklore. Young women talk longingly of going to 'French'. The communities accept them because of their wealth and possessions. Families may encourage their daughters to go to 'French' so that they can come back and help the family. Going to 'French' is ostensibly to work in chop bars or markets but everybody knows that the real business is prostitution. These prostitutes also introduce disease to other Ghanaian travellers. Ghanaian fishermen land their catches in neighbouring countries for bigger cash sales than they receive in Ghana. Because of language difficulties they prefer to visit Ghanaian-run brothels. Other businessmen, traders, and truck drivers also often prefer to visit their compatriots abroad. HIV-1 seropositive people are now being found among these and their sexual partners in Ghana.

Pilot intervention study

A second prostitute project was started in Accra in June 1987 (Lamptey *et al.* 1988). This was a pilot for a model intervention study. The project was conceived and funded by Family Health International (FHI) and the American Foundation for AIDS Research (AMFAR). The objective was to educate prostitutes about the risks and consequences of HIV infection and to offer condoms and spermicides as protection for those who continued to work as prostitutes. In this study six prostitutes who were judged to be articulate, to have leadership qualities, and to command respect from their peers were trained to be educators. They were then given educational materials and supplied with condoms and spermicides. Pamphlets were developed by FHI researchers and reviewed by the prostitutes before publication. The message was brief but explicit:

- AIDS IS DEADLY, THERE IS NO CURE.
- AIDS IS SPREAD BY SEX.
- PROTECT YOURSELF DURING SEX (THE MAN MUST WEAR A CONDOM. IF HE REFUSES USE A FOAM TABLET OR DO NOT HAVE SEX).
- YOU CAN GET AIDS EVEN IF YOUR PARTNER LOOKS HEALTHY.

Each of these six peer educators was asked to enrol ten colleagues and, with the help of the educational materials, reinforce the risks of HIV infection and the positive protective role of condoms and spermicides. The educators enrolled women who were interested in the study and supplied them with condoms and spermicides This was documented. Each educator was supervised by specially trained field-workers who served both to supply materials and to reinforce the message. The field-workers also documented supplies and enquired about complications or problems. A questionnaire was administered to each of seventy-two prostitutes enrolled and, with consent, blood samples were taken to facilitate testing for HIV infection. Analysis of the data from the questionnaire indicated very similar social characteristics to the first prostitute survey.

This exercise was considered to have been very successful in its impact on attitudes to condom use. It led to a significant increase in knowledge of AIDS and condom use by the prostitutes. Before the start of the project only 13 per cent of the women reported ever using condoms or spermicidal tablets. After three months, forty-seven women were interviewed and all reported that they were using condoms or spermicides regularly. When asked specifically about their use of condoms and spermicidal foam tablets in the past week, of the 268 reported sexual acts, 54 per cent were protected by condoms alone, 13 per cent by tablets alone, 27 per cent by both condoms and tablets, and only 6 per cent by neither. Twenty of the original seventy-two women could not be re-interviewed because they had travelled outside Acca and five were taken out of the study group because they tested as HIV seropositive or their HIV status was unclear. These five were counselled and asked to give up prostitution. At the end of the study, in January 1988, thirty-nine women were successfully re-interviewed. Two-thirds said they always used condoms with clients and only two said they never did so. The HIV serological tests initially conducted on the seventy-two women showed that two were HIV-1 infected and four others had indeterminate results, which may have indicated HIV-2 infection. Of the thirty-nine women who were re-interviewed only one was newly HIV-1 infected. This compared very favourably with another survey carried out concurrently with similar prostitutes who were not enrolled in the intervention programme. Eighteen per cent of these were by then HIV-1 seropositive. The success of this pilot project was encouraging enough for FHI to initiate similar projects in Cameroun and Mali. Why was this programme so successful? Was it the model approach of peer education? Was it the repeated attention given to the prostitutes by people who respected them? Was it the supply of free condoms and spermicides? The researchers believe that peer education may have been a major reason, as has been shown by Ngugi in Kenya and by subsequent experience in Accra (Ngugi and Plummer 1988). During the final re-evaluation it was possible to recruit some home-based women in preparation for the extended survey. The educator chosen in this group was a very articulate and intelligent woman. After her training she managed to convince the whole of her group to use condoms regularly. Their collective decision was taken at one of their regular meetings where they came for supplies. The educator used her initiative to buy supplies of condoms and retail to her group when the project ran out of supplies. This was very encouraging and it showed how such a project once initiated can be self-sustaining.

Conclusions

AIDS was first recognized in Ghana in 1986, and initially there was a marked female preponderance with a ratio of eleven infected females to one male. This was due to the influx of sick prostitutes returning from abroad, in particular from the Ivory Coast. At that time the seropositivity rate in prostitutes working locally was very low. However, without intervention programmes the number of those infected may rise very rapidly. Intervention programmes, as noted above, can reduce the spread of HIV infection into the general population. It is of vital importance to consider the social factors that lead women to become prostitutes and also that lead men to visit them. One of the most important is the lack of education for women, both formal and vocational, which means that they are often unskilled. Such women, if they have economic resources, traditionally engage in trading. If they have no such resources or lose them for some reason, they may have no alternative but to enter prostitution. One reason for loss of economic support is the death of a spouse or a marital split. Very often the husbands act as their wives' backers. This explains the relatively high number of widows and divorcées in the home-based study group. Another factor that leads to the poverty of women is the traditional method of inheritance in Ghana whereby a widow does not take over her husband's property and may be turned out of his house if he dies intestate. A new law remedying this situation has only recently been introduced. Prostitution can be therefore considered as a by-product of economic constraints in Ghana and generally in the developing world.

The migration of young people, especially men in search of work, for example to mining areas, to plantations, or to cities, leads to a situation in which they live in slums often without the support and guidance of their parents and families (Vail 1988). They may have many sexual partners under these circumstances. Due to the general economic situation, many young men have insufficient money to marry and may therefore feel the need to visit prostitutes. Young women, even those with some education, may be unable to find work. Those jobs which are available, for example clerical jobs, do not provide sufficient remuneration to live on. Part of the control strategy for AIDS must therefore include economic recovery programmes for developing countries such as Ghana, aiming to improve people's education, social circumstances, and financial standing.

Acknowledgements

The author acknowledges the help of his collaborators from FHI, Dr P. Lamptey, Ms S. Wein, and Dr M. Potts, and Dr J.E. Neequaye, Dr J.A.A. Mingle, and Dr D. Ofori-Adjei from the University of Ghana Medical School. Thanks are also due to the author's field-workers, Mr R. Mensah, Mr M. Doe, Mr P. Dzirasa, and Mr K. Malik. Miss G. Laryea is thanked for typing the manuscript so speedily and efficiently.

References

Denis, F., Gershy-Damet, G., Lhuillier, M., Leonard, G., Goudeau, A., Essex, M., Barin, F., Ray, J.-O., Mounier, M., Sangare, A., M'Boup, S., and Kanki, P. (1987) 'Prevalence of human T lymphotropic virus type III (HIV) and type IV in Ivory Coast', *Lancet* i: 408–11.

Kreiss J.K., Koech, D., Plummer, F.A., Holmes, K.K., Lightfoote, M., Piot, P., Ronald, A.R., Ndinya-Achola, J.O., D'Costa, L.J., Roberts, P., Ngugi, E.N., and Quinn, T.C. (1986) 'AIDS virus infection in Nairobi prostitutes: spread of the epidemic in East Africa', *New England Journal of Medicine* 314: 414–18.

Lamptey, P., Neequaye, A.R., Wein, S., and Polts, M. (1988) 'A model programme to reduce HIV infection among prostitutes in Africa', *Fifth International conference on AIDS*, Stockholm, p. 352.

Neequaye, J.E., Neequaye, A.R., Mingle, J.A.A., Ofori-Adjei, D., Osei-Kwasi, M., Grant, F., Hayami, M., Ishitawa, K., and Biggar, R.J. (1987a) 'Sexual habits and social factors in local Ghanaian prostitutes which could affect the spread of human immunodeficiency virus (HIV)', *Ghana Medical Journal* 23: 12–15.

Neequaye, A.R., Mingle, J.A.A., Neequaye, J.E., Agadzi, V.K., Nettley, V., Osei-Kwasi, M., Hayami, M., Ishitawa, K., Ankrah-Badu, D., Bertis, C., Asamoah-Adu, A., Aggrey, S.E., Ampofo, W., Brandful, J.A., Grant, F., and Biggar, R.J. (1987b) 'A report on human immunodeficiency virus (HIV) infection in Ghana up to December 1986', *Ghana Medical Journal* 23: 7–11.

Ngugi, E.N. and Plummer, F.A. (1988) 'Prevention of transmission of human immunodeficiency virus in Africa: effectiveness of condom promotion and health education among prostitutes', *Lancet* ii: 887–90.

Vail, L. (1988) 'HIV infection in Zaire', *New England Journal of Medicine* 319: 309.

Chapter eleven

Prostitution and AIDS in Spain

Pilar Estebanez Estebanez

Introduction

In Spain, as in some other developed countries, the number of women engaged in prostitution has been increasing. Current social and economic conditions appear to foster commercial sex. As indicated in earlier chapters, prostitution occurs in several different contexts. These include the streets, pick-up bars, discotheques, hotels, escort agencies, and massage parlours. In Spain, as elsewhere, there is a considerable variety of prostitution. The women who provide sexual services include those who work solely as prostitutes and others who engage in prostitution only to increase their family incomes at difficult times. There has also been an increase among younger women of those who turn to prostitution to raise money to purchase drugs.

Alongside the traditional means of practising prostitution, new, more sophisticated working styles have appeared. In most cities the traditional red light districts, with sex shops, brothels, and women working on the streets, continue to exist. The more 'modern' prostitutes work from pick-up bars, topless bars, discotheques, massage parlours, or through other methods. Such women may be found as much in the city centre as in the suburbs. In addition, prostitution is advertised through news-papers, magazines, and other mass media. Such advertising has been increasing, offering sex through 'massage parlours' or using other obvious yet euphemistic labels. It is also evident that there has been an increase in the number of women who work as prostitutes through hotels and escort agencies. Many of the clients of the latter are business executives and wealthy men.

From a socio-economic perspective three distinct subgroups of female prostitutes can be identified in Spain. First, there are those who work on the streets in red light districts. These women usually come from lower-class backgrounds and from large, problem families. Such women have generally received little formal education. Over 90 per cent are, for practical purposes, illiterate. Most have resorted to prostitution for purely economic reasons. Members of the second subgroup usually work from premises such as bars and hotels. They come from less deprived backgrounds and have usually received a basic education. Third, there are the 'call girls'. These have the highest level of education and often speak several languages.

The legal position of prostitution in Spain

On 3 March 1956 a law was introduced which ordered the closure of all brothels or houses of prostitution in Spain. This forced prostitution underground. It became illegal, but retained widespread social acceptance. Subsequently, prostitutes have lacked legal protection and have been targets for all types of exploitation.

During April 1989, at the International Workshop of Prostitution and AIDS, Cándido Conde Pumpido, the President of the District Court of Segovia, declared that:

> Faced with the hostile attitude of those in authority, who are usually in favour of its abolition, or at least its control, prostitution has throughout history found support paradoxically among religious institutions. In ancient Greece the 'Hetairas' devoted themselves to the goddess Aphrodite. In Babylon they were associated with the goddess Astarte. The church condemns prostitution from a moral point of view but for a long time it considered it necessary to protect the institution of marriage.

This reflects the ambivalence of both society and the law in relation to the sale and purchase of sexual services. International legislation relating to prostitution is based upon laws to suppress 'the trade in women and vices'. The agreement of 21 March 1950 revised earlier international agreements on this topic. The 1950 declaration was signed in Lake Juccess (New York) and is known as the 'Agreement to repress human trade and the exploitation of prostitution'. It also aimed to suppress all organized prostitution while ending the exploitation of individuals.

Spain became a signatory to the Agreement in 1962, having already introduced its own controls six years earlier. The 1956 legislation also created the Association for the Protection of Women. This aimed to support and rehabilitate women who had worked as prostitutes. These measures did not eradicate prostitution, as acknowledged by the Public Prosecutor of the Supreme Court several years later.

The 1956 legislation was amended in 1963. Under the new arrangements, which remain in force at the time of writing, prostitution is not a crime. No offence is committed by the sale or purchase of sexual services by consenting adults. The law penalizes any action that assists or persuades women under the age of 23 to engage in prostitution or to satisfy the sexual desires of a third person and helps and maintains such women in order that they can work as prostitutes.

In relation to women over the age of 23, the law proscribes any act that co-operates with or protects prostitution, any act of deceit, violence, or other form of coercion to encourage women to engage in prostitution or to force them to do so unwillingly. Pimping, deriving income from the earnings of prostitution, is illegal, as is the provision of premises for the practice of prostitution. The latter offence covers a wide range of activities. Any person working in such premises is subject to prosecution.

The legislation is rather anomalous since the age of majority in Spain is 18. The behaviours which are proscribed under the 1963 legislation are rather vaguely defined and courts have considerable discretion in relation to their interpretation. In addition, crimes such as rape, holding a person against his/her will, and physical abuse carry lighter punishments if related to prostitution than in relation to the general public.

Psychosocial aspects of Spanish prostitution

Many factors are involved in leading women to work as prostitutes. These include family background and life events. A number of features appear to be commonplace among women who engage in prostitution. Many such women left home at an early age, were institutionalized as children, had early sexual experiences, a low educational and/or intellectual level, and periods of anxiety and depression. Such problems, in particular lack of social support or economic opportunities, may be major barriers to a woman seeking to establish herself outside the world of prostitution.

Evidence suggests that family background may be the major factor associated with entry into prostitution. The absence of a father figure, due to alcohol or drug dependence or desertion, is a common feature in such families. Early sexual experiences also appear to exert an important influence on an individual's later relationships both with adults and with their own children. Other important factors which are often implicated in entry into prostitution include unplanned teenage pregnancy, especially if accompanied by family rejection; separation or divorce, especially if the woman has children to care for; sudden poverty due to illness, death, or desertion; and drug dependence.

A study carried out by the Instituto De la Mujer in 1986 indicated that women who had been prostitutes for more than six years regarded it as a way of life. In contrast, those who had been engaged in prostitution for only one or two years typically regarded it as purely a transitional phase in their lives. Several factors have been identified as encouraging women to remain in prostitution. These include the social conditions arising generally from this type of work and the stigmatized role of the prostitute in society, living and working in a ghetto, the difficulty of living part of one's life in other areas or with different people, the economic and health status of the clients, the attitudes of neighbours, the influence of pimps, and the association with crimes such as drug dealing, theft, and violence.

It is emphasized, as noted elsewhere in this book, that prostitutes do not conform to a single stereotype. They vary considerably. Some women become prostitutes after long periods of stressful life events, others adopt this form of employment because it offers an immediate answer to economic or other needs. The latter may include women who are drug dependent, migrants from rural areas, illegal immigrants from other countries, as well as older women who lead double lives as housewives in the suburbs.

Prostitution and health

As emphasized in earlier chapters, prostitution incurs a series of risks of sexually transmitted diseases. The author has earlier reported that 40 per cent of patients in a hospital for sexually transmitted diseases were prostitutes. Fifty-two per cent of these women had syphilis, 18.4 per cent had gonorrhoea, and 30.8 per cent had trichomonas (Estebanez Estebanez 1986). Other studies have indicated similar conclusions (Rosenthal and Vandow 1958; Conrad *et al.* 1981).

Hepatitis B is widespread among prostitutes who have used drugs intravenously. It is transmitted both by sharing infected injecting equipment and through sexual contact (Papaevangelou *et al.* 1974). Another condition that is commonplace among prostitutes is alcohol-related liver disease. This may be very serious, involving Ancient Australia Hepatitis aetiology. (HGAGS) (Henigst 1973).

Women who work as prostitutes often suffer from headaches and depression. Suicide is not uncommon among such women. A number of other health problems are associated with the general living conditions of those engaged in commercial sex. These include eating disorders (e.g. anorexia, bulimia) as well as lack of regular meals, mouth and dental problems, ulcers, bronchitis, asthma, and other respiratory infections, skin disorders associated with cosmetics, and back-ache due to standing for hours in high heels.

Adverse consequences due to drug use and the spread of HIV infection have further heightened the health risks associated with prostitution. Immune system disturbances associated with or caused by psychoactive drug use and infections due to poor diet and poor general health promote the development of other conditions such as genital herpes (Esteban *et al.* 1986).

Female prostitutes are also prone to infectious gynaecological and obstetric problems such as pelvic inflammatory disease. Their life-style increases the chances that they will give birth to premature, underweight babies or that their pregnancies will abort (Santamaria and Varios 1988). A study of a hundred prostitutes by *Solidaridad Democratica* indicated that forty of these women had undergone induced abortions. Three-quarters of the women in this study employed some form of contraception.

Many prostitutes have high anxiety levels, since some work in extremely stressful settings. The lack of companionship, rivalry with other prostitutes, and frequent drunkenness of clients combine to create an atmosphere of violence, constant threats, and frequent experience of physical abuse. As noted in Chapter 1, such circumstances may sometimes foster a heavy or abusive level of drinking or other forms of drug use, together with depression or other psychological disorders. Such problems are even more likely to occur if a prostitute is isolated from her family and lacks significant or supportive relationships. Such isolation is frequently intensified by social scorn, ridicule, and low esteem.

Many prostitutes live and work in ways that fail to protect or support them. Such women often live in boarding-houses and frequent bars or other settings in which alcohol and drug use are commonplace. Such an environment does little to assist women to resolve their problems. This situation is exacerbated by a lack of comradeship which is often evident among prostitutes.

It has been noted that many prostitutes were raised in families characterized by a lack of affection and a high level of violence (Santamaria and Varios 1988). Women coming from such backgrounds often leave home to escape and to find affection. They often have difficulty in expressing or satisfying their emotions.

Many women who work as prostitutes find it difficult to get out of the environment in which they work. It is normal for prostitutes to live in these areas. Only 13 per cent of the women studied at the author's centre in Madrid reported living and working in different districts. The lack of occupational and financial security, frequent moves from one city to another or from one area to another are major barriers to home ownership or to residence in one place for a long period. Prostitutes often reside in what amount to ghettos. Many prostitutes live, work, and relax in the same street or even the same building. Such environments are often characterized by drug dealing and violence, and may be difficult to escape from. Women who work as prostitutes, as already noted, often lack family contact or support. Most live alone, are single, separated, or divorced. Those who are mothers often do not have their children living with them. The women are also unprotected by the Social Security system, allowances, or state medical care. They are, accordingly, dependent upon private doctors or free clinics.

Alcohol and illicit drugs

The association between prostitution, alcohol, and illicit drugs has been discussed in Chapter 1. Drug dependence is certainly a reason for some women to embark upon prostitution. Furthermore, prostitution may foster the heavy or harmful use of both legal and illicit drugs. Sometimes, drug dealing networks overlap with those of prostitution. The precise levels of drug use among Spanish prostitutes are uncertain. Available information has been derived from surveys of small study groups. These include the survey by *Solidaridad Democratica* which related to a hundred prostitutes in Barcelona and Madrid. This investigation related solely to street workers. A quarter of these had used heroin or cocaine, a third used hypnotics, amphetamines, and cannabis regularly, and 54 per cent were regular drinkers (Santamaria and Varios 1988).

A quarter of a study group of 400 female prostitutes at a clinic in central Madrid were found to be drug dependent. Most of these women were also street workers. During 1986, the Direccion General de Policia (Main Police Office) conducted a survey of 200 prostitutes who worked in two different settings. Half of these women were street workers, the other half contacted their clients in pick-up bars. A third of the former were heroin users compared with only one individual out of the hundred bar workers.

The *Solidaridad Democratica* study involved interviewing a variety of people in contact with prostitutes. These indicated that they believed that 90 per cent of female drug dependants engaged in prostitution. It appears that male drug dependants typically steal to get money to buy drugs while their female counterparts turn to prostitution. Barbado *et al.* (1989) have concluded from a study in the Hospital La Paz in Madrid that 60 per cent of male drug dependants had been in prison in comparison with only 2 per cent of females.

The importance of drug dependence in relation to prostitution is further indicated by a study at a municipal clinic in Madrid. The youngest of the women studied, aged between 18 and 20, were drug dependent. These results were consistent with another study of female prostitutes attending a health centre in Pamplona of whom 51 per cent were intravenous drug users (Estebanez Estebanez 1986). Half of the drug users in the latter study were under the age of 24 in comparison with only 30 per cent of prostitutes who were not injectors or drug dependants.

Intravenous drug use incurs risks of a variety of infectious diseases. These include hepatitis B, HIV infection, staphylococcus, skin disorders, bronchopulmonary illnesses, and disorders related to poor nutrition.

As already noted, many intravenous drug users have criminal records. Among a group of male and female drug dependants at the author's health centre, more than half had been in prison and 70 per cent had experienced problems with the police.

HIV infection among prostitutes

Several studies have been conducted in Spain to examine the extent of HIV infection among prostitutes. These investigations have varied in relation to their methods, subjects, and geographical locations. Even so, they have all indicated that intravenous drug use is the most important risk factor related to the spread of HIV infection among female prostitutes. This is consistent with evidence presented in most of the preceding chapters. Recently, some evidence has been emerging of HIV infection among prostitutes who are not intravenous drug users. Before 1987 such women did not appear to have been infected.

During 1989 the author and Dr Victoria Zunzunegui reviewed the evidence on the extent of HIV infection among Spanish female prostitutes that had been produced since 1985. This review gathered together data on 2172 prostitutes who had been tested for HIV infection in eight different provinces. Information was collected from the following eleven locations: Alicante, Barcelona, Bilbao, Castilla-Leon, Cuenca, Madrid, Oviedo, Seville, Valencia, Vigo, and Zaragoza. The levels of intravenous drug use and HIV infection in these centres are shown in Table 11.1.

Table 11.1 HIV infection and intravenous drug use among female prostitutes in eleven locations

Study area	Year of data collection	N	Positive HIV results		Intravenous drug use	
			N	%	N	%
Alicante	1988	250	10	4	25	10
Barcelona	1988	75	8	11	5	6
Bilbao	1986–87	181	19	10	31	17
Castilla-Leon	1988–89	163	15	9	3	2
Cuenca	1987	100	12	12	20	20
Madrid	1986–88	246	63	26	94	38
Oviedo	1986–88	705	45	6	70	10
Seville	1986–88	70	6	9	11	16
Valencia	1986–88	216	20	9	25	12
Vigo	1988	37	2	5	2	5
Zaragoza	1987	129	4	3	5	4
Total		2172	204	9.5	291	13.4

As this table shows, 9.5 per cent of the 2172 women tested were HIV seropositive. Seroprevalence rates in the eleven study areas ranged from 3 to 26 per cent. Thirteen per cent of the women in these studies were intravenous drug users. The proportion of such drug users in the areas examined ranged from 2 to 38 per cent. It is noted that not all those who had used intravenous drugs were necessarily heavy, regular, or dependent users. The study group in Cuenca included some women who had injected drugs but none appeared to be drug dependent. None of the eleven study groups were necessarily representative of prostitutes in the general community, so the information in Table 11.1 may not provide a basis for generalization.

Other evidence reviewed by the author and Dr Zunzunegui indicated that levels of HIV infection among drug-injecting female prostitutes ranged from 3 per cent in Alicante to 67 per cent in Madrid. These variations coincided with levels of HIV infection among Spanish intravenous drug users.

Levels of HIV infection among female prostitutes who have not injected drugs ranged from 4 per cent in Alicante to 9 per cent in Cuenca. Only thirty-three of the prostitute women who were HIV seropositive stated that they had not used drugs intravenously. Ten of those had at some time had sexual partners who had injected drugs and two had engaged in sexual relations with clients from areas in which HIV infection was widespread. These were in Africa and the USA. It was not clear how the other twenty-one HIV seropositive women had been infected.

Analysis revealed that women who worked on the streets were more likely to have used drugs intravenously than were those who contacted clients in bars, hotels, or other locations. Street workers, accordingly, had higher rates of HIV infection than did other prostitutes. This is illustrated in Tables 11.2 and 11.3.

Table 11.2 Intravenous drug use and HIV infection among street prostitutes

Study area	Positive HIV test results		Intravenous drug users	
	N	%	N	%
Bilbao (N=181)	31	17	19	10
Madrid (N=246)	94	38	64	26
Zaragoza (N=129)	5	4	5	4
Total (N=556)	130	23.4	88	15.8

Table 11.3 Intravenous drug use and HIV infection among non-street-working prostitutes

Study area	Positive HIV test results		Intravenous drug users	
	N	%	N	%
Alicante (N=250)	10	4	25	10
Barcelona (N=75)	8	11	4	6
Castilla-Leon (N=163)	15	9	3	2
Cuenca (N=100)	12	12	20	20
Oviedo (N=205)	45	22	20	10
Seville (N=70)	6	9	10	15
Valencia (N=216)	20	9	26	12
Total (N=1079)	116	10.7	108	10.0

The author has calculated, on the basis of the thirty-three cases of HIV infection among apparently non-drug-injecting women, that the prevalence of infection among such women is approximately 19 per 1000. However, it is interesting to note that in the ports of Barcelona and Valencia the level of HIV infection among non-drug-injecting prostitutes was much higher at around 4 per cent. Studies of bar-working prostitutes in Castilla-Leon and Cuenca indicated an HIV infection rate of 9 per cent. These women were working around bars at highway intersections. Ten of these women worked as prostitutes in Ponferrada, a major road intersection. These studies indicated that, even among non-drug injectors, the HIV infection rate was 7.5 per cent.

This information supports the view that there is a slow spread of *heterosexually transmitted* HIV infection among female prostitutes in Spain. This spread may have been greatest in ports (Alicante, Barcelona, and Valencia) and at highway intersections (Cuenca, Ponferrada). This may be attributable to contact with transient clients from areas such as Africa, the Caribbean, or North America, in which there are high rates of HIV infection. These clients include sailors, service personnel, and long-distance lorry drivers. Such men have already been discussed in Chapter 1. It is also possible that HIV infection has been spread by heterosexual male clients who have become infected by sexual contact with drug-using prostitutes and then go on to infect non-drug-using prostitutes. Such conclusions must at present be tentative. Even so they do suggest new lines for research in relation to the possible spread of HIV infection among the general population.

Conclusions

The results of this review support the need for policies designed to improve the working conditions of prostitutes and the adoption of AIDS prevention strategies. The use of alcohol, tobacco, prescribed and illicit drugs is a conspicuous feature of the life-style of many prostitutes. Prostitution typically involves a life-style characterized by strong pressures to perpetuate it, making it difficult for women to enter or re-enter the mainstream of society.

AIDS prevention activities should be part of an overall programme designed to improve the general health of prostitutes. Such policies should be directed towards both the providers and the purchasers of commercial sex as well as to non-paying partners, pimps, and others involved with prostitution.

A multidisciplinary approach should be adopted to reduce the risks of HIV infection spreading through commercial sex. This needs to take into account the many factors which lead to prostitution and the fact that some of the associated health and social problems are attributable to a variety of causes. In other words, policy should consider not only biological but also psychological, social, and economic issues.

At the same time, any action designed to overcome such problems should form part of more general policy to promote community health. Following the famous Alma Ata Declaration, which advocated health promotion, disease prevention, medical care, rehabilitation, education, teaching, and research, such integration is important.

Policies should, as noted elsewhere in this book, aim to relieve the pressures not only on drug-using and/or HIV-infected prostitutes but on all prostitutes. Services for drug problems and HIV-related diseases should attempt to foster safer forms of drug use and to minimize drug- and AIDS-related risks. Coercion is not commended. Even so, services should recognize the importance of enabling those who are HIV seropositive to give up prostitution.

Research should be promoted which delineates those factors which influence the development of morbidity among HIV-infected people, as well as the co-factors which may influence the sexual transmission of infection. The different types of prostitution should be studied in order to identify behaviours which spread HIV infections as well as the geographical locations and socio-economic characteristics of prostitutes and clients which present the greatest risks.

There is a big responsibility to stop the incipient spread of AIDS through prostitution. This obligation rests upon the shoulders of health professionals as well as those who are responsible for AIDS policies and for health care. Available information already provides a guide to the likely future spread of the AIDS epidemic. This is advancing slowly but could still have even more disastrous consequences than anticipated, especially among groups as socially and medically unprotected as prostitutes and many of their clients.

The solution is in our hands. We know the virus, the means of transmission, the factors promoting the disease, and the preventive steps to be taken. Therefore, preventive action should be urgent and efficient because we have an obligation to control this epidemic. Moreover, society as a whole has an ethical duty to ensure that the fatal consequences of this disease do not fall upon those groups which are already afflicted by severe injustice and deprivation.

References

Barbado, E.J., Pena, J.M., Mostaza, J.M., Dominguez, A., Fernandez, J., and Vazquez, J.D. (1989) 'Complicacions infecciosas en ymujeres adictos a drogas por via paranteral en um hospital universitario del area de Madrid' (in press).

Conrad, G.L., Kleris, G.S., Rush, B., and Darrow, W.W. (1981) 'Sexually transmitted diseases among prostitutes and other sexual offenders', *Sexually Transmitted Diseases* 8: 241–4.

Esteban, R., Buti, M., Genesca, A., Gonzalez, V., and Vargos Garoia, J. (1986) 'Hepatitis en toxicomanios', *Anals de Medicina Interna* 5: 20–6.

Estebanez Estebanez, P. (1986) *Programa Diriqidu a Mujers Prostitutas en el Distrito Centro de Madrid 4th Congres o International de MSD*, Paris: JOR.

Henigst, W. (1973) 'Sexual transmission of infections associated with hepatitis B antigen', *Lancet* 2:1395.

Papaevangelou, G., Trichopaulous, D., Kremastinou, T., and Papontosakis, G. (1974) 'Prevalence of hepatitis B antigen and antibody in prostitutes', *British Medical Journal* 2: 256–8.

Rosenthal, T. and Vandow, J. (1958) 'Prevalence of venereal disease in prostitutes', *British Journal of Venereal Diseases* 34: 94–9.

Santamaria, C. and Varios, Y. (1988) *La Prostitucion en Espana*, Madrid: Instituto De la Mujer.

Chapter twelve

Conclusions and future strategies

Martin Plant

The contributors to this book have all undertaken this work because of their strong personal commitments to the women and men and children who are at risk from the AIDS epidemic. The success of the individual research projects reflects both the high levels of co-operation and mutual understanding between researchers and their subjects and the anxiety of the latter in relation to AIDS.

A number of remarkably coherent conclusions emerge from the preceding chapters. These are of particular value since the evidence upon which they are based has been collected by different methods in widely varied settings.

Available evidence indicates that 'sex workers' or 'prostitutes' are not necessarily vulnerable to HIV infection and that outside Africa and the Caribbean such infection among sex workers is mainly attributable to intravenous drug use rather than to sexual contact. Even so, there is also growing evidence of the sexual spread of HIV infection among prostitutes who are not intravenous drug users. It is emphasized that in all settings prostitutes, both male and female, are vastly outnumbered by their clients. Commercial sex is a world-wide phenomenon and reflects a remarkably high level of demand for paid sexual services.

The preceding chapters suggest that men and women who work as prostitutes are generally neither ignorant nor irresponsible. Many come from underprivileged backgrounds and work as prostitutes because of lack of education or alternative economic opportunities. Nevertheless, it is emphasized that prostitutes do not conform to a single stereotype. They differ considerably, both in relation to their socio-economic backgrounds and in relation to their working practices and general life-styles. Most prostitutes prefer to avoid engaging in high-risk sexual activities with their clients. In addition, many of those in the sex industry as well as many of their clients are both relatively well informed and worried about the risks of HIV infection and AIDS.

The evidence brought together in this volume confirms the established view that a high proportion of prostitutes are heavy and, in some cases, dependent users of alcohol and other drugs, such as cannabis (marijuana), heroin, and cocaine. It is also apparent that, at least in some areas, clients are frequently contacted in bars or other places in which alcohol and other forms of drug use are normative. Very often both the prostitute and the client are under the influence of legal or illicit psycho-active drugs. The role of drugs as disinhibitors has been emphasized throughout this book. HIV infection among prostitutes has so far, in Europe, Australia, and North America, been spread mainly by sharing infected injecting equipment. Only a minority of clients and prostitutes in many areas are intravenous drug users. Even so, as already noted, many are regular or heavy users of drugs such as alcohol, cannabis, and cocaine. Individuals are clearly less likely to implement 'safer sex' guide-lines when disinhibition from such substances is combined with the even stronger disinhibition of sexual arousal. The contributors to this book have highlighted two main sources of risk for sex workers. The first of these is the fact that a substantial proportion of clients choose to indulge in high-risk sexual activities. This demand has persisted in spite of extensive mass media publicity about AIDS. Some clients, probably a fairly small, but important, minority, deliberately seek prostitutes who are prepared to acquiesce to their requests for unsafe sex. Others even use threats or violence to force prostitutes to engage in such activities. It is very difficult to prescribe measures whereby such clients might modify their behaviours.

The second major source of risk for prostitutes is their clear preference for engaging in unprotected sex with their spouses, lovers, or other non-paying partners. As emphasized in several of the preceding chapters, many prostitutes use condoms as contraceptives, disease preventives, and to maintain a symbolic distance from their clients. This distance is not maintained with lovers, even if at least some of these are intravenous drug users or have multiple sexual partners.

Perhaps the uniformity of the results of the preceding studies simply reflects the fact that human sexuality varies little throughout the world. The evidence cited gains strength from the fact that it was produced in different locations using different methods. The whole subject of prostitution and its possible link with the spread of HIV infection is a very sensitive issue and is also difficult to investigate.

This book is an attempt to bring together an important selection of the studies into prostitution and its links with HIV infection and psychoactive drug use. The data presented are interesting as scientific and observational conclusions. The seriousness of the threat of AIDS necessitates far more than descriptive research, though, however fascinating it may be. Prompt and coherent action is needed to minimize AIDS risks and to limit the spread of this so far incurable, fatal disease.

AIDS is not 'just' a disease. It arouses fear, strong prejudices, and provokes a very different set of responses from those related to other afflictions such as cancer or heart disease. Much of this difference is attributable to the fact that AIDS is associated with sexual behaviour and drug use and that a considerable proportion of the initial victims of the epidemic were and remain homosexual males and intravenous drug users. For this reason some people have stated that AIDS is God's wrath or some form of moral punishment. People with AIDS have been ostracized, victimized, and discriminated against or treated as pariahs. In some countries mass media reports have been bigoted, inaccurate, and sensational in the extreme. Sadly, it is against such a background that AIDS prevention policies have to be formulated and implemented.

The evidence presented in this book emphasizes the fact that AIDS cannot realistically be dismissed as a problem only for deviant minority groups. Commercial sex together with 'unpaid' sexual activity link most of the population, directly or indirectly. The clients of prostitutes are often family men or have other sexual partners. Both prostitutes and their clients (in particular the latter) often travel and find sexual partners in different areas or different countries.

In some areas, notably Africa and the Caribbean, HIV infection has already become widespread and is mainly associated with heterosexual transmission. In other areas, Europe, North America, and Australia, for example, intravenous drug use by heterosexuals is now the fastest growing mode of spread. Prostitutes and their clients are clearly at risk of HIV infection. This is because most prostitutes and many of their clients have multiple sexual partners and because intravenous drug use is fairly commonplace among prostitutes in many areas. These risks need to be qualified. First, it is clear that many prostitutes and their clients do attempt to reduce risks by using condoms. Second, it is probable that some people who do not formally engage in prostitution also have numerous sexual partners. Some prostitutes have only a few clients and may encounter these infrequently. Many people may be only infrequent clients. Accordingly, 'promiscuity' and 'prostitution' are not necessarily synonymous. Even with these qualifications, available evidence strongly confirms that, because of the overlap between multiple sexual partners and intravenous drug use, prostitution may well be a means for accelerating the spread of HIV infection. Most of the authors contributing to this book have drawn attention to the fact that HIV infection already has a foothold, in some areas a firm foothold, among men and women who work as prostitutes. In spite of this, there is little general evidence to indicate whether or not such infection has originated from or has been passed on to clients and thereby on to the general population. Such spread has simply not yet been monitored so it is not possible to conclude whether or not it has occurred. In most countries only very limited HIV testing has been conducted, even among prostitutes. Studies not based upon clinical agencies have, as yet, seldom attempted to test for HIV seropositivity. Surveys have typically asked people if they have been tested and, if so, with what result. Such information is valuable, but is less informative than blood or saliva test results.

Some, but not all, of the contributors to this book have concluded that 'street prostitution' is most likely to be associated with intravenous drug use, HIV infection, and high-risk activities. Street workers may certainly be more vulnerable to persuasion, coercion, or violence from clients than workers in 'organized' settings such as brothels, massage parlours, or saunas. It would appear that there is considerable local and national variation in the way that prostitution is organized. At present, far more information has been collected about female prostitutes than about males. It is not obvious why this has been so, especially since males may be more likely to engage in anal sex. Evidence is rather contradictory in relation to which types of prostitution are least likely to incur high levels of risk. In spite of this, there is a clear consensus that health policy will only be hindered by any attempt to proscribe prostitution or to penalize those involved. Past experience suggests that repressive measures do not eradicate prostitution. They simply make it even more stigmatized and covert than it is already.

Health policy has to be negotiated in accordance with the law and with social mores. It is unrealistic to expect all countries to adopt a single policy, such as that in Holland. It is also unrealistic somehow to insulate health policy from views of morality or the fact that people do have to accept a measure of responsibility for their own behaviour. The AIDS epidemic has exploded into several overlapping and very sensitive areas.

Prostitution, homosexuality, drug use, and drinking are each individually politicized and controversial areas. The fact that these are interrelated with the spread of a sexually transmitted disease has accentuated the problems of legal, social, and health care response. Established policies may now be completely counterproductive. Accordingly, AIDS compels us to re-examine 'traditional' methods of responding to drug use and to commercial sex. Long-established policies must be reconsidered urgently in the light of a new imperative: AIDS IS A MUCH BIGGER THREAT TO SOCIETY THAN EITHER DRUGS OR PROSTITUTION.

It is not easy to change people's behaviours but it is possible to do so. Already the tragedies of the AIDS epidemic have prompted many gay men to revolutionize their sexual repertoires. Sadly, there is no more forceful form of health education than the terminal illness and death of a friend or lover. Many people, as yet, persist in regarding AIDS as being purely a problem for homosexual males or intravenous drug users. Human sexual interchange means that AIDS will not be contained within such subgroups: in effect, anyone who engages in a high-risk activity or who has sex with someone who has in turn had sex with another person is at risk.

As noted earlier, it is unrealistic and would probably be counterproductive to attempt to discourage, reduce, or even ban prostitution. Such a policy would have adverse effects for AIDS prevention since it would inevitably deter people from seeking proper health care. Measures are needed to greatly increase contact between prostitutes, their clients, and health services. People should be encouraged to seek regular check-ups with a guarantee of a 'user-friendly' confidential service. In areas in which prostitution is extensive, specialist health workers should be appointed who should, if necessary, seek out prostitutes to enlist their participation in health checks and AIDS prevention activities.

Many prostitutes and clients are reasonably well informed about HIV infection and AIDS, but many are also woefully ignorant. There is a pressing need for clear and explicit educational messages to be prepared and delivered directly to both prostitutes and their clients. Some promising initiatives have already been launched. These include several in which prostitutes and clients have played a leading role both in preparing materials and in disseminating them. 'Outreach work' is important in this context since it is unlikely that all prostitutes or clients will visit clinics/offices, etc., for either medical checks or information. In many ways clients are a harder group to reach than prostitutes. Clients may often regard their encounters with prostitutes as furtive and somehow 'not part of real life'. Ways have to be found to contact, inform, and influence clients, not only when they are aroused or intoxicated but also in the cold, sober light of day.

AIDS education should be accompanied by policies designed to foster condom use. This may involve, as in Liverpool or Amsterdam, free condom supplies or may simply involve increasing the availability of condoms for sale. Condom vending machines should be located in key areas such as streets, bars, hotels, saunas, massage parlours, or other places in which prostitutes work. At present, in some areas, possession of condoms may be used as evidence of prostitution or related offences. Such policies have no legitimacy in the age of AIDS. They should rapidly be replaced by strategies to encourage condom use.

In many areas the main route of HIV infection among prostitutes is through intravenous drug use. There has never been a consensus on the best way to manage drug dependence, and AIDS has further confused this situation. In some localities, such as Edinburgh, it is even possible that traditional drug control policies may have encouraged the spread of HIV infection through restriction of the supply of needles and syringes. This may have encouraged 'needle sharing'.

Policies are needed to discourage such dangerous sharing practices. The best way to avoid such risks is not to inject drugs. It has to be acknowledged that some drug users do not wish to abstain, but that many of these can be enabled to avoid needle sharing if they can be provided with injecting equipment. A number of experimental injecting equipment exchanges have been established in Britain, Australia, Holland, Switzerland, the Federal Republic of Germany, and the USA. The effectiveness of such agencies needs to be carefully assessed. Available evidence does suggest that they have led to a reduction in needle sharing.

In conclusion, prostitutes are not problems. They are people. Prostitution is an ancient and very well-established occupation. It is fostered by a huge demand and by a multiplicity of social, psychological, and economic factors. It is not necessary or even particularly useful to measure the precise extent of prostitution. Some prostitute–client interactions have little relevance for AIDS because they are protected by condoms or involve low-/no-risk activities. In spite of this, prostitution, because of its ubiquity and its scale, is a potential 'flash point' from which HIV infection could spread more generally than it *appears* to have done so far.

AIDS presents a huge challenge to humanity. The measures of our success will be two-fold. First, will it be possible to prevent the spread of HIV-related diseases? Second, will it be possible to respond to the AIDS crisis pragmatically yet at the same time recognizing that all people have a right to be respected and treated in a humane manner? Fears about AIDS are understandable; they must be acknowledged and, if possible, allayed. Such fears must not be allowed to prevent proper care for or safeguard of the basic human rights of people with AIDS and their families. Little will be gained and much may be lost by scapegoating or victim-blaming. If 'prostitution spreads AIDS' then this is because of something very basic in sexuality, especially in that of the human male. It is not enough to dismiss AIDS as a problem only for a 'deviant' few. It is a problem for us all, and for our children.

Name index

Subject index